WAR OF THE WORDS

WAR OF THE WORDS

*The Office Revolution That
Transformed the Lives of Women
and the Men They Worked For*

CAROL KARELS

FCP

Full Court Press
Englewood Cliffs, New Jersey

First Edition

Copyright © 2025 by Carol Karels

Published in the United States of America
by Full Court Press, 601 Palisade Avenue,
Englewood Cliffs, NJ 07632
fullcourtpress.com

.

ISBN 978-1-953728-43-2
Library of Congress Control No. 2025908930

Editing and book design by Barry Sheinkopf

Back cover author photo Casey Boyd

Cover design Deepak Malhotra

DEDICATION

To Hank Karels (Dad)
And Surender Goel

- It's gotta be small and nimble—otherwise expenses balloon.
- Each crucial task has to be undertaken by a superstar with light in their eyes—otherwise no "value proposition."
- The superstars have to be compatible and their home life has to understand/support them in their endeavors—otherwise explosion.
- For these to be true over a period like a decade or more is rare. The ultimate survivors typically "professionalize" their management, ultimately driving out the superstars, or extinguishing the light, which amounts to the same.

ACKNOWLEDGMENTS

I am grateful to my father, who took a chance on me. I am grateful to my mother, who always used her words to give encouragement and advice to my father, brother, me, and others fortunate to have crossed her path. I'm grateful to those who extended their hands and hearts as I wrote this book, providing editorial advice, design guidance and proofing, financial assistance, and/or moral support. These include Kathy and Bob Cartwright, Pam Nelson, Surender Goel, Bonnie LaScola, Kathy Nichols, Barry Sheinkopf, and Kevin Tremble. And finally, thanks to all who shared their MECollections for this book. Together they make the story come alive. Most of all, I am grateful to be "Mom" to Beth and "Grandma" to Hallie and Tessa, my greatest loves.

FOREWORD

James G. Meade, Ph.D.

THIS IS THE BOOK I WOULD LOVE to have written back in 1985. I almost did. And I had high hopes it would be a bestseller and make me, a journalist who covered the Information Age revolution, rich and famous.

It's the story of two Texas brothers, Hank and Everett Karels, who founded Microsystems Engineering Corporation (MEC) in the late '70s. Over the next decade, they developed a powerhouse of a word processor called MASS-11, which ran on Digital Equipment Corporation's (DEC) VAX minicomputer and IBM PC and compatibles.

MASS-11: Maybe a clunky name, but it was feature-packed, its performance was like a Porsche, and its customer base was the *Who's Who* of the Fortune 500. It was the best word processor you've never heard of.

If you used it, then it's likely that you were one of the thousands of engineers, scientists, or secretaries worldwide who needed to create lengthy, complex documents filled with scientific equations, graphics, and tables. The Patriot Missile, new drugs such as Zoloft, Zithromycin, and Prozac, the Hubble telescope, the Alaska pipeline, and the first HIV test—all were documented with MASS-11, software that helped get these products to market in record time.

It was a fascinating field, and the mid-'80s was a boom time in office automation and electronic publishing. DEC, the second-largest computer company in the world, was looking to lead the charge and set the pace in office automation with its All-in-1 and WPS-Plus word processing software on their VAX. But pesky little, family-run MEC beat them to the chase, outperforming, out-featuring, and out-wowing everyone they gave a demo to. MEC was eating DEC's lunch as DEC looked to leverage its size against MEC's adaptability, performance, and customer-driven design.

As a journalist, I was very intrigued by MEC's founders, who saw before DEC how the VAX could be harnessed for office automation and revolutionize how big companies operated. They were able to tackle a huge segment of the market better than DEC! It was obvious that DEC alternated being cooperative with, and antagonistic toward, MEC. Yet MEC kept charging ahead, making inroads into both established DEC accounts and opening new ones.

MEC, the little engine that could, listened to what its customers wanted whereas DEC designed its software in an ivory tower. MEC defied DEC when they ported their VAX word processor to the IBM PC after DEC said they'd crush MEC if they dared to do so. It was a wise decision on MEC's part to listen to their customers.

I loved the romantic, swashbuckling path MEC was taking, and I wanted to capture the spirit of their company in the magazine articles I wrote, and hopefully, *a book*.

Instead, the book on MEC would be written forty years later, by Hank's daughter, Carol, a nurse who left the profession to work for her family company for a decade. Like me, she felt it was a story that had to be told. She asked if I would write this Foreword.

What story does she tell? The ridiculous transformation that happened in the workplace in the 1980s as computers, office automation, and (leading the pack) word processing changed the character of the office. She provides an inside story of the lively changes in an industry that influenced and transformed all of society. She recreated the wrenching childbirth experience that happened as word processors were introduced into the office, against great resistance from mighty IBM, champion of the engineering marvel that was the Selectric typewriter.

Carol catches the full flavor of that fur-flying, heartbreaking, millionaire-making decade, and does it with such revealing detail that it feels as if the page is 3-D as the times come to life before you. She recreates the history of a time and place that rarely, if ever, is the stuff of history—the humdrum life of the workaday world before office automation—a world before word processing, email, the worldwide web, fax machines, and cell phones. She writes of the Sisyphean world of secretaries, typing from nine to five, then retyping it all the next day if there were corrections to be made.

She and her brother, John, whom she loves to death, tear each other apart, as we watch, in excruciating detail. Hank and Everett? Get a ringside seat if you dare. DEC and MEC? The battle ensues, and our commentator, a Hemingway armed with word processing, renders every blow and every response, but objectively, fairly, and lovingly. She also touches on the unusual spiritual journey both brothers were on as they led MEC. Both were dedicated seekers of the Absolute, the field of pure consciousness underlying everything.

Enough. I wanted to give you this mouthful from another voice than Carol's. I envy you. You have this adventure about to happen, this artistically rendered narrative from a born writer who discovered the tool she needed to achieve her aspirations while working for her family company. Surrender to her story of Hank, Everett, Surender, and even me a little bit, as we changed the world back in those darkest 1980s.

Part One

Introduction

WRITING A MEMOIR REQUIRES patience, perspective, and forgiveness, none of which I had when our successful family company, Microsystems Engineering Corporation, also known as MEC, was sold for peanuts in 1992.

Our flagship product MASS-11 (Microsystems Administrative Support System for the PDP-11 computer) was initially a word processing system that replaced the IBM Selectric in offices. A decade later, we were innovators in office automation and electronic publishing products, and our products were used worldwide on a powerful computer (the Digital VAX) designed for engineers and scientists.

As an ER nurse, I was an unlikely, but undisputed part of our company's success. In the decade I'd work for MEC, I'd written a million words using MASS-11, mostly user manuals, ads, marketing materials, and sales guides. I also traveled the world as I trained and sold our product. When our company was sold, I needed to write to distract myself. Instead of writing the amazing story of MEC, I joined a writing class and wrote a memoir about my years as a nurse at Chicago's famous Cook County Hospital in the early '70s. I self-published *Cooked: An Inner City Nursing Memoir* in 2004.

My father, who lived in four refurbished Maersk shipping

containers in a Douglas Fir forest, read my memoir and replied by email:

> *Great job! I wish you'd write a book about MEC now. It's a helluva David and Goliath story! And you're the only one who could write it. You were there through it all.*

My brother John, who lived in a cabin with a wood-fired stove in an unglaciated area of Wisconsin, read it too and emailed:

> *Your book brought tears to my eyes. Why not write a book that is funny for a change? MEC was the most hilarious company, especially at the end. Why not write a good fictional novel based on it as a parody of modern corporate life? It would be an instant bestseller. I would be happy to collaborate with you on the memories as it was going down the drain. MEC's demise was an endless source of entertainment for me. Love, John*

The two most important men in my life, my father and brother, were encouraging me to write about our family company: one about the astonishing success we had in the '80s, and the other about the heartbreaking crash landing in the early '90s.

In February 2005, just a few months after it was released, my nursing memoir received a 2005 Book of the Year award from the *American Journal of Nursing*. I sent an email to friends and family who had read the book, telling them of the news. I asked if they'd write a review on Amazon.

Within minutes, most had responded to my email, offering congratulations and promising they'd write a review. My brother was the last to reply to the group.

Hi all, I cannot endorse my sister's book. If it's so good, why does she need us to write a review? The book should stand on its own merits. This reeks of nepotism. John

Later that night, he sent us all another email:

Hi All. Please read the review that I have posted of my sister's book on Amazon.com. Nepotism is the beginning of the end of free societies. John

His review, from "Honest Brother John," discouraged potential readers from buying my book. "I'm giving it one star, and only because she's my sister." That review, and an even more hurtful one he posted the next day, were both removed by Amazon after family members pressed the "inappropriate" button numerous times.

I felt as if I was under attack by a cyber-terrorist who lived in a shack in the woods, yet he had been a graduate of the U.S. Naval Academy, a well-respected officer in the Navy, a nuclear engineer, and the product development manager at MEC. But after he left MEC, he had become a recluse.

I was terrified that his Amazon posts might become a daily occurrence and that my unhinged brother would continue to toy with me like a cat and mouse. But why?

"This is war!" Dad said. "Use all the ammunition you can to fight him. I'll do whatever I can to help."

I just wanted to be happy and excited about my book's award; I didn't want to go to war with my brother over it. Anyhow, how could Dad help? Our family company MEC was over; their father-son relationship was over; their lifelong war of words was over. I didn't want to start a new one.

I called an uncle who was a trained mediator. His advice was to send him an email and tell him to stop.

And so I did. "John, please STOP."

In the morning, he finally replied by email.

"OK, I'll stop, but only if you get over your nursing book and write the book about MEC."

A WEEK LATER, MY FATHER DIED UNEXPECTEDLY. In one short week, I went from ecstasy over winning a book award to despair over losing both my father and my brother. The only thing they both agreed on before his death was that I should write the book about MEC. And twenty years later, I have.

My story starts with the office of the '70s, one filled with the humdrum sounds of typing secretaries, using either manual typewriters or IBM Selectrics. It was a world I knew nothing about when my father asked me to write a beginner's manual for our word processor with the odd name of MASS-11.

For the next decade I had a front row seat during the explosive office automation revolution of the '80s. MEC would not only play a major role in it, but we set the bar high.

We were also decades ahead of the business world when it came to providing a workplace environment conducive to creativity and work/life balance. Thanks to all who shared their memories with me so this remarkable story of a company, way ahead of its time, could finally be told.

A Diamond in the Rough

THE EARLIEST MEMORIES I HAVE of my dad, Hank Karels, are of him hovering over a drafting board in our two-bedroom, one-bath, crackerbox house in Davenport, Iowa, on the banks of the mighty Mississippi River. The board was in my parent's bedroom, and there, he designed computerized corn-processing plants by hand on drafting paper. My brother John and I were forbidden to go in their room or to touch that board filled with his hand-drawn mysterious engineering diagrams.

The year was 1956, and my parents had moved us there from an unfinished basement apartment on Chicago's north side, just two blocks south of the famous Riverview Amusement Park. I was three and John one.

Dad was an electrical engineer who had just completed six years of night school at the Illinois Institute of Technology. He had been hired by Foxboro Engineering, a computer company based in Massachusetts, to sell 'direct digital process control systems' to corn-processing plants in Iowa and southern Illinois.

Dad was on the road five days a week for the next five years. When he was home on weekends, his mind was on his work, and he had a short fuse with all of us. John and I had to be on our best behavior,

Mom insisted; the slightest noise or squabble between me and my brother might cause Dad to have a "fit," an expletive-filled outburst, one similar to a microburst in its power and brevity.

Mom, who was a stay-at-home mom like all the other women in the neighborhood, ignored his fits, which were infrequent but made an unforgettable impression. She'd send us outside to play, where we had a swing set, a giant pile of sand, and numerous pets—our mutt Studs, cats Muffy and Fluffy, hamsters Lixie and Pixie, a house mouse we called Hunkamunka, and a goldfish named Gloria. John and I were both relieved when he went back on the road Monday morning. Our life was back to normal with Mom.

I remember my Aunt Lee once said to Mom, after witnessing one of his outbursts, "Henry is too hard on Carol and John! They're such good kids! Can't you talk to him?"

To which Mom replied, "He's never laid a hand on them. He's got some hard edges, but he had a tough upbringing. I handle him like a feral cat, with kid gloves. He needs a lot of attention and stroking. He's a diamond in the rough."

Mom once told me, when I was old enough to understand, that the only silver lining in Dad's childhood was his mother Johnie, the paternal grandmother I had never met.

"I met Johnie after we married," Mom said, "just before she died of metastatic breast cancer. She was soft-spoken, played classical piano, and was a writer. She hoped to publish her short stories someday."

Mom added, "More importantly, she was committed to getting her kids, who were all smart as whips, a good education. She once told your father, when he was about to leave home to join the navy, 'Your father will be remembered for *his* deeds after he dies. I will be remembered for *yours*.' Dad has never forgotten her words. He is driven to make her proud."

When I was eight, Dad was promoted to branch manager, and we moved from Iowa back to the Chicago area. My parents bought a new three-bedroom split-level home in the Chicago suburb of Streamwood for $15,000. The yellow, aluminum-shingled house had a quarter-acre yard that overlooked a wooded, marshy area filled with wildlife. The elementary school, town pool, playground, and town dump were all within walking distance. We had achieved the "American Dream."

Dad continued to work hard and travel while fighting demons both known (his regional manager) and unknown (his traumatic childhood in Texas). Around age forty, he had an epiphany that he was an overweight workaholic, taking handfuls of antacids to calm his stomach, and facing a diagnosis of high blood pressure. He resisted Dr. McNeil's suggestion he get on blood pressure meds. With that suggestion, Dr. McNeil and the entire medical profession became "the enemy," and Dad vowed to improve his life naturally, and to never visit a doctor again.

He also decided to take his work life into his own hands. He aspired to leave the corporate environment and to start his own business. He wanted to be an entrepreneur. He had a partner in mind, a fellow named John Taylor.

Mom was vehemently against him starting his own business with the Taylor guy while we were still in school. Mom wanted a secure income source until we were out of high school. They never fought in front of us. But a fight was brewing, and for Easter break, my brother and I were both sent on the train to Temple, Texas, to stay with Grampa Karels and his new wife Minnie for a few days. John and I were perhaps nine and eleven at the time. Mom said she and Dad would drive down and pick us up mid-week. An elderly train porter promised Mom he'd look after us.

Grampa and Minnie did their best to entertain us, and to stop our thumb-sucking habit. We ate all our meals in the Village Cafe, which Grampa owned, and in which Minnie was the cook and cashier. We watched Grampa play dominoes with his friends in the cafe every afternoon and hung out in his adjacent tool sharpening shop or Minnie's ceramics gift store. And at bedtime, instead of a warm glass of milk we were used to getting, Grampa put hot pepper sauce on our thumbs.

After Mom and Dad picked us up, we drove to Big Bend National Park. Mom and Dad must have resolved their differences on the child–free drive down. Mom won that battle, for Dad continued working at Foxboro, and our life went on as usual.

DAD SPENT THE NEXT DECADE preparing mentally, physically, and spiritually for the next chapter of his life. He devoured books on fitness, nutrition, and living a self-sufficient life. He started jogging before it was popular, converted the grassy backyard into an organic vegetable garden, and became an outings leader for the Sierra Club. He began each day with the positive mantra, "This is the best day ever!"

During those years, we also started to travel more as a family. We took a road trip in our Volkswagen camper every Christmas break, first stopping at Grampa's house for a Christmas Day barbecue dinner, then heading out to explore a different area of America's Wild West: Carlsbad Caverns in New Mexico, the Superstition Mountains in Arizona, or Pikes Peak in Colorado.

Making the annual Christmas trip to Robinson was Mom's suggestion, as Grampa was our only living grandparent. But watching the two men interact, I suspected Dad would have been fine to never see his father again.

On these trips, we saved money by sleeping inside the camper after Dad had permanently removed the middle seat. We also took our first trip out of the country when we took a train trip from Nuevo Laredo to Mexico City, learned a few words of Spanish, and spent a few pesos.

Every summer during my teen years, we also took a week-long wilderness canoe adventure in the Canadian Boundary Waters. And on most weekends between Memorial Day and Labor Day, we canoed on the wild rivers of the midwest: the Current in Missouri, the Tippecanoe in Indiana, the Wisconsin, and the Upper Iowa were favorites.

My brother was my paddling partner, and even though he was younger, he always paddled stern. While floating downstream, often past grazing cattle and swallow's nests on cliffs, we daydreamed.

Joining us on the canoe trips were family, friends, and guests from all walks of life. The regulars who brought their families included Ken, the editor of *Who's Who in the Midwest;* Warren, the president of the Audubon Society; and Eben, a math professor at Northwestern. Four unmarried women: Audrey (an heiress), Marilyn (a college history professor), Mary (a lawyer and author of a book on ethics), and Jean (a librarian) also joined us.

Most were well-traveled, and well-versed in the arts, philosophy, and politics. The conversations around the bonfire were always stimulating, and filled with laughter fueled by shots of port wine. We kids were always included, in both the conversations and the sips of port.

Although many of the guests who signed up for these Sierra Club outings were powerful business leaders seeking a nature break, Dad was always the "alpha male," and the trips he led were immensely popular.

When I was around fourteen, Dad asked my brother and me how we'd like to take a trip around the world. *How could we afford that?* I thought we were poor! My clothes were hand-me-downs from my cousins. We didn't even own a washer or dryer; Mom went to the laundromat weekly. And we only went to the Riverview Amusement Park on "nickel day."

"That's my job to figure out how to pay for it," he said. So for the next several months we planned a three-week itinerary around the world and learned about the countries we planned to visit. Part of the planning was attending travelogues held at nearby Barrington High School. We could afford it, Dad said, by staying in hostels and riding the local buses and trains.

Ultimately we didn't go, but there was a valid reason that had to do with Dad's job. None of us felt let down; it meant a lot to hear, from both my parents, that anything is possible in life, including a trip around the world! (And that we weren't poor!) It planted the seeds of future travel for both of us. From that experience, I learned my dad dreamed big, and my mom supported his dreams. Most of them, that is. Starting his own company would have to wait though.

A Fire in Their Bellies

At THE SAME TIME, DAD'S YOUNGER BROTHER Everett was also entertaining thoughts of starting his own business. An electrical engineer by training, just like Dad, Everett was employed by Avco, an aerospace company that developed missile systems for the Air Force.

Avco was situated on Route 128 in Massachusetts, where, in the late sixties, hundreds of start-up high-tech companies were sprouting up. These companies included Digital Equipment Corporation (DEC), Data General, Wang, Prime, Honeywell, MASSCOMP, and Apollo. The Boston-area universities, including MIT, Boston University, and Harvard, were the incubators of talent for these new tech companies.

In 1971, when the Air Force canceled numerous multi-million dollar contracts that fueled the local New England economy, many of the scientists and engineers testing nuclear weapons at companies such as Avco and Honeywell would soon be out of a job.

In 1972, five thousand of Avco's seven thousand employees were terminated. Many were unemployable since they knew everything about testing nuclear warheads but nothing about the exciting new science of computers. The Information Age was in its infancy.

Everett was retained at Avco, but saw the writing on the wall; he wanted to be either employable or entrepreneurial. In the '70s, both required knowledge of computer hardware or software; bits and bytes were where the new money was. So Everett started learning how to "program." He and Dad discussed the possibility of Everett developing application software and Dad selling it.

In anticipation, in 1975 they came up with a name for their company: Microsystems Engineering Corporation, or MEC for short. The only problem was they had no investment capital, so both had to continue working. But they did have enough seed money to purchase a used PDP-11 minicomputer, made by Digital Equipment Corporation (DEC).

While still working at Avco, Everett bid (as MEC) on a proposal for an altimeter for a NASA space shuttle at Edwards Air Force Base in California. He wrote a proposal to NASA, with a price of $65,000. The backup-bidder was Lockheed, with a bid of $2 million. As the low bidder, MEC was awarded the contract; the procurement officer said he had no other legal option. If MEC failed to deliver the solution in the required six months, they would re-award the contract to Lockheed.

The project was more difficult than Everett anticipated. Dad told him he worked with a brilliant programmer at Staley, one of his corn-processing clients in Decatur, Illinois. This programmer, whose name was Surender, might be willing to give it a try, he said. Surender met with Everett, reviewed the project, and replied, "Sure, I can do this." In less than a week Surender had hand-written the code. He then loaded it into their PDP-11.

Just two weeks after the contract was awarded, the three of them delivered the finished product to NASA at Edwards Air Force Base. The NASA guys took the contraption over to their environmental chamber, hooked it up to the various sensors, and then simulated the hypersonic reentry scenario. To everyone's amazement, it worked!

A few months later they received a check for $65,000. With "a fire in his belly," Everett quit Avco in late 1976 and became a business partner with my father.

(Almost) All Hands on Deck!

To save money, once Dad committed to becoming an entrepreneur, I attended the affordable Cook County School of Nursing on Chicago's West Side instead of the University of Illinois Circle Campus, which did not offer student housing. Mom was a volunteer at Cook County Hospital, had checked out the school, and was hoping I'd consider the more affordable option. "It's the best nursing school in the world!" she assured me.

"You can live in the city, have a room of your own in the nurses' residence, and in three years, you'll have a well-paying job as a nurse!" she said. "Then, if you still want a degree, you can afford to attend the university."

I took her advice, and even though I had no interest in becoming a nurse, I was captivated by the strangeness of that behemoth medical wilderness from the moment I stepped foot in the place. Everything about it was foreign, and fascinating.

My parents gave me forty dollars a month to help pay the six-hundred dollar annual tuition, room, and board. I worked as a student assistant on one of the hospital wards three evenings a week to raise the balance, and develop hands-on skills. In 1974, I graduated from their "diploma program" and passed my nursing boards.

My brother planned to follow in Dad's footsteps when, at seventeen, he applied to and was accepted to IIT's electrical engineering program. If he didn't get a full scholarship, Mom suggested he try to get a nomination from our senator for the U.S. Naval Academy.

"It can't hurt to ask," she said. "You can study engineering at Annapolis and see the world after you graduate. After you've done your service, you can get a job anywhere as an engineer."

Like me, he took her advice and got the nomination. Four years later, in 1977, he graduated and spent the next six years as a commissioned officer seeing the world from the deck of a destroyer in the Middle East.

In one of the dozens of letters he sent me from his ship, he wrote, "One great quality of our family is that we never give up just because the going gets a little rough. Also we stick together as a family and support and help the others no matter what happens. That's the #1 guiding law in my life."

In this spirit, he helped Dad's entrepreneurial dream by loaning him $3,000 from his high school job savings; he continued to support Dad with a second loan of $6,000 in 1976.

Both Dad and Everett were working hard. *Crazy hard.*

Unlike my mother, who would be fine with either feast or famine, Everett's wife Doris was *not* fully "on-deck" with *her* husband's burning desire to be an entrepreneur. Doris, a physicist before she became a wife and mother, preferred order to chaos, yet her life as an entrepreneur's wife was anything but. Instead of smooth sailing, her life more resembled a rowboat adrift in a storm.

The stress of living with a rocket engineer with no regular source of income, and raising two young and rambunctious children became overwhelming. She had a series of mental health crises, and was hospitalized more than once. Their daughter Lisa, who was around ten at the time, recalled her family as one in chaos, and falling apart, as her mother struggled with mental illness while her father struggled to be an entrepreneur.

Everett hired a single mom to feed the kids and help around the house. In the office, he handled support questions, fielded sales inquiries, and wrote an instruction manual. Dad was traveling Monday to Friday. Both tried to keep the other in the loop. And both realized they needed help getting the word out about their product There were now three word processing competitors on the PDP-11.

Finding Surender

T HE PROGRAMMER WHO HAD HELPED MEC win the $65,000 bid at NASA was Surender Goel. He and Dad had met at the Staley corn processing plant in Decatur, Illinois, in 1976. That's where Dad first witnessed Surender's extraordinary programming feats. He would eventually become MEC's third partner, and play an instrumental role in MEC's future success.

Surender grew up in Delhi, India, the youngest of four, and the only one who became a programmer. His father was a fourth-grade teacher making a very modest salary, his mother a stay-at-home mom.

MECollection: Surender Goel

As a teacher, my father had to be proficient in every subject: language, geography, history, and math. He supplemented his income by writing textbooks that were approved for use in all the grammar schools in Delhi. The revenues from those books made it possible for all his children to go to university. In 1967, I graduated with a degree in Mechanical Engineering. After that, I moved to Berkeley, California, where I got my Master's degree in Industrial Engineering.

Moving to California was the first time I had ever left my family or flown in an airplane. I was naive, spoke English poorly, and had no idea what to expect in the United States. But I settled in, made friends, graduated, married my wife Manju in 1971, and was hired by the National Cash Register (NCR), which was headquartered in Dayton, Ohio. We moved to Dayton, where I began work as an Industrial Engineer, and raised three kids: sons Rajeev and Ajay, and daughter Nirupa.

In those early days at NCR, computers were a novelty. They were the size of a dining room table and had one-hundredth the power of today's laptops. One of those computers sat in a corner of my department. I started fooling around with it and asked if I could go to a one-week programming class. After six months I was programming full-time.

NCR sent me to more classes; after those, I became a bona-fide programmer, the only one from the engineering department to have learned these skills. Programmers were ranked Level 1-4; I was the only programmer to achieve the highest rank of 4. I stayed at NCR for seven years, then left to join Staley in Decatur.

At Staley, I was one of many programmers who worked in a big hall. It was in that hall where I met Hank Karels, in early 1976. He mentioned he was trying to start his own business with his brother. He asked if I'd be interested in solving a programming puzzle at NASA, and I said, "Sure, I'll give it a try." Hank paid for my flight to Edwards Air Force Base in California, where Everett showed me the program he was working on. It was a lucrative side job if I could get it to work. And I did, fairly quickly. It was all very exciting!

After the success at NASA, Hank asked if I could develop a general-purpose inventory system for him. I didn't have a computer, so I wrote the code on paper and then drove to Chicago on weekends, where I programmed it into their PDP 11–03, a very small floppy disk-based computer in Hank's basement.

After I completed the inventory system, Hank asked for a mail merge system—an automated program to merge names and addresses and print them, for a bus company in California. They started very simple with 30-line letters for merging and printing. After that, we got a contract from a large insurance firm in New Hampshire for a form letter generator, basically a simple word processor that worked with a database manager. Little by little we developed a rudimentary word processing and database management system.

They called their product MASS-11: Microsystems Administrative Support System for the PDP-11 computer.

Faith, Freedom, and Fun

MY PARENTS HAD VASTLY DIFFERENT upbringings. Dad was a country boy from Texas; Mom was a big-city Chicago girl. Dad was the oldest of three, and spent most of his childhood dreaming of freedom—from his abusive father, the endless farm chores, and the hot summers he and his sister Joyce spent picking cotton in Texas.

At eighteen, he left home to join the Navy. He was stationed at Great Lakes Naval Training Station, just north of Chicago. He was one of thousands of young men being prepared to invade Japan until his mission ended after the atomic bomb was dropped on Hiroshima. After being honorably discharged, he worked various, mostly low-paying jobs while attending the Illinois Institute of Technology (IIT) on Chicago's near South Side. He met Mom at the Aragon Ballroom, where she taught ballroom dancing and he had two left feet. They eloped a few months after they met.

By contrast, Mom was the youngest of nine. Her father, P.J. Kelly, had been a prosperous businessman who had seven patents for valves but had lost everything in the Depression when Mom was two. Unlike her eight siblings, she had never been gifted with new toys and school clothes. She and her sisters were given a nickel every Saturday to ride the El train downtown to attend the matinee at the Chicago Theater.

She understood freedom and knew how to "make do" and have fun with very little. She saw money as transitory. "Sometimes you have it, sometimes you don't. But life goes on. You gotta have faith, laugh at the dumb things, and make the best of it!" She took that upbeat attitude into her marriage.

Mom was raised Catholic; Dad Baptist. But those differences didn't affect their marriage. Each had formed their own beliefs. Mom was more interested in Mary than Jesus and his male disciples. She believed in the "divine feminine," and that women held the true "keys to the kingdom."

Dad prided himself on being "one step beyond" what the Baptist preacher taught on Sunday. He was a spiritual seeker, and from a young age was drawn to the esoteric teachings of mystics and transcendentalists.

My grandmother Johnie was also a spiritual seeker of sorts. She had read the Bible several times, and was a member of the Robinson Methodist church, which her husband built. But she also subscribed to the *Daily Word*, a monthly pamphlet of affirmations and prayers first published by the Unity Church of Christ (not Unitarian) in 1924. She corresponded with Unity's founder, Charles Fillmore, at Unity Village in Kansas, and always carried Unity's *Prayer for Protection* in her purse.

The light of God surrounds us; The love of God enfolds us; The power of God protects us; The presence of God watches over us; Wherever we are, God is.

BY AGE TWENTY-TWO, DAD HAD READ the entire works of the transcendentalist writer Ralph Waldo Emerson. Among Dad's favorite essays was the one on self-reliance, learning to trust yourself, and listening to your inner voice.

"Conformity to social expectations is the greatest obstacle to self-reliance," Emerson wrote. "We must be prepared to go against the grain of popular opinion to follow our intuition." Dad was an advocate of going against the grain!

Two other Ralphs were instrumental in Dad's outlook on life: Ralph Parlette and Ralph Hazlett. Ralph Parlette was the author of *The University of Hard Knocks: The School That Completes Our Education*. The book was compiled in 1917 based on lectures given by Parlette on the Lyceum Circuit that was popular in those days.

Among the lectures included in the book were "Sweet Are the Uses of Adversity," "How We Become Great," "Preparing Children for Life," "Help People to Help Themselves," "You Must Earn What You Own," and "How We Decide Our Destinies: Why the Big Ones Shake Up and the Little Ones Shake Down." Dad often told my brother and me that he would be proud of us if we lived our lives based on the universal truths from Parlette's book.

THE THIRD RALPH WAS THE OCTOGENARIAN Ralph Hazlett, a self-professed expert on human potential and personal growth. In the mid-'70s, Dad had discovered his teachings and reached out to him, offering to create videos of his talks to preserve his legacy. For a couple of years, Mr. Hazlett spent most every Sunday morning sitting in our living room in deep philosophical discussions with Dad. Hazlett died before the project was completed, and never paid Dad for the equipment (cameras, lighting) purchased for the project.

ALTHOUGH MY PARENTS WEREN'T RELIGIOUS *per se*, they wanted my brother and me to learn about God and the great spiritual masters Abraham, Jesus, Buddha, and Mohammed. They sent us to the closest church every Sunday. The first was the Pilgrim Congregational Church, a block from our home, where we were both baptized. (We asked, my parents didn't suggest.) When that church folded, we walked an extra block to St. John the Evangelist, the new Catholic church, which was housed in a circus tent.

They exposed us to other cultures and religions by joining the Chicago International Hospitality Center and inviting Indian doctors, Filipina nurses, and Japanese engineers to our home on weekends and some holidays for several years.

Neither had strong political beliefs, although when we lived in Iowa, they took us to the political rallies of both presidential candidates Richard Nixon and John F. Kennedy. They didn't belong to a political party, but never failed to vote, and never shared with us, or with each other, who they were voting for.

My parents gave each other the freedom to explore and enjoy life on their terms. For Mom, that meant being a fun-loving mother who took her kids on adventures, a gourmet cook, a supportive wife even if it meant primitive camping and exploring wild caves, a neighbor with a sympathetic ear, and an animal-whisperer who provided a backyard haven for wildlife. My brother and I rightly sensed Mom could manage emotionally with or without Dad; she was self-confident, and very little rocked her world, as long as he brought home the bacon!

For Dad, freedom meant jogging around the neighborhood at 6:00 a.m. before it was fashionable, leading Sierra Club canoe outings, spending time in his organic flower and vegetable garden, photographing nature, and reading books on the unlimited potential of the human mind and expanding consciousness. To him, the universe was a great unknown, and he desired to explore every aspect of it, seeking the outer limits of possibility.

MEC, the company he and his brother started, would be a superb vehicle to help him with this exploration, and once she was on board, Mom was the best support system an entrepreneur could ask for. She understood Dad's ambitions and his spiritually-seeking nature, and never discouraged or ridiculed him. She made it clear she would be his rock whether he was successful or not.

A Unique Niche

IN THOSE EARLY DAYS, SURENDER OFTEN spent weekends with my parents. He stayed in our home, and Mom and Dad frequently took him downtown to Chinatown for dinner on Saturday nights. After dinner, Dad would drive north along the lake and they would then have coffee and dessert at Lutz's Bakery, a German cafe and bakery on Montrose Avenue. I occasionally joined them if I wasn't working.

As a new nurse with my own interesting life in Chicago's largest medical center, I had little curiosity about Dad's new business. My world consisted of nurses, doctors, and patients with gunshot wounds, drug overdoses, and cardiac arrests. Word processing, database managers, and minicomputers were foreign concepts.

If anyone asked what my father did for a living, I said he invented something called a "word processor." I later grew to understand that there were many word processors on the market before ours.

I was also unaware, at the time, that three types of computers could be purchased. The most expensive were *mainframe* computers, which were high-end commercial computers designed for high-speed calculations and database management. They were produced by companies such as IBM, NCR, Control Data Corporation, and

Honeywell, and sold to large corporations.

The next class was the minicomputers, midrange computers with a price tag under $30,000. The most popular in 1979 were DEC's PDP series of minicomputers and the Data General Nova. Multiple users could access the computer and share data. These minicomputers were primarily purchased by corporations, universities, or small businesses.

Also available were home computers, most notably the Apple II, the Altair 8800, the Commodore PET, TRS-80, and the Atari 400. Offering games and basic programming capabilities, they appealed primarily to computer geeks and could be purchased by mail-order from computer magazines or in stores such as ComputerLand. Except for Apple II, most sold for under $200. The first IBM personal computer would not be released until 1981, with a starting price of $1,565.

In 1979, an estimated 250,000 people were using a standalone word processor in the U.S., mostly in large corporations or law firms. They were a novel concept in most companies then; most secretaries still used the IBM Selectric typewriter, which had been released in 1961.

In June of 1979, the relatively new International Word Processing Association held their convention in Chicago; twenty-thousand people attended. On display were optical scanners, facsimile machines, high-speed printers, micrographic equipment, and computer terminals.

One of the first systems marketed as a word processor was IBM's MT/ST, or the Magnetic Tape/Selectric typewriter. Released in 1964, it was a machine in which text could be edited without printing out a hard copy; the text was stored on a half-inch magnetic tape.

More than a decade later came a product called Electric Pencil for the Altair, an early word processor for home computers. It was also the first to feature "word wrap," in which lines are adjusted as words are inserted and deleted.

In 1977, Apple released its Apple II microcomputer, with a 4K memory card. The price tag of $1,295 was too expensive for most middle-class households and didn't include the monitor or disk drive. It wasn't until 1979 that the AppleWrite word processor was released.

That same year, MicroPro released a word processor called WordStar for the CPM/M-80, later DOS, operating system. Wordstar became a bestseller on the IBM PC; millions of copies were sold to individuals in retail stores such as Radio Shack or ComputerLand.

In 1980, DEC released their standalone word processor, a floppy disk-based DECmate computer that came bundled with basic word processing software. It was followed by the DECmate II, III, and III+.

The following year, Atari released a product called Atari Word Processor. Then Commodore released the Commodore 64, featuring a word processor called Paper Clip. Thirty million Commodores were sold between 1981 and 1993. The use of simple word processors on home computers was exploding.

Then came small-storage, single-user systems that pioneered the way for word processing in the office: Wang, NBI, Lanier, CPT, and Vydec were among the best known. Wang was the most successful, becoming a $3 billion company employing 33,000 people at its peak in the '80s.

The products mentioned above were all stand-alone dedicated systems: one machine, one user. MASS-11 was a *shared* word processor, one where several people could work on one "host" PDP-11 computer simultaneously. We had a unique niche!

Sitting on a Gold Mine

D EC WAS THE KING OF THE MINICOMPUTER WORLD and was in a good position to sell thousands of PDP-11s as long as there were software developers such as MEC writing value-added application software such as MASS-11.

Hundreds of software entrepreneurs tossed their hats in the ring in search of software success on that PDP-11; MEC was among them. One magazine editor likened the scene to the 1890s Gold Rush.

The early purchasers of the PDP-11 were research and scientific centers within corporations and universities. The concept of multiple users creating, editing, and *sharing* documents on a PDP-11 was still a novel one in 1979, and many system managers feared that putting word processing software on their computer would bring the system to a grinding halt. Increased memory, storage space, and tight programming were key to making "shared" word processing a success.

Besides targeting research and scientific firms, DEC had a network of resellers, also known as OEMs, who sold specialized turnkey systems to, for example, law firms, insurance firms, and accounting firms. The brothers placed a small ad in *Computer World* magazine looking for DEC resellers who might be interested in including their MASS-11 word processor as part of their turnkey systems; they received 300 inquiries. Both gave demos to dealers who visited their Streamwood office on a regular basis. Within a year, MEC had thirty-one DEC resellers on board.

Many resellers made the trip to MEC's two-room home office to sign on the dotted line and then learn the product from Dad or Everett. To celebrate their new "partnership," Dad would invite new resellers to join him and Mom for dinner, often at their favorite restaurants in the city. He often gave them a quick tour of downtown Chicago after dinner, driving along the lakefront, past Buckingham Fountain, so they could view the stunning skyline at night. Dad and Mom never grew tired of the view. If my parents were unavailable, Dad occasionally asked *me* to take them out, and if I wasn't working, I willingly agreed.

"My daughter's a Chicago tour guide," he'd proudly tell them. I wasn't an official tour guide, but besides nursing, I was a trained docent at the Chicago Historical Society, leading both gallery tours and historic neighborhood tours. I'd always ask these distributors what they were most interested in seeing, or eating.

On one of these occasions I took two resellers from South Dakota to Miomir's Serbian Club on the north side of Chicago. The only request from these guys was a restaurant that they wouldn't find in North Dakota. There were hundreds that could fit that bill, but I chose Miomir's because it had a gypsy orchestra.

There, the resellers and I shared a heaping platter of grilled meats, vegetables, and rice. After finishing off a bottle of wine, one of the resellers leaned over and said, "You know your dad is sitting on a gold mine, don't you? Office automation is all the rage, and MASS-11 is going to take off like a rocket and make your family rich. *Very rich!*"

The other guy nodded his head and added, "The digital revolution has begun! DEC is going to sell thousands of those damn PDP-11's. And every company is going to want a word processor on theirs. Standalone word processors like NBI and Wang will go the way of the dodo once companies see the cost savings of shared word processing on a minicomputer."

"Yeah," the first one agreed. "*Shared* word processing is definitely the wave of the future. All MEC has to do is ride that wave and hang on."

Blood rushed to my face. I didn't know how to respond—with thanks, humility, or astonishment. I felt comfortable discussing the *American* revolution, but was clueless about this *digital* revolution they referred to. I thought about their predictions as I drove them back to their hotel in my eight-year-old Oldsmobile Cutlass; it was Dad's former company car. *Was MEC really poised for that kind of success?*

Maybe, I thought, I should show a little more interest in what they were doing.

The Paperless Office

TWO MOMENTOUS EVENTS OCCURRED for the Karels brothers in 1979. The first was an invitation to the grand opening of *The Paperless Office* in Washington D.C. It was a gala event held May 3 and 4 on the plaza of the infamous Watergate Hotel, where the future of technology was on full display. Office automation products from sixteen firms, including MEC's MASS-11, were represented.

Dad said he had extra tickets for the event and asked if I'd like to go, and I did. Dad, Everett, Surender, Mom, and I attended the event on Saturday.

We enjoyed the day immensely and had lunch on the Watergate Plaza. Unfortunately, we weren't invited to the Paperless Office gala reception held Saturday evening, where the keynote speakers were Ronald Reagan *and* futurist author Alvin Toffler. Toffler had just published his new book *The Third Wave,* and all attendees were given an advance copy. The evening reception was attended by reporters from most of the nation's major newspapers.

"World Without Paper!" was the headline in the Sunday business edition of the *Washington Post.* The event made a huge impression on everyone who attended, especially Dad.

The founder of the Paperless Office was computer whiz and serial entrepreneur Larry Stockett, a 32-year-old multi-millionaire who was also the president of the consulting firm MicroNet. Micronet advised businesses on how to automate their offices and did market research for computer firms.

Stockett was quoted as saying, "I have $2 million worth of equipment here: computer output microfilm recorders, optical scanners, desktop microfiche display screens, word processing software, and minicomputers. They are linked in a system that quickly converts paper business correspondence, market research, personnel records—all kinds of paper—into computer talk so that the paper can be thrown away. The Paperless Office is the office of the near future. All our equipment is state of the art!

"The Paperless Office," Stockett continued, "could have a major impact on the pillars of the American economy: secretaries!" For National Secretaries Week, he proclaimed, "With new tools such as word processors, secretaries would not be forced into the same drudgery as with using a typewriter. There will still be lots of keyboard work," he said, "but not quite so many repetitive, boring tasks. No more typing the same letter fifty times! Office automation tools such as word processors will liberate secretaries."

Stockett noted that factory output was up 84% in the past decade, but office efficiency only rose by 4%. He proclaimed that would all change with office automation.

He told the *Washington Post* reporter he was attempting to integrate the concept of a paperless office into his lifestyle as well, so he could work remotely. "I have a computer terminal in my home," he said, "which I can connect via telephone with the office information bank."

Word Processing. Office Automation. Paperless Offices. These keywords were exactly what Dad and Everett were promoting! Both realized they were on the cusp of something big—a digital revolution that could change the way Americans worked. They had just met the office automation prophet Larry Stockett; the brothers saw themselves as office automation pioneers. With their word processor installed on a PDP-11 computer at the Paperless Office, they were eager to help spread Stockett's office automation credo far and wide. *They could dare to dream!*

THE SECOND MOMENTOUS EVENT was in December 1979, when the brothers leased a spacious suite in a new office building in suburban Hoffman Estates. Suite 400, at 2400 W. Hassell Road, had four large offices with windows, a central area, and a warehouse in the back. It was conveniently located just twenty minutes from O'Hare Airport, right off the expressway. Dad would tell future visitors, "There's only one red light between the airport and us."

On December 30, they held an open house for friends, family, former coworkers, neighbors, and clients. Surender and his family drove up. It was a well-attended and festive end-of-year event, with catered food and drinks. After three years of hard work and perseverance, they had confidence that their product was on its way to being a success. All made a toast to success in the decade ahead.

To MEC! To The '80s! To The Information Age!

More than a dozen of those friends, neighbors, and family in attendance would eventually be employed by MEC—as writers, trainers, sales reps, shippers, printers, support staff, or managers. *I would be one of them.*

As MEC grew, it would lease all eight suites of that building, *as well as* an entire new building across the street. But on New Year's Day 1980, it was just two-and-a-half men—Dad, Everett, and part-time Surender—each hoping that MEC would be the one business out of twenty that would someday achieve the lofty status of sales over $2 million per year. They had survived four years!

1980: Catching the Third Wave

D AD AND EVERETT WERE BOTH GIVEN pre-release copies of Alvin Toffler's new book *The Third Wave* at the Paperless Office event. And both had completed it before they moved into the new office space, and were riveted by what they read.

More than a decade before the 'World Wide Web' was invented, Toffler predicted the "third wave" would usher in a tidal wave of changes in the office environment. This "third wave," or *Information Age,* he said, would replace the "second wave," or *Industrial Age.*

Like Larry Stockett, he predicted the word processor, also referred to as a "smart typewriter" or a "text editor," would be just one of several new office technologies that would rock the conventional "second wave office," and that the largest makers of computers, including IBM and Exxon, would compete for what could be a $10 billion market in the upcoming '80s decade.

Dad and Everett were also intrigued about his predictions in the chapter entitled "The Electronic Cottage," where Toffler espoused the concept of telecommuting, a revolutionary concept where employees could work out of their homes if given the tools needed to be productive: a terminal, a modem, a phone line, and a connection.

Toffler predicted this new work environment would result in

positive changes for humanity—enhancing work, play, and the raising of families. The electronic cottage concept would, according to Toffler, "reduce commuting, energy consumption, pollution of the environment, and building investments and maintenance." It could also enable mothers to work from home, he wrote, leading to "greater community and family stability, greater participation in community life, and a boost in productivity."

Among his many predictions were cheaper electronics and computers, de-massification of the media, and electronic storage of all media that could be accessed by anyone. He even devoted several pages in his book to the Paperless Office in Washington D.C. Toffler concluded by predicting the Information Age would change the way of working, loving, and living.

After reading and rereading the book, especially the part where he wrote that workers would be more creative if they could work on their terms, both agreed that MEC's new goal was to be financially successful while *also* achieving and maintaining a company culture of empowerment.

Dad bought a dozen copies of the book, took them on his travels, and passed them out to every potential client he met. Like the Paperless Office and its near futuristic view of office automation, Dad and Everett became "third wave" evangelists.

We're surfing the wave! Even though they were only a two-and-a-half-man company, the future described in Toffler's second book wasn't *shocking* but one worth celebrating. His predictions would define MEC's trajectory for the next decade.

DEC's NEWEST AND GREATEST MINICOMPUTER, the VAX, developed in 1977, would also play a major role in MEC's future success. The VAX-780 was a 32-bit minicomputer that was revolutionary in terms of its power, price, and potential. It offered upward mobility from the PDP-11 and was considered the most successful computer in history.

MEC's engineering customers, as well as the research departments of universities, were upgrading to VAXes as fast as they could get their hands on them.

Surender recalled, "Hank asked if I could make MASS-11 work on the VAX. MEC couldn't afford one, so Hank made a deal with Purdue University, which was using MASS-11 on a handful of PDP-11 computers. Hank's friend and Foxboro colleague, Al Rayshich, was a Purdue graduate and knew many key players there. We gave them a site license for their PDP-11s in exchange for using their VAX for development. They put MASS-11 on at least a hundred PDP-11s nationwide, and we got MASS-11 working on the VAX."

Dad then struck a deal with a very large and prestigious law firm in Ohio, one that was considering migrating from their standalone Wang word processors to a VAX with MASS-11 for their office automation needs. Their only objection was that MASS-11 lacked the more sophisticated legal features they currently had on their Wang system. *Could MEC provide those features they needed?*

Dad asked if they were willing to write the functional specs, and they agreed. Surender, who had moved back to Dayton and had returned to NCR, told Dad it would be difficult for him to program using a 300-baud modem. So Dad asked the law firm if they would let Surender use their VAX for developing the next version of MASS-11, which would include their legal specs, and they agreed. The estimated time to finish the job was six months.

Dad and Surender spent many weekends at the law firm reviewing and programming the legal features they had requested. If everything worked to their satisfaction, this large law firm would be a valuable legal reference.

MECollection: Surender Goel

Someone would let us into the computer room on Saturday morning and we loaded the tape with the source code. I programmed and Hank tested. On Saturday night, we removed the tape and deleted it from their system so nobody could copy our source code. On Sunday morning, we loaded it up again, then took it down when we left Sunday afternoon.

We finished the job in three months. The law firm was very happy with the finished product and with the speed of implementation. Hank and I then realized there was a market for a general-purpose word processing product on the VAX that was not being met by DEC. We figured, if a big law firm is happy with MASS-11, maybe we could sell it to other large corporations, even Fortune 500 companies!

While we were together, Hank and I dreamed big, and we both hoped MEC would make enough money to bring me on board full-time. That was a big 'if' at the time. Over breakfast, we talked about developing the best word processor in the world, one so powerful that it justified the purchase of a VAX to run it.

The brothers' optimism was short-lived when, in the fall of 1980, they were sued for commercial fraud in Federal Court in Washington, D.C.! The lawsuit was brought by a lawyer who used MASS-11 on his PDP-11 for his small law practice. In the lawsuit, the lawyer claimed the system did not live up to what was promised. He was using an early version developed by Everett. The lawsuit put a hard stop to their forward momentum as entrepreneurs.

During that time, neither brother took a salary. An added expense was that Everett had to fly frequently to Washington, D.C. to attend court hearings. The cost of airfare, hotels, and meals quickly added up. They couldn't tighten their belts much more and survive.

An added complication was that, as long as they were being sued, they couldn't apply for any business loans to grow the company. Fortunately, Al Rayshich, Dad's former boss at Foxboro, came to their rescue and lent them $50,000.

"You've worked too hard to lose it all like this, Hank," he said. "This loan will buy you some time. Use it however you need to, to pay the rent, buy some ads, or just pay the airfare to Washington D.C. during the trial. MASS-11 is a winner; the sales will come!"

With Al's financial help and optimism, the brothers vowed to stick to their goal of developing and selling *the best word processor in the world!*

Unsolicited Advice

S HORTLY AFTER THE NEWS OF THE LAWSUIT, I had a conversation with Dave Aberson, the lawyer Dad and Everett had hired to represent them in federal court. Dave was from Encino, California, used MASS-11 in his immigration law practice, and was thrilled with the new legal features that Surender had recently completed. Dave insisted it was a bogus lawsuit; he would happily and confidently defend MEC *pro bono*.

It was the first time I had met Dave, who, with his bald head and neatly trimmed salt-and-pepper beard, appeared to be in his late fifties. He was a colorful raconteur who enjoyed the free-wheeling conversations held at my parent's home, where every subject under the sun was tossed about. Dave loved discussing technology, the Information Age, and *The Third Wave* book with Dad.

Like a good lawyer, Dave asked me a lot of questions, many of them personal. I told him that I'd just broken up with a surgical resident when I realized there was no future for us. I was the wrong nationality and religion; it was earth-shattering to hear that.

Then I told him I had recently applied to, and been accepted into, two law schools downtown. After a few minutes, Dave asked *why* I wanted to be a lawyer, and I replied, "Maybe I can represent my family's business if they're sued."

Dave, who had been a lawyer for over thirty years, replied, "Let me handle the lawsuits, Carol."

Then he asked, "Do you have a *passion* for the law?"

"Not really," I replied. I needed a distraction from my recent breakup.

Dave continued, "Three intense years of study, then the bar exam, paying off hefty student loans? I don't mean to discourage you from the law. It pays well, and there's job security, but what your dad is doing is fun, creative, dynamic, exciting, *and the future*! If I was younger, I'd leave law in a hot minute to be an entrepreneur in this field. I just think you'd have a helluva lot more fun, and it would be far more interesting, if you worked for him, than going to law school."

I'd never considered working in a business, let alone for my father, who I hardly knew due to him being a workaholic. What little I knew of computers, software, word processing, and office automation didn't light my fire. But neither had the thought of attending nursing school a decade earlier. I also doubted that my skills as a nurse would transfer to computers, software, or whatever he did. But at twenty-eight, I was at a crossroads, and all ears. *What could I lose?*

Over dessert, Dave said, "From our conversation, I gather you're burned out from working as a nurse. And good decisions aren't made when you are in that state. I know this is presumptuous of me, but let me suggest you take whatever money you've saved for law school and take a trip overseas. Eat exotic foods. Visit exotic temples. Hang out with people who dress differently than you. I have always found that travel is great for sorting out your life."

His unsolicited advice to travel was *exactly* what I needed at that moment! The saying 'Travel Broadens One' applied to me. My first trip to the British Isles in 1976 inspired me to get a BA in History. The trip to Mexico in 1977 led to my learning Spanish by immersion and eventually becoming a nurse translator in the U of I OB-GYN clinic.

My trip to the Soviet Union in 1979 revealed to me the crushing consequences of Communism. I studied both Russian and American history after that.

I told Dave I had recently looked over a travel brochure from the Chicago Council on Foreign Relations featuring a two-week trip to Egypt. What could be more exotic than sailing down the Nile while surrounded by pyramids and men wearing *galabeyas*?

Dad didn't miss an opportunity.

"If that interests you, I'll pay for half of it if you'll consider writing a MASS-11 beginner's manual for secretaries."

"You've got to be kidding Dad," I replied. "How could I, an ER nurse, possibly write such a manual?"

"For Chrissakes, Carol," he replied. "You're limiting yourself by saying you're *just a nurse*. I wish I had *half* your talent. Your skills as a nurse could transfer to any profession.

"Learning MASS-11 and writing a manual about it may or may not the right career move for you," he added. "But right now we urgently need a beginner's manual written. And I'm starting to think you may be the best goddamn person to write it. I'm not suggesting you quit your nursing job. This manual should take a couple of months at most."

In high school, I aspired to be a journalist. I was the News Editor of the high school paper. I also had a weekly column with a by-line for the local newspaper all through high school. But I hadn't written anything in years. Being a nurse left no time for anything but writing nursing care plans and nursing notes.

Mom, who was serving dessert, listened intently. She knew I'd always wanted to be a writer.

"It may open doors you never dreamed of," she said. "It's only three months. You can't go wrong. And maybe, after you write *this* manual, you'll write about something more interesting. You just gotta jump in the river and get your feet wet."

Dad's suggestion, and Mom's encouragement, led me to eventually accept his offer. The deal was that I would continue working as an ER nurse in the evenings, and work at MEC a few days a week. No salary, just the half payment for the trip to Egypt until the project was finished.

In early December of 1980, I "jumped in" and started working part-time at MEC. It was a decision that eventually led to the end of one exciting chapter of my life (nursing) and the beginning of an even more exciting one (office automation), but only after an exotic interlude in Egypt.

Modern-Day Sisyphus

SUSPECTED THE REASON DAD WAS so gung-ho about my writing a beginner's manual was that the current one, written by Everett, was very technical and filled with computer jargon more targeted toward engineers and scientists. Dad had said they were both overwhelmed with phone questions on the basics—how to use the simplest features of the product.

Everett bristled whenever customers complained on the phone. "The secretaries say the documentation is too technical." Dad tried to make Everett understand that someone was needed to write in plain English, *for secretaries,* not engineers. It would be the secretaries, *not their bosses,* who would be using MASS-11, he said. After all, men didn't type in the '80s. If the secretaries weren't happy, their use of MASS-11 would be short-lived.

I imagined Everett, an electrical engineer who had started his career as a technical writer, was somewhat miffed that his business partner/brother wanted to hire his daughter, an ER nurse, to replace him in this task. I was certain he secretly hoped I'd last just long enough to finish the manual.

Dad handed me the instructions Everett had written for secretaries, explaining what MASS-11 was:

MASS-11 stands for Microsystems Administrative Support System. Written in the Fortran language, it's a command-driven shared-logic word/list processing system for the RSTS operating system, which works exclusively on Digital Equipment Corporation's PDP-11 minicomputer. When using MASS-11, you will be typing on a keyboard attached to a "dumb" VT-100 terminal. It supports ANSI escape codes so you can see where the cursor is on the screen at all times, and it allows for smooth scrolling. Multiple users can connect to the host computer.

I didn't understand a word of it and got nervous. "I'm not sure I can learn this. Do secretaries understand it?"

"Hell, no! But that's how Everett writes," he replied. "He thinks everyone's a goddamn rocket scientist. This will make secretaries bawl their eyes out, even though MASS-11 will ultimately free them."

"Free them from what?"

"From all the repetitive typing they do all day on their IBM Selectric typewriters," he said. "How would you like to spend your entire morning taking dictation, then your entire afternoon transcribing a seventy-page document only to have your boss show up at four and say, 'Sorry, but I made lots of changes, and I need it by noon tomorrow for a 1:00 p.m. meeting. And this time, can you make sure everything is spelled correctly?' Using a typewriter would require them to retype the whole damned thing until he changes his mind again," Dad explained.

"How do you know what secretaries do all day?" I asked.

"Because *I* was that asshole boss who couldn't type and endlessly marked up documents, until my secretary, Betty, put me in my place by explaining what the secretarial pool had to go through when I made all those changes. When I became Branch Manager, I proposed *she* become the Office Manager, because she was the best qualified. But upper management wouldn't hear of it. 'A woman has never been an Office Manager. That's a position for a man!' But I fought for her, and Betty became the first female office manager at Foxboro. And she was a damned good one!"

In my naivete about the office world, I didn't know *what* secretaries did other than type letters, make coffee, and answer phones. It was similar to what I had thought about nurses when I was in high school—that they made beds, gave bed baths and shots, and took orders from doctors. The only thing nurses had in common with secretaries at the time was that they were primarily female professionals, and their superiors were primarily male.

Being a secretary, I thought, reminded me of the character Sisyphus in Greek mythology—one tasked with pushing a boulder up a mountain but, when he reached the top, it rolled down, and he had to start all over. Every day. For eternity. Typing and retyping.

THAT FIRST WEEK DAD TAUGHT ME MASS-11 and answered my few questions. There weren't many because I didn't know what to ask.

He started with the basics. "There's a terminal (monitor) and a keyboard." After he turned on the monitor, a cascading menu of options was displayed on the screen: Create New Document, followed by Edit, Rename, Delete, and Copy Document. Dad pressed "Create New" and a blank screen appeared.

"Just begin typing as fast as you can. It will keep up with you," he said.

He, who could only hunt and peck, was just typing gibberish, which automatically wrapped to the next line. *That was interesting!* No stopping to hit a carriage return bar.

"Now watch this," he said. "If you want to add a word in the middle of a sentence, just put the cursor on the space and start typing. Everything moves over automatically. It's called 'Quick Edit mode.' Try it."

I felt like Eliza Doolittle in *My Fair Lady,* learning a whole new language, not from Henry Higgins, but from Henry Karels. Unlike Eliza, who was learning how to properly speak the English language, I was learning the language of word processing: 'Headers and Footers, Search and Replace. Copy or Cut—then PASTE!'

No more carriage returns, ribbon changes, or Wite-Out. No more adding a new sheet of paper at the end of every page, or retyping the entire document if I changed my mind. No more throwing wads of wasted paper on the floor.

Damn! Damn! *Damn!* as Henry Higgins would shout. I realized that these were the reasons I hadn't done any creative writing since high school. Getting my thoughts onto paper was just too frustrating. Writing by hand with a pen was too slow for my thought process; fixing mistakes on the typewriter interrupted my train of thought.

Dad said I'd have to use MASS-11 to write the documentation since there were no typewriters in the office.

No. Typewriters. *Ever. Again.* Yes! By George, *I got it!*

1981: A New Sense of Direction

ON JANUARY 20, 1981, RONALD REAGAN was inaugurated as President of the United States. At the time, the U.S. was in a recession that would last until 1983. But for the rest of the 1980s, the economy would explode.

Three days after his inauguration, I left for Egypt, and had a wonderful adventure cruising on the Nile, exploring Cairo, Luxor, Karnak, and the Valley of the Kings. Our guide Nabil was a retired Egyptian Air Force pilot turned Egyptologist; he had the gift of transporting you into ancient and romantic worlds with his stories. Horus, Tutankhamun, Ramses, and Nefertiti were just some of the Egyptian characters he introduced to us.

Egyptian men, young and old, as well as children of all ages, tried to sell us everything they could get their hands on: papyrus paintings of Isis, *scarabs*, spices, gold cartouches, *jalabiyas*, leather slippers, glass sand bottles, and hand-sewn dolls, always with a big smile. "Ancient" tomb treasures were the most popular. Nobody begged; everyone was selling. Instead of brushing them away, I bought their trinkets. They were all giving me a lesson on being an entrepreneur.

It was a fun and informative trip, and just what I needed before I joined my father on this entrepreneurial odyssey!

WHEN I RETURNED FROM EGYPT, my head was clear, I had a new sense of direction, and I dove head first into writing the beginners manual. Two other part-time employees started the same day: my parents' next-door neighbor Lisa, who had been hired for data entry three mornings a week; and Terry, a relative who was a Chicago cop on short-term disability. Dad found useful work for him, as he did for many family members and neighbors who needed help throughout his life.

I asked Dad if there was a book on word processing that I could reference. He said no, that *I* was writing the book. This was before the Internet, so I couldn't just search "word processor" and discover other products such as Electric Pencil, Wang, and Wordstar. There was no mention of word processing in the *Encyclopedia Britannica*, which was the Wikipedia of those days. The library had no books on the subject, nor did the local book store. I just got puzzled looks when I asked if they had any books on word processing.

Perhaps there wasn't a book on word processing *in 1981*, but if I had waited, an excellent one by Peter A. McWilliams, released in 1982, quickly became a *New York Times* bestseller! In one year, "word processing" had gone from obscure to almost a household word. But by then, I had finished writing my MASS-11 beginner's manual. And, I only learned about the McWilliams book a decade later.

I wasn't technical and I didn't read computer magazines or tech journals. So I knew nothing about word processing in 1981 as I worked diligently at writing documentation for what, *I thought,* was the first word processor known to man, on the only computer I'd ever heard of: DEC's PDP-11.

Over the next few weeks I would come to understand that a word processor is a noun phrase that can apply to a person, a machine, or a software program. After understanding the function of a word processor, I learned there were others, but what made MASS-11 different was that ours was a *shared* word processor, not a *standalone* one like Wang, Electric Pencil, and WordStar. Because no diskettes were involved, secretaries didn't have to worry about misplacing, deleting, or storing diskettes—a common fear among all, I later learned.

SURENDER MAY HAVE BEEN SURFING the "third wave" as he worked from his home in Dayton and transferred his code by 300-baud modem to the home office via phone line. But I was still operating in the "second wave."

I used a lot of gas when I reverse-commuted an hour from the city to MEC's office in the northwest suburbs every morning. I worked at MEC till two, then drove back into the city for my 3:00-to-11:00 p.m. ER job at the University of Illinois Hospital, where I changed into scrubs, and changed gears from 'cut-and-paste' to 'cuts-and-scrapes.'

Every day, and occasionally late into the night at MEC's office, I practiced using MASS-11 and wrote about how to use it. It wasn't creative writing by any stretch, just, "Press this key. Observe how the text shifts to the right. Now press this key, followed by that key."

Just as I thought I was almost finished with the manual, Surender added new features or fixed a feature that required changing the instructions. After three months, I worried I'd *never* finish the manual! But I just kept at it.

Writing documentation, I quickly discovered, was a lonely job. I was often the only one in the office, sometimes working late into the night when I had an evening off from nursing. Working seven days a week, my only social life was the Chinese buffets I organized every Saturday night in the ER. *All-you-can-eat for $5!* I would order twenty or so dishes from Wing Wah in Chinatown, pick up the food on my dinner break, and set it out on the tables in the Psychiatric room. All the on-call docs came down for it.

Besides *writing* the manual, I was also responsible for *producing* it. That meant I had to print out what I wrote on a line printer, deliver it to a typesetter (a human), and then create a "mechanical" from the sheets of type. Dad gave me the tools I needed to create the mechanical—a light board, an X-acto knife, a rub-down tool, a blue pencil, and wax adhesive.

Once the mechanicals were complete and Dad approved them, I drove them to the local printer, who photographed the camera-ready copy with a stat camera, produced plates, and then printed the pages, uncollated, on a small offset printer. This very detailed process, and all the terms associated with it, was new, and eye-opening for me as well.

Finally, the books had to be assembled. Dad had set up several wooden sawhorses covered with plywood in the warehouse, where I laid out all the pages, perhaps sixty at the start, then went round and around the table, manually collating, page-by-page, one book at a time. I then three-hole punched the books and put each in a three-ring caramel-colored binder. I then inserted a pre-cut, pre-printed card into the spine, which indicated this was the *MASS-11 Beginners Manual.* Each book took fifteen minutes to assemble. Thankfully, Dad soon hired another neighbor to take over that job.

Thoughts Become Things, So. . .

O UR NICHE MARKET IN 1981 was a mid-size office, university, or high-tech lab with a PDP-11 computer. Their secretaries typically typed documents, form letters, and labels using the IBM Selectric, which was still the most widely used office machine for creating correspondence, legal documents, insurance contracts, and research papers. It would be discontinued in 1986 after twenty-five years and thirteen million had been sold.

Office managers or system managers would make the buying decisions; their secretaries would be the primary users. Our MASS-11 software would be sharing the computer with other applications such as spreadsheets, the most commonly used computer application before word processing.

Dad and Everett were in and out of the office, handling the phones, training, and selling. Dad spent most of his time giving demos at government agencies in Washington, D.C., aerospace companies in California, the military and space industry in Texas, and high-tech firms in Massachusetts.

As a result of his travels, customers who purchased MASS-11 in early 1981 included MASS General Hospital, MIT, and Raytheon in Massachusetts; Lawrence Livermore Labs, Hughes Aircraft, and

Lockheed in California; Micronet (the Paperless Office guy), the U.S. Fish and Wildlife Service, the U.S.D.A, and the U.S. Postal Service in Washington, D.C.; and NASA, Fort Sam Houston, and Lackland Air Force Base in Texas. The decision-makers were primarily Information Technology (IT) managers.

In the office, phones went unanswered, messages piled up, support questions went unanswered, and inquiries were not followed up. When all three of us were in the office, which was rare, we'd go out to lunch at a Greek diner called Scorpio's, and I'd listen as each brought the other up-to-date and prioritized projects.

At one lunch session, Dad had expressed concern that Everett was keeping a private notebook of his conversations with Surender and customers but didn't share that information with him. Dad added that he knew clients were reporting problems and shipping errors, and that there were unreturned calls from potential clients, but no log of any of these. When the three of us went out for lunch, Dad worked diligently, and diplomatically, between bites of gyros and Greek salad, to get Everett to recall conversations he'd had, or deals he'd made, when Dad was on the road.

"I just spoke to the decision maker at Hughes Aircraft," Dad said, "and he hasn't gotten the demo tape yet. I promised that a month ago."

"You'll have to ask the girls in shipping about that," Everett replied.

"I did," Dad replied. "They said they didn't know anything about it. And I just got off the phone with the decision maker at the U.S. Fish and Wildlife office. He's been testing MASS-11 list processing and has some technical issues. Last we spoke, you said you'd give him a call to walk him through it. That was over a month ago, and he still hasn't heard from you. He's pissed, and so am I. In the meantime, the Word-11 people are trying to get in the door." [Word-11 was a competitor on the PDP-11.]

Dad continued with his frustrations. "And our good friend Dr. Will at MIT said you told him you'd be adding some custom features for him by the end of the month. When were you planning to tell me about that decision? I felt like a fool talking to him, saying I wasn't sure that was something we could do, and having no idea what you'd promised."

Everett was rattled about the lawsuit, and his domestic situation was less than ideal. Doris was back home, but both kids, now teens, were in and out of rehab programs. Lisa spent her teen years recovering in a group home in Minnesota. She recalled, "I was wild and independent. My mom was home, and doing well, and my dad said it was best I stayed in Minnesota."

If Dad criticized him for anything, Everett's lower lip would quiver and he'd tersely respond, "I'm just one man." And I often thought that Everett believed he *was* just a one-man company. He didn't see the need to share what was in his business diary with his business partner.

At one lunch, Everett criticized Dad for spending too much money on fancy ads and manuals. Dad had recently hired a local graphic designer to design an ad, and of course, we paid a typesetter for the "fancy" manual I was writing. Everett surmised that customers would be just as happy with his hi-tech instructions printed off the sheet feeder printer and corner-stapled instead of three-hole punched, typeset instructions in a vinyl binder. Dad reminded Everett that we had been getting fewer support calls since we started shipping the new manuals.

I listened and learned. Most of the conversations were technical, but some were on marketing strategies, which I understood more. Dad wanted to project the best image possible of MEC. We had received over a hundred leads from our recent ad, but Dad pointed out there was no system in place to respond to these leads.

Everett, the frugal and technical brother, was often uncomfortable with Dad's spending to enhance MEC's image. He had no qualms about spending money on Surender; Surender was a genius, a rare bird that both agreed was worth the expense.

"Surender ran rings around the other programmers at Staley," Dad recalled. "You can give him any problem, and he can figure it out. What would take others weeks or months, Surender did in days or hours!"

I wasn't getting paid yet, and I felt sure Everett would be happy to hear me say I was turning in the towel. Who, besides me, was willing to work for nothing?

In time Everett became more comfortable with Dad's mantras, "You Have to Spend Money to Make Money," and "Thoughts Become Things," so think big thoughts.

Training on the Horizon

THE BEGINNER MANUAL WAS HELPFUL, but most new customers now requested training. A training session for a dozen users could last three days, too long for either of the brothers to be away from phones and potential clients.

Everett also had to travel to Washington, D.C. every few weeks because of the lawsuit. So there was a high probability, I realized, that I would soon be adding training and demos to my repertoire.

Until they could afford to hire more help, I couldn't just quit. They couldn't even pay me a salary, but I was family, and in mid-1981, I was committed to helping my family business however I could, even if I wasn't paid. If I couldn't be their lawyer, I'd be their documentation writer and trainer. And being a trainer would mean travel—and lots of it, I suspected!

I shadowed Dad during some in-house training sessions to see his technique. He did his best, considering he could only hunt and peck with one finger while teaching secretaries who typically typed eighty words a minute. I watched and listened to how he answered their questions.

I also observed both brothers give demos to visiting clients and resellers in-house and accompanied them to local customer sites. Everett wasn't keen on me shadowing him and told Dad as much. But how else was I to learn and update the manuals, if I couldn't observe and ask questions?

Out of respect for Everett's concerns, I shadowed Dad only, who was a master at sales technique, having spent much of his life perfecting his craft. For him, sales success meant a win-win situation for both the vendor and the client. He called this method *consultative selling*. "It's all about listening and asking questions," he said.

Demos of MASS-11 had to be done with sensitivity, he added. Secretaries who had previously used typewriters were being introduced to a product that would ultimately *help* them, but many, he noted, were afraid it might *replace* them. Typically their managers had seen, and liked the first demonstration; they understood how much time and money could be saved and repetition avoided. The secretaries were only then brought in for *their* feedback.

All new concepts. All new terminology. And not just for me, the nurse, but for these secretaries, many of whom thought they were too old to transition from a "tried and true typewriter" to a *"what if I'm too old to learn it?"* word processor. It was a whole new (office) world.

Dad customized his demos around expressed needs. He scrutinized faces as he gave his demos—what made faces light up, what made brows furrow, and what elicited looks of amazement. I was relieved to observe more nods, smiles, and laughs than tears.

He answered questions as they came up. Many often started with, "This is probably a dumb question, but..." and then asked a question such as, "Why did the words disappear when you typed past the bottom of the screen?" Scrolling was a difficult concept to explain to someone used to a typewriter and panicked at the thought of words disappearing. So was "word wrap." I made a point to include these explanations when I edited the documentation.

If the demo went well, everyone left thinking they'd attended a magic show filled with useful tricks that they could easily master. But it wasn't just the tricks. It was the fact that he was able to extract from prospective customers, both the secretaries and their managers, *exactly* what they needed to make their jobs more productive and less frustrating. So I learned both how to train and how to give demonstrations of MASS-11.

We continued to get requests for demos at the customer site. Once Dad and I realized that I would be doing many of them, he suggested I apply for American Airlines' new Aadvantage Frequent Flyer program.

"You get a free First Class trip to Hawaii after you've flown 30,000 miles," he said.

30,000 miles! I'll never fly that much! I thought. But I was wrong. In 1981 alone, after Egypt, I traveled for MEC to London and Sydney, Australia, as well as domestic trips to San Antonio, New York City, New Orleans, Boston, and Washington, D.C. I earned enough Frequent Flyer miles for *two* first-class trips to Hawaii! And eventually, I took them!

DAD ARRANGED FOR ME TO ATTEND DEXPO (a DEC vendor show) in New Orleans. "Check it out and get to know our competitors. [There were three at the time: Saturn, Word-11 and WordMarc] Ask for their promo pieces. Attend some workshops. DEXPO is a great place to learn about the DEC market!"

I had never been to a trade show. I walked through the entire place in a daze and left after a couple of hours. *Who could I, an ER nurse, talk to, and about what?* The only technical words I knew had to do with word processing: cut and paste, search and replace, headers and footers.

That experience reminded me of my first evening working as a student assistant in Cook County Hospital's Emergency Room. *Suction, lavage, GI bleed. . .*I didn't understand what anyone was talking about. The language of these technical people in their booths was foreign to me, as were the products they were promoting. Frankly, that trip was a waste of MEC's money. But future trips, which came one right after the other, weren't.

Jetsetter!

L ONDON: My FIRST OVERSEAS TRIP was to train the sales rep
and trainer of our first international dealer, whose offices were
located in London's financial district. I had to demonstrate
MASS-11 at an upcoming trade show at Wembley Exposition Center.

Dad arranged it, and a week before I was supposed to leave, he
asked if I'd made my hotel arrangements with the contact he'd given
me. I told him I hadn't, justifying it by saying, "Isn't that an expensive
phone call?" Seeing Dad's appalled look, I realized I had a lot to learn
about business!

"When you call, ask them what they want you to wear in the
booth. Do you have a suit?"

I hadn't even thought about what to wear. No, I didn't own a suit,
or any business clothes for that matter, I told him. I spent most of my
waking hours in hospital scrubs.

"Then buy yourself a decent suit, and make sure it fits right," he
said. He handed me a fifty-dollar bill.

So I went to Marshall Fields' bargain basement downtown and
bought an Evan-Picone lavender linen suit and a lavender print blouse.
Both were on the clearance rack and fortunately my size. The outfit
became, over the years I worked at MEC, my "lucky lavender linen

suit." I always stood out from other businesswomen in their navy pinstriped pantsuits that were popular in the '80s.

After arriving in London, it was hard getting the Londoners up to speed on all the features because, except for the trade show, "business" for them ended at noon! One tech guy flippantly said, "All our afternoon's wages go to the government authorities, so we commence Happy Hour early." The work fridge was stocked with beer! After working in the morning, the trainee took me out to lunch, then shopping and sightseeing at places like Piccadilly Square, Harrods, and Hyde Park.

While we were at the trade show, I overheard the sales rep, Gordon, misrepresenting our product to a prospect. I took him aside and said, "Gordon, MASS-11 can't do that. You're going to get us in trouble by saying we have that feature."

His smug reply was, "I'm sure you'll have it by the time they purchase it, Carol. Giving them a teaser is how you get in the door."

But I knew Dad and Everett were already dealing with a stressful and potentially costly lawsuit for allegedly "overpromising and under-delivering" and had no desire to go through another, even if the U.K. had a different system of justice.

That night, I called Dad and explained the situation. I felt bad because I knew he was very optimistic about this dealer. He'd spent a lot of time with them at their U.S. office in Hoboken, New Jersey, getting them up to speed. The next day, he discussed his concerns with the CEO, and said they had come to "an understanding."

TEXAS: MY SECOND TRIP was to Lackland Air Force Base in San Antonio, Texas for two weeks of training secretaries at Wilford Hall Medical Center, during a Texas heat wave.

The IT Manager there, a captain looking dapper in his Air Force blues, suggested places to eat and local attractions to visit, including the spring-fed Comal River in nearby New Braunfels, where locals spent their weekends tubing. I grew very fond of San Antonio and the Texas Hill Country, despite the heat!

The captain explained that the secretaries would have two weeks to make the transition from their IBM Selectrics to MASS-11 and that he'd be training the next groups of secretaries. At Wilford Hall, I learned first-hand what secretaries do. I told them I was a nurse, and that this was my first training assignment, and I too was fairly new to word processing.

I worried that there might be lots of tears during the training, as many secretaries looked to be in their forties or older. And there were some, in the morning. But I was blessed, as a new trainer, to have a cheerleader in the class who, throughout the morning, assured the others, "This is so much better than the IBM Selectric!" She caught on quickly and helped the others.

Soon the entire class was having fun moving text around, and setting up multiple margins and different types of tabs: left indent, right indent, decimal, and wrap tabs. At the end of the day, one of the older women in the class blurted, "This product is a Godsend!"

The secretaries at Wilford Hall helped make *me* a believer in the value of word processing. When I returned to the office, I began writing a training tutorial, and each time I returned from a training session, I updated it, in the hope that more trainers would eventually be hired and, once trained, they could hit the ground running with this manual.

For a fleeting moment, while training these secretaries in a hospital environment in my lavender linen suit, surrounded by busy nurses and doctors in scrubs, I asked myself, "What the heck am I doing here training secretaries how to use a word processor? *I'm a nurse!*" But as I learned about the repetitive work they did and realized how I was helping free them from that, I felt I *was* being a nurse, helping them transition from a "toxic" office to a "therapeutic" office.

The captain sat in on the training sessions and presented me with a page of questions at the end of each day, which I promised to have answers to the following morning. So instead of cooling off in the La Quinta pool with a bunch of truckers, I spent my evenings speaking to Dad or Everett on the room phone, racking up long-distance phone charges, while the motel's window AC unit struggled and sputtered to keep the room temperature below eighty.

NEW YORK CITY: I ALSO MADE TWO TRIPS to New York in the summer of 1981. The first was to train users at the *New Yorker* magazine on how to use our mail merge feature to maintain their subscriber database. Mike, the IT Manager, lobbed endless technical questions at me during the training, most of which I couldn't answer; I felt like an idiot at the end of every day.

Once again, I had to make numerous calls back to the office to get clarification from Everett on how certain new features worked, but Mike wanted instant answers and was willing to interrupt the training to get them. The silver lining was that my evenings in the city were free to attend a Broadway show or the Metropolitan Opera.

AUSTRALIA: AND FINALLY, LESS THAN A YEAR after I'd started at MEC (nine months longer than the estimated three months), Dad had asked if I could give demos for our new Australian dealer, in Melbourne and Sydney, the week before Christmas. Their potential clients included the largest broadcasting company in Australia and the Australian stock market.

"Are you sure, Dad?" I asked. I'd never given a sales demo on my own. He insisted neither he nor Everett had the time for a ten-day trip that would require a major adjustment due to jet lag both ways.

I was in a daze when I arrived after the eighteen-hour flight. There was a twelve-hour time difference *and* a season change, from winter to summer. I was met by two reps from the dealer. The male one, Gavin, said, "So good to finally meet you, Carol. You must be exhausted! But we have to head straight away to the broadcasting company. This is the only day they were all available for your demo. ABC (Australian Broadcasting Company) is potentially a huge sale for both of us."

I could barely keep my eyes open on the drive from the airport to ABC. December in Australia was mid-summer; it was hot, the country was in a drought, and had rolling brownouts. Only the "up" escalators worked in the building. Our only concern was that the power might go off during the demo. But the demo was a great success and resulted in a huge order. It was worth suffering jet lag.

I spent the first half of the week in Melbourne giving demos between escorted side trips to the beach and rain forest to see penguins, kangaroos, koalas, and pink cockatiels. From Melbourne, I flew to Sydney, by which time I was finally adjusted to the time and season change, and feeling myself again. There, I was met by the Sydney sales reps who introduced me to *their* prospective clients.

Once again, the demos went well, and I was finally able to answer most of their technical questions. Once I got over my initial nervousness about giving demos, I felt like a performer on stage receiving thunderous applause during the curtain call.

Dad had taught me well, how to read the room, figure out who the key decision makers were, and make sure the lead secretary would give a thumbs up to her boss at the end of the demo.

On the weekend, the sales manager and his wife took me to dinner after we'd spent the day sailing in Sydney Harbor, past the famed Sydney Opera House and the expansive white sand beaches. We were both ecstatic over the positive reception we'd had all week, which would result in numerous sales of both hardware and software. I had so much fun and enjoyed the Australian people *so much*, that I briefly considered moving to Australia—until the sold-out sixteen-hour flight home. Australia was, I realized, so close to my heart but *so* far away!

Staying Afloat

D ESPITE MY HIGH FROM THE SUCCESS of the Australian trip, Dad was doing his best to keep MEC afloat financially. After reviewing all the requests for training and demos, and the sales figures, he came to the conclusion we desperately needed more sales and more sales help. The three of us were stretched to the max, and if MEC was going to grow, some drastic changes had to be made. While Dad and I were on the road, Everett was handling all the phone calls—inquiries, support questions, demo requests—as well as suggestions and complaints from dealers.

A week or so after I returned from Australia, Everett took me aside and said, "Going forward, you're going to have to share your training assignments with others who would like the opportunity to travel too."

His statement took me aback. He had agreed with Dad that I should be the one to go to Australia the week before Christmas, and London before that.

But he didn't mean *himself*; the "other" was the single mother who helped Everett with his kids, and also worked part-time shipping disks. Everett taught her how to make labels and type letters using MASS-11. She told Everett she would love to travel overseas like Hank's daughter.

I shrugged and later told Dad, who was already riled up about

Everett not sharing critical information with him, and various other shenanigans that went on while he was out of the office.

"Travel and training are two different animals!" Dad snorted. "He's delusional to think we can send part-time shipping staff out on the road to train our customers! I need to have a talk with him! I already have a long list to review with him."

In September, he and Everett made time to review all of Dad's concerns.

"We're drowning!" Dad told him. "We have to make changes if we're going to stay afloat." Both came to an agreement that any important phone calls with customers or dealers who gave recommendations, or feedback on our products, would be tape-recorded and transcribed, so both brothers had access to the information. Before promises were made, the transcriptions would be reviewed by both. Only then would they call Surender, and it would always be a joint call.

Nobody would represent MEC as a MASS-11 trainer or demonstrator, in-house or out, unless they were thoroughly trained in all aspects of the product and willing to be on the road, non-stop, for up to two weeks. Changes would be made. *MEC had to survive!*

IN THE FALL OF 1981, DESPITE MY HEAVY travel schedule, I had saved the date for my ten-year high school reunion. There I ran into a former classmate, Bonnie (Keating) LaScola. I remembered Bonnie as smart, no-nonsense, organized, and efficient.

In the first five minutes, I learned that Bonnie had attended, but not completed, college, had been married five years to a divorced man with two sons that he had full custody of, and that his job kept him on the road full-time. Bonnie was stressed working as a secretary to a vice president of a manufacturing company while being responsible for her two young stepsons. Within twenty minutes of catching up with her, I knew we had to hire her.

MECollection: Bonnie LaScola

The job description was a perfect fit for me; it sounded like a dream come true. Carol wasted no time, and I interviewed with her father the next day. We hit it off right away. I guess he figured, if Carol trusted me, so could he. He also assured me if one of my stepsons was sick, I could pick them up at school and stay home with them. Being a good parent trumped everything, he said.

When I started, Hank said, "Here's your desk, here's your computer, there's the phone—do your thing." I had never worked on a computer. Most secretaries hadn't back then; we all used typewriters. Hank assured me Carol would get me up to speed on MASS-11, and she did.

I soon learned there was no office to organize, no forms to file. Phone messages, purchase orders, and questions from clients were scattered all over on bits of paper. No dates, often no return numbers. One week Everett was in the office and Hank on the road; the next week Hank was in the office. Usually one didn't know what the other had done and what needed to be handled.

For me, the first couple of months was just trying to figure out how I could best help bring order from chaos. I could see that, if they wanted to grow, and Hank assured me they did, they couldn't continue in such a haphazard way.

In the third month, I realized what my most important role was. I had to be the go-between for the brothers. First I took over all incoming phone calls. I took copious notes and passed the call info to the correct brother. I had to follow what each was doing, who they were seeing, what their travel schedules were, and what they needed done in the office while they were gone. I learned on the fly what MASS-11 was all about, how it was produced, how it got to the customer, what problems the customers had, and how to handle those problems. I learned a lot by asking questions—constantly.

Hank would always say, before he went on a trip, "Make sure you take care of this, that, and whatever while we're gone." I had to hold down the fort, but first I had to create the fort. And they gave me free rein to do that.

But Hank was loud and swore a lot, not at me, but out of frustration. I wasn't used to a boss who swore, and I cried a lot. Hank wasn't used to a woman who cried. He finally sat me down and told me I had to be strong. He wanted me to be successful but said he couldn't deal with a woman who cried. He wanted me to be confident and handle things on my own like his wife did at home. But what he ultimately taught me was to believe in myself—that my power was within.

With the hiring of Bonnie came more good news. In early 1982 the lawsuit was settled. The brothers were fortunate to have hired Dave Aberson, who was quite experienced with computer law, to represent them. It also helped that the presiding federal judge was Harold Greene, who was concurrently conducting the antitrust trial against AT&T in the same courtroom. Although he ruled *against* AT&T in their case, he ruled *for* MEC in ours.

With the lawsuit settled and Bonnie onboard, bringing order from chaos, the MEC train was back on track. I was finally paid a monthly salary, (not enough to quit my nursing job though), and moving full-steam ahead in 1982.

1982: A Window of Opportunity

I N LATE 1981, MEC's BRITISH DEALER had the exclusive rights to sell MASS-11 on the VAX in the United Kingdom and New York City, where they had an office. But that agreement was canceled for a couple of reasons.

First, they insisted on having a copy of our source code, the "keys to the kingdom." Second, Gordon, the sales rep who had misrepresented our product at the London trade show, insisted that MASS-11 was "not ready for prime time" in either London or New York City.

"It's just not sophisticated enough for the big banks," he insisted in his thick British accent. "I *won't* be humiliated."

We didn't know what features the big banks needed and had no idea whether MASS-11 was ready or not for prime time in New York. The *New Yorker* magazine was thrilled with us, but they only used our mail merge feature to maintain their subscription list.

Regardless, Dad renegotiated the contract, allowing them to resell MASS-11 in the U.K. and New York but *not* with *exclusive* rights. That was a wise decision, for soon after, we started getting requests for demonstrations, not only from the New York City DEC office, but from DEC offices *all over the U.S.*

Overnight, it seemed, DEC sales reps were very curious about MASS-11. Office automation was the next big thing for offices, and a key element was word processing. DEC didn't offer a word processing product for their PDP-11 *or* the new VAX. But their customers were telling them that MEC did.

If a client wanted word processing, DEC sales reps recommended their stand-alone DECmate, which was a decent enough standalone word processor. But if the clients wanted a *shared* word-processing system, one where secretaries could easily share documents with their bosses, DEC had no solution. They referred their customers to us.

Once MASS-11 was available on the VAX, articles and great reviews appeared in the DEC-oriented press, which included, at that time, *DEC Professional, Digital Review, Digital News,* and *Hardcopy.* These magazines were targeted solely to DEC customers who used PDP-11 and VAX computers.

The office automation managers in DEC's regional offices took notice of the powerful combination of the VAX and MASS-11 at their scientific and engineering sites, including Hughes Aircraft, Lawrence Livermore Labs, Sandia Labs, and MIT's Whitaker Lab.

With the successful installation of MASS-11 on the VAXes at the Ohio law firm, word spread. DEC office automation managers soon saw the potential for selling VAXes to not only law firms, but the big commercial and investment banks, and Big Eight accounting firms that weren't previously on their radar as office automation prospects. Maybe MASS-11 *was* ready for prime time in Manhattan!

My first invitation to give a joint demo, in a DEC office, was in January 1982. DEC's Office Automation Specialist in Manhattan rolled out the red carpet for me. She met me at LaGuardia Airport, drove me to DEC's midtown office at 1 Penn Plaza, and took me out to dinner. She was intense as she reviewed the needs of several potential clients she'd arranged for me to meet with over the next three days. I assured her that MASS-11 could do 90% of what she was asking for.

"We are so close to a sale at all of these accounts, but their sophisticated requirements for word processing are beyond what we can offer," she said. We both hoped I could provide the solutions they were seeking.

She introduced me to the salespeople for each account, all wearing navy suits, the demo specialist, and their technical team. We'd be meeting with five banks and a Big Eight accounting firm, she said. It reminded me of my trip to Australia. If it's Tuesday, it's Chase Bank and Chemical Bank. I just followed along.

As we passed the cubicles in DEC's midtown office, I sensed the DEC people were watching me, and whispering, "That's the MASS-11 rep." I was approached by a number of them with questions about MASS-11's functionality. Most of my answers were "Yes. Yes. And yes!" I sensed they had all been frustrated by past demos where the answers were "No. Not yet. Or Soon."

The Office Automation manager prepped me, warning that, if the customer asked if *we*, MEC and DEC, worked together as a team, I was to respond in the affirmative. She told me most Fortune 500 companies wanted one vendor to provide and support the whole office automation package. That became a strategic problem for DEC, as we were a "third-party vendor."

If I was asked whether MASS-11 was integrated with All-in-1, I was to say, "It's a top priority and we are working on it." All-in-1 was DEC's office automation umbrella that would allow users to access all their VAX software products using one interface. Word processing just wasn't one of them yet. And DEC hadn't yet given us access to their All-in-1 code.

At the demos I gave that week, in skyscrapers uptown and down, each was packed with decision makers—the office manager, the lead secretary, the IT manager, and several curious DEC reps, all anxious for the winning solution to miraculously appear.

All eyes were glued to the blinking cursor on the terminal.

Projection devices from the terminal had not yet been invented, so those sitting next to me, with the best views of the screen, were typically the lead secretaries. DEC reps who watched my demos spread the word back at the office.

Being competitive with Wang feature-wise made the VAX/MASS-11 combination a strong competitor in Manhattan's office automation arena. Word got around to other DEC offices. *Just call MEC, and they'll send a rep to show MASS-11.*

Back in the MEC home office, Bonnie answered calls from DEC offices all over the country requesting on-site demos. Dad told her to only schedule an in-person demo if it was a Fortune 500 company. In those large corporations were opportunities to sell not just one, but *several* VAXes with MASS-11 licenses. In my mind, we had to strike while the iron was hot and cooperate as much as we could with DEC. Time was of the essence! Who knew if DEC programmers were working feverishly behind the scenes on their own word processor for the VAX? But at that moment, the combination of MASS-11 and the VAX was unbeatable!

Making the Switch. . .to MASS-11

O NE QUESTION I OFTEN RECEIVED was about MASS-11's performance on the VAX with multiple users. How could we, a small company that didn't yet own a VAX, guarantee it would work well in a large corporate environment with multiple word processing users?

I told them that, although we could never do that type of testing in-house, several universities who used MASS-11 on the PDP-11 had offered to be beta test sites for our VAX version, including MIT's well-respected Whitaker Labs. Dr. Will Gilbert, the manager of the lab, agreed to test our latest VAX beta version—to find bugs and do performance tests.

In addition to MIT, the University of Dayton, Purdue, Baylor, Northwestern, and the University of North Carolina were also beta test sites for the VAX product and provided us with invaluable feedback on how MASS-11 performed in various situations and configurations.

Another question we frequently got from DEC salesreps was on how to make the transition from standalone DECmates to MASS-11 easier, as the commands used for functions were completely different. At the time, the majority of MASS-11 users were still secretaries. The documentation I had written was geared toward those secretaries, as was our marketing pitch.

And with increasing frequency, decision-makers were making requests like this one, which was taped, transcribed by Bonnie, and taken seriously by the brothers:

IT Manager:

We're not so much interested in word processing as an administrative tool to write letters or maintain lists. We're interested in word processing to solve a researcher's manuscript problem. We need the ability to create very large documents. We want it to produce scientific manuscripts, requests for proposals (RFPs), and grant requests—really big documents that many different people work at and contribute to.

Also, our engineers hunt and peck using the EDT editor [a technical editor that came with the VAX]. We'd like our engineers to use the same word processor as the secretaries, and we're leaning towards MASS-11. But the engineers are balking. EDT doesn't have the powerful functionality of MASS-11, but these guys are used to it. They don't want to learn something new. I'd like you to give some thought to being able to toggle the numeric keypad so it emulates the EDT editor. I think you'll hear this from other research environments such as ours if that's your target market, and I think it is.

Hank:

I think that's going to be typical of most of our target VAX installations. Creating a toggle for the EDT editor is a brilliant idea. And while we're talking about toggling the keypad, maybe we can create a second toggle that emulates the DECmate's 'Gold Key' editor. That might incentivize secretaries using DECmates to switch.

Everett:

Up to now, our marketing strategy has been to target secretaries converting from typewriters. But you make an excellent point. A lot of engineers are learning how to type and may prefer typing their first drafts. We'll take your suggestions very seriously.

The brothers discussed these suggestions with Surender, and they jointly agreed to make that happen. The default editor would be our mnemonic commands (PF1 C for copy, as an example). Secretaries switching to MASS-11 from standalone DECmates could toggle the keypad to the Gold Key editor. And engineers and scientists could toggle it to an EDT editor.

That toggle feature alone was a great incentive for engineers, scientists, and DECmate users to get on board with MASS-11. New doors opened and goodwill was made with both DEC and the scientific community as a result.

Armed with the EDT editor toggle, the engineers and scientists now clamored for two more features: a scientific equation editor and a spell checker. These men could design space-age weapons, but most couldn't spell. Surender was working diligently on the equation editor but expressed concern that a spell checker with thousands of words in the dictionary might stall the system. *And that would be a deal breaker!*

Dad recalled that the University of North Carolina School of Public Health in Chapel Hill had a spell checker on their PDP-11. He arranged to meet with Ken Crossen, who had programmed it. Ken, an MIT-trained electrical engineer, designed specialized research electronics for EPA environmental monitoring at the School of Public Health.

MECollection: Ken Crossen

My boss Harvey was a terrible speller, so I had developed a spell-check program for him on our PDP-11. We had a new VAX, and we were testing an early release of MASS-11 on the VAX. Harvey liked it but wanted my spell checker to work on the VAX version of MASS-11. Hank met with Harvey and said, 'We'll give you MASS-11 if you put Ken's spell checker on it.' They made a handshake deal.

Hank arranged for Surender to come down to Chapel Hill, and the two of us spent a week in a cubicle at the university, alternating working and sleeping on a row of three chairs, in 12-hour shifts. While I worked, Surender slept. Surender and I both spoke Fortran [a programming language], and we worked it out. We successfully got the spell checker onto MASS-11 for the VAX.

That was one problem solved. The other was performance. Although it was better than its competitors at the time, you could barely get eight MASS-11 users on a VAX, which came out to around $30K per word processing user. The Wang standalone word processor, the Cadillac of word processing at that time, cost $32K per user.

Harvey told Hank, 'I love MASS-11, but you need to make it more efficient on the VAX.'

I had access to the school's VAX after hours and spent my nights testing ideas, potentially crashing the VAX only when nobody was around to be affected by it.

Once again, Surender came down and we worked around the clock for five days. When we finished and put it to the test, MASS-11 could support thirty-two users, which put it way ahead of Wang cost-wise. That high-performance boost made the VAX with MASS-11 an unbeatable option for word processing, especially in technical environments.

MECollection: Surender Goel

Besides the spell checker, Ken wrote routines to speed up the display on the terminal, improve system performance, and integrate MASS-11 files with other software products. The last feature made it possible for system managers to create a common user interface to integrate several software products.

He also made it possible to create documents of unlimited size, which is what our research users were begging for. We also simplified the whole file naming and retrieving process. In that short time, the two of us transformed MASS-11 from good to great!

Desperate for Purchase Orders

B Y THE END OF 1982, WE HAD DOZENS of VAX demo tapes in the field. Every engineer, scientist, and DEC office was testing it, it seemed. Surender and Ken had done their part, producing a spell checker, a scientific equation editor, and improving efficiency.

Now we needed purchase orders and a big, fat end-of-the-year check. Dad made dozens of calls to see who might be ready to close. One evaluation site, a large research lab in Iowa where I had given a demo, was close to making a decision, he discovered. They were 95% committed to standardizing on MASS-11 for numerous VAXes, they told him.

"What do we need to do to close the deal by the end of the year?" Dad asked. He wisely didn't tell them, "We need an order to keep our doors open."

They told him they still had concerns. "Let's get together and hammer them out," Dad offered. So on a Saturday in mid-November, a group of decision-makers, four men and a woman, flew by private plane to meet with Dad, Everett, and me at MEC.

Dad had brought in a couple of folding tables from the warehouse and set them up with eight folding chairs in the middle of the office, between the copy machine and the pantry.

Mom had woken up early, her usual 5 a.m., to pick up a pecan coffee cake from her favorite bakery in Elk Grove Village, a half-hour drive from home. She'd arrived at the office before us to empty the trash cans, slice the coffee cake, and put on a large pot of coffee. Before leaving, she checked to make sure the toilet was clean and the bathroom was supplied with toilet paper, paper towels, and hand soap. At lunchtime, she dropped off two large pizzas, some meatball subs, and a large Italian salad, all from nearby Fio Rito's Pizzeria.

During the intense five-hour meeting, they reviewed their list of requests that needed to be implemented by January 3, 1983—*just a month and a half away!* If we were going to get that purchase order, *there was no time to waste.*

Dad and Everett had Surender on standby and called him throughout the day to review their requests. Surender assured them they were all reasonable, that they would enhance our product, and that he could provide these additions by their deadline.

During lunch, the subject of the source code also came up. Of course, they wanted a copy of it in escrow, in case anything happened to MEC or Surender. They weren't the first, or the last, to ask for this. Though we were desperate for their business, Dad and Everett made it very clear that they would *not* give the source code to *anyone,* even in escrow. The source code was MEC's crown jewel.

Dad added that, if we agreed to implement the customized features they needed in that very short time frame, we would need a purchase order and a hefty down payment by mid-December. They agreed and said they would expedite this.

Then, just as the meeting was coming to a close, and Dad asked if there were any more questions, the woman brought up documentation. It would also have to be ready by January 3, she insisted, since they'd be beginning internal training shortly after that.

"Does MEC have someone on staff to write this?" she asked. Her request stopped the forward momentum. It meant that one of us would have to work non-stop through the Christmas/New Year holiday week *after* Surender had completed the programming part.

I quickly reviewed my holiday plans in my head. I could have made double time and a half working as a nurse during the Christmas holidays. But I volunteered to do it, knowing there would be no overtime or bonus pay from MEC. Everyone expressed relief except the woman, who was frowning.

"You give great demos, Carol," she said, "but you're a nurse. How are you qualified to write this technical documentation? Do you even have a college degree?" Her condescending questions, implying that I was merely a demo dolly, brought a chill over the room.

Before I could answer, Dad replied, "Carol has written all of our documentation. She knows the product cold, and I'm surprised and grateful she volunteered to do this over the holidays. I know she had other plans. And Everett and I sure as hell don't have time to do it!"

I sensed that wasn't what this woman wanted to hear—the boss defending his "unqualified" daughter. After a moment of silence, I replied, "If having a degree is your only concern about who writes the documentation, I *do* have one."

I noticed Everett had a surprised look on his face. I'm not sure he or Dad even knew I had a degree. Neither had ever asked to see my non-existent resume. But one of the perks of working as a nurse at the University of Illinois Hospital was three free classes per quarter, in any subject, at U of I's Circle Campus, just down the street. At the time I'd been interested in history. Taking a guided tour through Westminster Abbey in London ignited my passion for it in 1975.

When I returned from that trip, I took the maximum credits allowed, most in History, and some in Geography, a subject that also interested me. I took these classes during the day and worked the evening shift in the ER.

One summer day, like King Midas, I counted up my credits from both the U of I, and Chicago's junior colleges I had attended including

Loop College downtown, Malcolm X on the west side, and Wright on the north side. I went to the admission office and they agreed I had enough for a Bachelor's degree in history. There was no congratulatory dinner or graduation ceremony—just a diploma mailed to me in late August. Getting that B.A. degree was far easier than three straight years of nursing school!

With all objections met Dad ended the meeting with handshakes all around and drove them back to the local airport. Surender and I had our work cut out for us.

After Surender finished his programming work in late December, I had no time to waste. I worked throughout the holiday week, alone in the office, speaking on the phone only with Surender, and taking time off only to have Christmas lunch with my parents at the Golden Ox Restaurant on Chicago's north side. It had become our Christmas Day tradition after I'd become a nurse, dining on appetizers of *hackepeter* (raw ground sirloin with onions and capers), and liver dumpling soup, then feasting on roast duck, sauerbraten, and pork loin. The festive Christmas lunch made up for my stoicism for the rest of the holiday.

I put the final touches on the documentation around 10 p.m. on New Year's Eve. I had been invited by Dan, our ER pharmacist, to a New Year's Eve party at his apartment a few blocks away. I told him I'd make it if I finished a project I was working on. I did. It was a fifteen-minute walk in the freshly fallen snow to his place.

Once there, I chatted mostly with my ER co-workers, but while waiting in line for the one bathroom, one of the pharmacist's friends initiated a conversation with me.

"How do you know Dan?" he asked.

"I'm a nurse," I told him. "We work together in the ER. What about you?"

"I went to college with him," he replied. "I live in New York City now. I sell computers."

I didn't ask what kind of computers. Nurses wouldn't know that. And I didn't tell him I had a side gig selling word processing software for the Digital VAX.

I was exhausted, and after spending my entire holiday writing about software, computers were the last thing I wanted to discuss. At the party's end, the out-of-town friend handed me his card and said, "If you're ever in New York City, give me a call."

I didn't say, "Sure, I'll be there in a couple of weeks to give some MASS-11 demos! We can hang out." I figured I'd never see him again. After I got home, I looked at his card. *He was a DEC sales rep!*

1983: Automate or Perish!

Office automation was the big buzzword in 1983. *The New York Times* published an article in January 1982 on the concept, predicting every white-collar office worker, both boss and secretary, would soon have a terminal or PC on their desk, all wired together, eliminating telephone tag and reducing travel via teleconferencing. But time savings weren't enough to justify the expense. If office automation was to take off, it would have to help the business be more profitable.

An analyst with Paine Webber was quoted, *"There is no doubt in my mind that within a realistic time horizon, all large companies will require office automation to survive."*

In 1983, I was intensely focused on the window of opportunity we had to help DEC offices sell VAXes with MASS-11. That year, we released a version of MASS-11 that included a scientific equation editor, multiple numbering styles, and composite documents to meet the needs of R&D and aerospace firms.

Later in the year, we released a version that included multiple legal features such as floating footnotes, table of contents, redlining, split screen editing, and indexing. With those features, we were poised to replace all stand-alone word processors!

Time was of of the essence, and I gave joint demos with DEC sales reps in New York City and twenty-one other cities in the U.S. I also spent considerable time at the Canadian DEC offices in Calgary and Vancouver. I'm sure Dad and Everett's travel schedules were just as hectic as mine. We rarely saw each other. I accumulated thousands of Frequent Flyer miles.

MY FIRST OFFICE AUTOMATION DEMO of 1983 was in midtown Manhattan, at Manufacturers Hanover Bank, in the second week of January. Six VAX sales hinged on how well MASS-11 was received as a part of DEC's office automation strategy. The Manager of Information Systems was ready to toss DEC out for not coming up with a decent word-processing solution. *Could MEC save this relationship?* The answer rested on how well MASS-11 would be received by the secretarial staff. DEC's office automation specialist warned me that the audience might be skeptical.

I first met with the bank's office manager and VAX system manager, who offered scowls, not smiles, when they shook my hand. I proceeded to give a demo to a roomful of people. Dad had taught me that the attention span of most people at a demo is about ten seconds. "If you don't grab them in ten seconds," he'd said, "they'll be thinking about what to make for dinner."

I had created my demo routine with a 300-page document, mostly a page of text pasted three hundred times with some hidden words on pages 79 and 240. I opened the document, asked if speed was important to them (and it always was), and pressed [PF1] B. The cursor reached the bottom in a split second. All jaws dropped. *I had their attention.* I knew that it would take about ten minutes of whirring and churning for any other word processor, including DEC's DECmate, to do that.

It was a successful demo, converting scowls into smiles on all the right people's faces. I looked up from my keyboard and was astonished to see the guy I'd met at the New Year's Eve party in Chicago, two weeks earlier, standing in the back of the room.

He approached me and asked, with a perplexed look on his face, "I thought you were a nurse."

"I am," I replied, "but I also help out at my father's company."

"Your father owns MEC?"

He whistled through his teeth. "Manny Hanny is my account. And based on what I just witnessed, I think your father's company just helped me make my quota for the year, and then some!"

It was a serendipitous meeting; one even hard for me to believe. He asked if I had plans that evening. I told him I did. My passion was selling MASS-11. I didn't want to jeopardize my relationship with DEC in Manhattan by dating one of their sales reps.

"Next time, give me a heads up when you come back to New York," he said. "I'll be on the lookout for you." Once again, he handed me his business card.

One-Woman Support Department

OST OF OUR DEMOS AT DEC OFFICES eventually resulted in large sales, but MEC didn't get the purchase order until after the VAX had been bought and installed, which could take six months to a year. We were the last to get our piece of the pie paid for. All we got from DEC in the early part of the year were phone calls with endless questions. Bonnie was the one answering all the phones.

MECollection: Bonnie LaScola

The phones took up most of my time. There were three lines, and they'd ring constantly, mostly with support questions and requests for demos—and a few orders, thankfully. I put the demo requests on Hank's desk and the support messages on Everett's. After one hectic trip, Everett declared, "I can't travel and handle support calls anymore!"

Hank asked if I would be willing to handle the support calls. I told him I knew MASS-11 but nothing about the operating system, or printing, which were the questions we mostly got. Hank said Everett would teach me. But he didn't.

Once Hank told him I'd handle all support calls, Everett

just dropped all the messages on my desk and told me to call everyone back. That's how I got into technical support. It was like being dropped into the deep end of the pool before learning how to swim.

I became a one-woman support department. I learned as much as I could on the fly, and if I was stumped, I would call the VAX system manager at Loyola University, who used MASS-11. He generously offered his assistance. But within a few weeks, I was going crazy with phone calls from irate customers if I couldn't solve their problems. I couldn't keep calling the Loyola guy for help.

So I tearfully told Hank, "Support can't be handled by one person!" His reply was, in typical Hank fashion, "For Chrissakes, Bonnie, you gotta stand up for yourself. You're so efficient, so good at what you do. How the hell am I supposed to know you're overwhelmed if you don't tell me? If you need help, you have to ask for it. Stop paddling upstream! Drop the oars and hire some more people."

I didn't know hiring more help was an option. All I had to do was ask? So that was my next project. Hiring! I hired a woman to handle just order processing—Barb Gossen.

MECollection: Barb Gossen

I believe I was the seventh employee in the company. Bonnie was a Jill-of-all-trades, like a mother hen; she was very organized. I was a small-town girl from Iowa who hadn't been out of the Midwest. My experience was trading commodities.

Like Hank, I knew a lot about Staley Corn Processing Plant, where he and Surender had met. When Hank later heard I had experience selling commodities, he said, 'Barb, you should be in sales.' So he put me in charge of handling international sales out of the home office. At that time we had a Telex international line and I spent an hour every morning reading email messages from Australia, Norway, and England, among others who used or sold MASS-11.

My desk was outside both Hank and Everett's offices. The two were so different; you wouldn't know they were related. Everett was always "the smartest person" in the room, and often arrogant to us; Hank was so down to Earth.

MECollection: Bonnie LaScola

When Hank moved Barb into Inside Sales, I had to hire more people to help with the phones. I focused on interviewing, hiring, and teaching support people. Back then, not too many folks knew computers and had a friendly, calm phone presence. I hired three young people I hoped would fit the bill. They eventually worked well together, did a good job, and freed me for another project at MEC.

Before I was hired, Hank brought in friends, neighbors, and family for short-term projects. But once I was onboard, he dropped his own oars. He felt comfortable turning projects over to me that he no longer had time for. Managing projects was what he and I discovered I did best. And he had lots of them! Big ones, little ones. Every few months he gave me a new one, and I'd figure out a way to get it done.

He often said, "That's not how I would have done it, Bonnie, but you got it done, and that's all that matters. Are you ready for another one?'"

It was like the TV show Star Trek: The Next Generation. Hank was Captain Picard, who was in charge of the Enterprise. I was his #1. When Captain Picard wanted his #1 to take over, he'd say '#1–Make it So.' And I did.

The Company That Listens

I N 1983, OUR TARGET CLIENTELE WERE FORTUNE 500 companies and universities—large installations with complex requirements that required long, technical conversations with both Dad and Everett, on the phone and in person, about future directions we might take.

Numerous start-up software companies, even those with ample financial backing, had gone belly up in the '80s by putting all their eggs in the wrong basket, supporting a product or operating system that didn't live up to the hype. Dad and Everett *could not* afford to make one bad decision.

One of the best decisions they made was to form a Steering Committee, comprised of a handful of our most knowledgeable and technically advanced customers who advised the brothers on future development. Most were beta test sites for both MASS-11 and DEC's hardware products.

The first official committee was held in the fall of 1982 at the Broadmoor, a five-star resort in Colorado Springs. A roomful of sixteen scientists, engineers, and MIS Managers gathered for two days—all experts in their fields, all responsible for purchasing decisions, and most importantly, all willing to help us, which would ultimately help *them* meet their office automation objectives.

At this playpen of technological brilliance, Everett would discuss features being developed, and the steering committee members would give us feedback—what features and products to add, and what printers, platforms, and software to support.

These men had all gone out on a limb by recommending MASS-11 as their flagship word processor on the VAX. We were, after all, just a two-man operation, a small start-up with no venture capital money, and a programmer with an unusual name whom no one had ever met. It was a secret that Surender was still working full-time at NCR and would until 1984 when the brothers could finally afford to hire him full-time.

I'm sure most wondered: *Are the brothers trustworthy? Could MEC deliver all they promised?*

The answer to many of these questions came in 1983, when we released, to great fanfare, two major releases which were feature-rich, clean (mostly bug-free), efficient (didn't hog the memory), and timely (available ahead of the promised release date).

The releases confirmed that we could be trusted to deliver what we promised. Everyone wanted to meet the mysterious Surender the same way they all wanted a copy of the source code, in case something happened to him. But very few did, and nobody got the source code.

Surender recalled, "Everett and Hank always conferred with me about implementing future features. They never put me in a position of not being able to keep commitments. And once I assured them I could do something, they never gave me a deadline, which I appreciated."

We had developed the nickname "The Company That Listens" from our customers because. . .*we did!* Besides the law firm that wrote the functional specs for our legal features, our steering committee members were designing our products, providing the details needed for Surender to program each feature.

MECollection: Gary Mauler, Westinghouse

Westinghouse was an early user of MASS-11, and as I was its champion, I was selected to represent Westinghouse at MEC's steering committee. It was great fun being on that committee.

At Westinghouse, we were pushing technology along with other aerospace companies. There were a lot of aerospace guys on the steering committee. Lockheed, Raytheon, and Boeing were all represented. We were all competitors one day and partners the next, but we all had the same objectives: to guide them on the directions they should take that would help us meet our corporate objectives. The value of my representing Westinghouse was that my opinions were taken seriously and would ultimately benefit Westinghouse.

During meals, you could share ideas with MEC's programmers and hear what attendees from other industries needed. We were all basically on the same mission: to produce heavy-duty documents that looked like they'd been professionally typeset. It just was an amazing opportunity to be able to guide the developers and watch them knock it out of the park!

After taking copious notes at the meeting, Everett would reveal all the enhancements that had been made at the next meeting. It was amazing! Nothing fazed those guys. No matter what we asked for, it was delivered in the next release. It was an exciting time; the whole aerospace industry was using VAXes and MASS-11 to create those complicated documents while saving a tremendous amount of time and energy, in a way that just a few years earlier would be unheard of. It was the '80s, and we were all there at the right time.

Although there were occasional differences of opinion on priorities and timelines at these meetings, one direction all agreed on at the inaugural meeting was that MASS-11 had to be ported to the IBM PC and compatibles. It would also have to support PC networks, with seamless communication between the PC and VAX. The IT Manager of GM Research offered to help with that, as they had numerous VAXes and PCs and intended to standardize on MASS-11—but only if MASS-11 worked on the PC.

"We'll take your suggestions into consideration," Everett replied.

Until then, the IBM PC was not on the brothers' radar, even though IBM released its first personal computer, Model 5150, with 16 KB RAM, a Color Graphics Adaptor, and no disk drives, in August 1981. The top-secret project took one year to develop, had an open architecture, and sold for $1,565. The operating system, DOS, was provided by Bill Gates's startup company Microsoft, also developed in secret. DOS soon took the world by storm.

In 1982, the personal computer was selected as *Time* magazine's "Man of the Year." It was the first time the magazine selected a non-human recipient for the award. *PC Magazine* was also first published in 1982. It would become the bible for PC users in the next decade.

However, personal computer users were not MEC's target market in 1982. Not until 1984, when the IBM PC AT (Advanced Technology) was released, would the PC have enough memory and storage to handle a robust word-processing product such as ours.

Our target market was not a home user; it was Fortune 500 companies seeking office automation solutions. But when those large companies began purchasing PCs as part of their office automation strategy, the big question was, could we accommodate them?

Porting the program to the PC would be a challenge, and not just a programming one. Everett explained to the steering committee members that DEC and MEC were working well together, that DEC was bringing us into their key Fortune 500 accounts, and that, at their last meeting with DEC's VP of Office Automation strategies, he requested that we develop MASS-11 exclusively on DEC's newly released microcomputers: the Pro350 and the Rainbow. And Not The IBM PC!

The brothers had refused to shake on the deal. They were angry and torn. Members of the steering committee who had beta-tested DEC's PCs warned the brothers that the Pro350 was a dog and incompatible with the IBM PC. Nobody in their right mind would buy it, they insisted. They warned that, if we went the route DEC insisted on, and not the IBM PC route, it could be the end for us.

But was it worth defying DEC when we had such a win-win situation with them? The entire U.S. DEC sales force was opening doors for us. Our informal agreement with them was a winning strategy.

A few of our members mentioned, on the QT, that DEC was working on its word processor for the VAX, but that no date had been set for release. This revelation shocked nobody in the room, and nobody seemed to care. They liked working with us and the mysterious, mountain-moving Surender.

Dad and Everett trusted their customers more than DEC, and they made the risky decision to port MASS-11 to the IBM PC. The next big question was, *who* could do it?

Surender suggested Ken, the programmer in Chapel Hill who had been instrumental in implementing the spell checker and improving performance. The brothers agreed. The only negative was that Ken would not be able to work out of his home. He and his wife Cynthia were "back-to-the-landers" who lived off-the-grid in a 600-square-foot cabin, with no running water or electricity. Dad did some homework, then flew down to meet with him.

MECollection: Ken Crossen

My boss Harvey had been promoted, and the UNC administration put me in charge of supporting MASS-11 on campus. I missed working for Harvey because he was like

Hank—he was supportive and helped people reach their potential. Surender and I had kept in touch since our first meetings; he saw I was unhappy in this new position and spoke to Hank about it. Hank flew down to visit and, over dinner at a fancy restaurant, offered me the job.

At the time the IBM PC was very primitive compared to the VAX. Trying to shoehorn MASS-11 onto the first IBM PC was a very odd experience, and I worried about my future, with a wife and a child on the way. I had a contract with UNC and a state pension, and I couldn't be fired. If I worked for MEC, I wouldn't be able to work out of my home due to no electricity. All my previous work had been done in the university's computer center, where I had unlimited access to the VAX and printers.

I expressed my concerns to Hank about leaving UNC, and he said, 'I'll double your salary, so you don't have to worry about money. I did some homework, and there's an office building across the street where you can rent space.'

I then began to think of life as an adventure. I had some savings, and my land was paid off. So I accepted the offer. My dad used to say, 'There are so few problems that money can solve. When you find one, throw money at it.' This was a case where money was needed.

The Power of Deliberate Intent

M ONEY WAS FINALLY ROLLING IN, and it was a good thing! Bonnie desperately needed help in the office. Dad needed help with sales. Everett needed help with product development. And I desperately needed help with both training and the training documentation.

I was spending most of my weekends updating it, while still working evenings as a nurse. We all put on our thinking caps, hoping to find qualified employees to help us grow. Bonnie placed an ad in the local paper for a part-time documentation writer. A local woman named Pam Nelson responded to it.

MECollection: Pam Nelson

In 1983, my third child was ready to start pre-school and it was time for me to step back into the workforce. I focused my job search on three criteria: (a) close to home, (b) part-time, and (c) making use of my writing skills. I was interested in computers and technology and thought, 'I want to hop on that train.'

I interviewed with MEC's Office Manager, Bonnie, and then with Hank, both of whom I would describe as hardworking and no-nonsense with an underlying humanity. The job fit my criteria, and Hank offered it to me on the spot. I accepted, and Bonnie showed me my desk while informing me that I was their sixth employee.

I was hired part-time, but part-time lasted only a few weeks. I learned MASS-11 quickly and thought about what freedom you have as a writer when you use an intuitive word processor such as this! Things mushroomed pretty quickly. Within weeks, Hank had made me an offer for a full-time position, which I gladly accepted.

To me, MASS-11 was the bomb. I remember excitedly describing to my father all the incredible things you could do with word processing that you couldn't do on a typewriter or even an IBM Selectric. MASS-11 had word wrap, move, copy, and paste! The list seemed endless and bordered on miraculous. I was smitten!

Though I can't say exactly when, my initial duties— writing, editing, proofing, and general office assistance— quickly morphed into larger and tighter responsibilities that included training and writing the training documentation. And eventually hiring more trainers.

Besides Pam, who had been hired to write training documentation, Dad hired two family friends as trainers: Sue Dewalt, who like me was an RN, and Kathy Rayshich, an industrial engineer. Both were unlikely choices but became training rockstars!

Sue's family joined ours on an annual summer vacation canoeing in the Canadian Boundary Waters. Her father, Warren, was President of the Illinois Audubon Society; they lived on a wooded estate with a sunken pool, property bequeathed to the Audubon Society. Their home would later be where many MEC company picnics would be held.

Kathy was like a little sister to me. Her father, Al, had been the one who had faith in Dad's business dreams early on and lent us money when we needed it in 1981.

MECollection: Kathy Rayshich Cartwright

In 1983, I had just graduated from Purdue University with a degree in Industrial Engineering, so being a trainer for MEC was not on my horizon. A year earlier I had done an internship at McDonnell Douglas in California and was hired as a Product Manager.

But during spring break 1983, my family home in Streamwood burned down, apparently from a short in an electric blanket. I lost all my prized teenage possessions, including my Elvis collection and my prom dress. I returned home to help my parents. Since I'd missed the window of opportunity to start at McDonnell Douglas, Uncle Henry offered me a job for the summer as a trainer.

He trained me on MASS-11 and even taught me some rudimentary VMS system management. Then I went out with Carol a few times, and she taught me how to train customers. We had a great time driving up and down the East Coast, training at DuPont and Westinghouse, staying in 'mom and pop' motels, and sharing biscuits and gravy for breakfast. This was before cell phones, so we also spent a lot of time at gas stations, where Carol used pay phones to return calls, set up future training dates, and confirm visits. We went from sunup to bedtime, it seemed. I took lots of notes.

I trained a lot of customers in the midwest and on both coasts—aerospace, financial, pharmaceutical, and legal. Only once was there a problem, when I had food poisoning and couldn't complete the class.

I was on the road non-stop for two years, from 1983 to 1985, before I transferred to sales. I learned a lot from Hank and Carol. I enjoyed the work; it was both fun and challenging, and I never thought about quitting to pursue a job I was better educated for.

Business Lessons

I N 1983, MEC WAS IN THE RIGHT PLACE at the right time. We had found our niche—working with DEC to help Fortune 500 companies implement office automation. Unfortunately, we encountered lies and deceit along the path to success.

Trainer Kathy Rayshich recalled one such instance that Dad had shared with her. "It was one of the many business lessons I learned while at MEC," she said, "which helped me with my own tech business that my husband and I later formed. This particular lesson was 'Never. Discuss. Business. On a Plane!'"

MEC's trajectory was heading straight up, like a rocket, with the help of local and regional DEC office automation managers who brought us into large accounts. They pushed for MASS-11 to be a DEC-supported product, one that DEC could sell and support directly to avoid any finger-pointing if something didn't work. Many expressed a desire for DEC to outright purchase MEC.

Perhaps Dad anticipated this when they received a call from a higher-up at DEC who requested a meeting to discuss strategic directions. DEC was a giant, a multi-billion dollar company, the #2 computer maker behind IBM. But our top customers warned us that DEC was covertly developing its own word processing product, one tentatively called WPS-Plus, to compete with us.

Carl Marbach, editor of *DEC Professional* magazine, recalled that period. "DEC was very proprietary," he said. "They felt they had to develop everything in-house. They never understood that third-party software developers were what made the IBM PC so popular, just as apps are designed for cellphones today. Sadly, DEC ate its children—all the software developers such as MEC. Why did they feel the need to reinvent the wheel with their own word processor, which would never come close to MASS-11 in power and functionality?"

Dad and Everett agreed to meet with these managers at DEC's headquarters in Merrimack, New Hampshire. On the flight there, Dad overheard bits of conversation between two men sitting in front of him. They were talking about MEC, and how they planned to get in as many doors as they could with MASS-11, get customers excited about a total DEC office automation solution with All-in-1, and how it would tie all their software products together. Then, by the time the customer made a purchasing decision, DEC would have their own WPS-Plus ready and they would do a bait-and-switch.

The two men also joked about how MEC had only one programmer, some 'top-secret Indian guy' who MEC kept hidden in an underground bunker somewhere in Ohio. By contrast, they concurred, DEC had dozens of programmers working on WPS-Plus and for that reason alone, their product would surely run rings around MASS-11. And even if their word processor wasn't as feature-rich as MASS-11 getting out the starting gate, the fact that it was fully integrated with All-in-1 would make prospects more likely to choose an all-DEC solution. But in the interim, they'd have to make it sound like they were best buddies with MEC.

What are the odds that Dad was seated on the plane within hearing distance of the "higher-ups" he'd be meeting with later in the day?

Dad summarized the meeting when he returned. He said the manager spoke highly of MASS-11, and they made small talk about the successes of some of our shared accounts. He then asked the brothers about the progress MEC was making with integrating MASS-11 with All-in-1, which had just been released.

"We told him we were working on it."

"And how about the progress with MASS-11 on the Rainbow and Pro-350?" the DEC manager had asked.

"Everett told them MEC was almost done with the Rainbow, but our customers weren't interested in the Pro-350, just the IBM PC."

"If we don't address that, we'll be out of business in a year," Everett had said.

To which the DEC higher-up blurted, "I don't give a damn if MEC goes out of business. We have an agreement. And it's over if you put MASS-11 on the IBM PC!"

With that, the meeting came to an abrupt end when Dad and Everett walked out. In the parking lot, Dad told Everett, "DEC can't be trusted. We can't put all our eggs in DEC's basket. We have to get the IBM PC version out as quickly as possible. And we can't count on their sales force to sell our product. We have to create our own."

And just like that, at the height of our success working alongside DEC sales reps to get orders, we were at war with DEC. A corporate edict was issued that DEC sales reps were no longer to have any contact with MEC.

Dad's attitude was "Screw 'em!"

I was nervous. Dad was taking a big gamble. How could we afford a salesforce to compete against DEC's?

Trade Show Success

N 1983, BESIDES HIRING MORE HELP, we could finally afford to have a booth at the Fall DEXPO trade show in Las Vegas. DEXPO was a trade show for DEC's third-party vendors. Our drawing card was MASS-11 Version 3-E, which received favorable reviews in all the DEC-oriented magazines.

One enhancement, the 'composite document' feature, made it possible to use a series of commands to string together multiple chapters for unlimited-size documents, with continuous pagination, headers, and footers.

Producing lengthy scientific documents finally became a true collaboration between engineers and their secretaries: no more handwritten documents full of scratched-out text, no more dictation, no more typing, revising, and retyping lengthy scientific documents. It was liberating, time-saving, and cost-effective for everyone working on a project requiring massive and complex documents.

It quickly became apparent that our booth was too small, and that we needed more help, for we were inundated with prospects and existing customers from the moment the doors opened until the show closed.

Our conversations with prospects continued long into the evening.

From that gathering of excited MASS-11 users, our first National MASS-11 Users Group was formed. They agreed to convene at every DEXPO show and give us a list of the top ten features voted on. We committed to include their wishes in the next release.

That Las Vegas show was the last one at which we had a small booth. The DEXPO sales rep, Natalie Kaye, noticed ours was always packed, and worked on Dad every day to increase the size of it for the next show.

Natalie knew the DEC market. She was also tuned in to the buzz at the show, and she told us it was all about office automation and MEC's MASS-11. She told Dad, "Hank, you need to move closer to the front of the hall. Be seen. Make a bold statement." Dad was all ears.

By the last day of the show, with Everett in agreement, Dad signed off on the largest booth for the next DEXPO, a 30' x 50' one opposite the entrance. It was more than twice the size of our current one!

Dad told Everett and me, "DEC can go to hell. We'll show them we're a force to be reckoned with. I'm planning to hire some of their best people."

By the end of the year, he had hired two DEC sales reps that he had worked with on large accounts in California and New Mexico. He hired an experienced DEC marketing specialist who was very familiar with DEC's office automation strategies to be our VP of Marketing. "All three are DEC superstars," he assured us.

Dad was flying high. Future sales success was all in his imagination at the Las Vegas show, but he knew that thoughts create reality, so he thought big thoughts. The brothers' dream of creating the best word processor in the world was becoming a reality!

Come Fly With Me!

ITH MONEY FINALLY ROLLING IN, Dad spent it on new people and tradeshows; Everett spent it on his passion, a four-seater V-tailed Bonanza plane dubbed "MECAir," which he leased in 1983. A trained pilot, he welcomed any opportunity to fly—to tradeshows, customer sites, or to visit our programmers.

Only once did Everett ask me to fly with him in his airplane. It was the morning we departed DEXPO Las Vegas. The show had been another successful one for MEC; the stars, the moon, and the constellations were lined up, pointing to MEC's future success. I agreed to accompany him after he said we'd be flying over some spectacular Utah scenery.

Dad asked if I was sure I wanted to go with Everett; he said he had upgraded our flight home to First Class. He seemed surprised and, uncharacteristically for him, a little nervous. Although he didn't say anything, I imagine he might have been concerned that his business partner/brother and his only daughter would be spending a day flying over Colorado's mighty Rocky Mountains in a fully loaded four-seater propeller plane.

After breakfast in the hotel, Dad was silent as he helped Everett load the plane. The backseat was filled with computers, printers, boxes of marketing materials, and our suitcases. We barely fit everything in.

"We should get back to DuPage Airport by dinnertime," Everett told Dad. Dad said he and Mom would pick me up, and we'd go out to dinner.

"We'll be making two pit stops for food, fuel, and bathroom breaks," Everett told me as we prepared for take-off. "Boulder, Colorado, and Omaha, Nebraska." I didn't think to look at the flight map. Everett knew what he was doing, I assumed.

The first leg of the trip, over the Utah canyons, was stunning. We took lots of photos, and then refueled in Boulder, in the western foothills of the Rockies. While Everett logged the flight plan from Boulder to Omaha, I looked at photos of different airplanes on the wall and noted the maximum weight and altitude of each one. *How much did our plane weigh with all those computers?* I wondered if Everett even knew.

About forty minutes into our flight, when we had reached our peak altitude, I realized we were circling back quite a bit over the Rockies. Everett said that was because we couldn't reach the altitude needed to get through the passes—perhaps, he suggested, due to the plane's weight. *Did he say that for the shock effect?* If so, he did make me quite nervous with that statement. I kept looking down at the peaks below. But we eventually made it over the peaks and flew toward Omaha. A big "whew!"

Sixty miles from Omaha, the engine died mid-air. The fuel gauge was on empty! Everett laughed it off, saying there were two tanks, and he switched to the auxiliary tank, which restarted the plane mid-air. But that fuel gauge also read empty! Everett said that gauge was broken, and nothing to worry about. He'd been meaning to get it fixed.

So how much gas did we have? I wondered, as we flew in eerie silence (between us) for the next thirty minutes over Route 80 during Friday rush hour.

"Did you fill both tanks?" I asked.

He replied he hadn't, because that would have made the plane too heavy going over the mountains. So he had no idea how much fuel we had used circling back over those mountains. I thought I'd faint from fear of crashing into the neighborhoods adjacent to the road.

Three miles out, the flight controller radioed to Everett, "Bonanza 321, you are cleared for landing from the east."

"Roger," replied Everett.

"No!" I shouted. "It has to be from the west!"

Everett shot me an angry look when the flight controller asked, "What's your situation, pilot?"

"We may have a fuel situation," Everett replied.

"Permission granted for emergency landing from the west," the flight controller replied.

The minute we landed, two flight engineers ran out to meet us after the plane came to a halt. They pushed our plane to the fuel tank and started pumping.

"Seventy-nine and three-quarters gallons!" stated the engineer after filling it, "in an eighty-gallon tank! I'll have to write a report. You know you could lose your pilot's license for this."

Everett glared at me. But even he had to silently acknowledge that the circumstances might be different if we landed from the east.

"Don't tell your dad," Everett later muttered as we made the final leg of our trip to Chicago.

Later, after we'd landed at the DuPage Airport, Dad asked, "How was your flight?" and expressed relief that we'd made it home safe and sound. It was so unlike him to worry. I *so* wanted to tell him the truth as we rode home in the car. I was just glad to be alive.

Later that evening, over dinner, Mom said, "Tell Carol about your premonition, Dad."

"Oh," he said. "I was hoping not to, but I'm relieved it was just a premonition. I had a horrible headache this morning, Carol. That's unusual for me unless my blood pressure is elevated, but I checked it and it was fine.

"It was an anxious feeling I couldn't shake," he continued, "that something bad might happen to the two of you. After breakfast, I went to return the rental car, and a woman ran a red light and crashed into my car—right on the airport property. Nobody was hurt, but I felt such immense relief that *I* was the victim of an accident and not the both of you. I hugged and thanked the woman for hitting me!"

I could feel my tears welling up and turned my head so he couldn't see them. But I didn't tell Dad about that flight from Vegas for many years. I suspected it might cause a rift between him and Everett, which I didn't want at the height of MEC's success.

It wouldn't have been the first rift, or the last, between them, but his brother/business partner taking unnecessary risks with his daughter's life might have been the final straw. So I kept my mouth shut. *I was alive,* after all.

When I finally *did* tell Dad, in 1990, he went silent. After a few moments, he confirmed what I had suspected years before. He said it would have been the end of his relationship with Everett, and ultimately MEC. "If I can't trust my brother with my own daughter's life, how could I trust him with the well-being of our employees, or trust his judgment with running the company?"

In the months after that flight, I felt I'd been given a second chance at life. And I began questioning what it was I wanted from life. At thirty, I loved what I was doing, working for MEC, and jet-setting all around the country promoting MASS-11. But how long would the thrill of working for MEC last? I was a thirty-year-old workaholic working two jobs. I had no social life. And who would want to date someone who was never home? *Did I want children?* I hadn't thought about having children since I started working at MEC. But the clock was ticking.

An Unexpected Invitation

WORD OF OUR SUCCESS AT THE LAS VEGAS DEXPO show must have gotten back to the corporate managers at DEC. Perhaps it was pressure from local office automation managers, or from their top customers that prompted DEC to invite us to participate in the Scientific Solutions Center of DECWorld 1983, held at the World Trade Center in Boston.

Unlike DEXPO, which was a trade show for third-party vendors, DECWorld was a DEC marketing extravaganza that every DEC sales rep and their top customers attended. There, the latest and greatest innovations from DEC were on display.

All the booths were manned by DEC's top salespeople and tech geeks. Customers and potential customers from all over the world were invited to attend the lavish event. Attendees filled all of Boston's hotel rooms, and cruise ships were brought in when the hotels became overbooked. DEC reps stayed four-to-a-room in nearby motels. DEC reserved rooms for us at the elegant Copley Plaza Hotel, in Boston's prestigious Back Bay neighborhood. I remember having curried shrimp in the hotel's dining room.

Our latest release had all the advanced features required for scientific users. And its performance on the VAX was dazzling. The fact that we had been invited to demonstrate our new release proved, to Dad and Everett, that DEC was desperate. If their own WPS-Plus was even close to being ready, they would have shown it, or a prototype, at DECWorld. But they hadn't.

The booth manager told us the ground rules. We weren't allowed to exchange business cards with potential customers at DECWorld. If a client was interested in MASS-11, any future demos would have to be arranged through a DEC sales rep. And we were not to mention that we were developing a product for the IBM PC.

Even with these restrictions, DECWorld was an unparalleled networking opportunity. While at the show, Dad introduced me to the two DEC sales reps and the marketing person to whom he'd made offers. All three women, dressed for success, agreed that MASS-11 was the hottest product in office automation.

On the plane back to Chicago, he and Everett were both in upbeat moods, and for good reason. MASS-11 had been the star at the Scientific Solutions booth, the missing link in DEC's offerings. And the three DEC sales and marketing superstars had accepted Dad's offers of employment and would start working for MEC in 1984.

On the plane, Dad suggested I move to the East coast since I spent the majority of my time there selling to banks, accounting firms, and pharmaceutical firms in New York, New Jersey, and Delaware.

He also noted I might have a better chance of finding a potential mate if I wasn't flying all over the world all the time. The only problem was I was still working as a nurse, still doing training, and keeping the documentation up to date as new features were introduced.

"It's time you become an official MASS-11 sales rep," he said. "We'll find someone who can do the documentation for you, and we'll give you a raise so you can finally quit your nursing job, if that's what you want. The next time you're out there, check out places to live. Find an apartment where you can give demos and do training. We'll pay your rent. You can fly back to see Mom and me, and your friends, whenever you want. Try it for a year and see how it goes."

Finally, we were making money, enough to hire new sales and marketing people. We were staying in nicer hotels and eating the breakfast buffet instead of sharing the biscuits and gravy. It would be a huge change for me, but I was ready. *New York, New York!*

1984: Unprecedented Growth!

A YEAR OF UNPRECEDENTED GROWTH, 1984 was, when Surender, Ken, and I were hired full-time. I quit my nursing job and in March, moved to Fort Lee, New Jersey, a mile as the crow flies from upper Manhattan. Surender quit his job at NCR in Dayton, and Ken quit his at UNC. Both programmers began telecommuting full-time, Surender from his home, and Ken from the newly leased office in Chapel Hill.

Four versions of MASS-11 WP were released, and included increased support for proportional spacing on laser printers, the latest "must have" feature. Perhaps of most importance to our base, we introduced MASS-11 on two personal computers—the DEC Rainbow and the IBM PC AT—the latter in defiance of DEC. The PC AT sold for $6,000, too expensive for most home users.

If DEC had been smart, they would have made an offer to purchase MEC in 1984. But there was still bad blood between the two, and no offer was made. I doubt Dad and Everett were interested in selling MEC. They were finally having fun with its success!

Our strategy was to continue selling our total office automation solution on VAXes and PCs directly to Fortune 500 companies via direct sales, with or without DEC, and not to retail stores.

Across the pond, DEC U.K. announced *they* would be selling and supporting MASS-11. They published an eight-page, four-color brochure lauding the strengths of our product:

"The Word Processing System
Designed By Professionals for Professionals"

That is why Digital Equipment Corporation Limited, the world's second-largest computer manufacturer, has combined with MEC, the USA's foremost name in word processing software, to bring you MASS-11, for legal, financial, and technical professionals.

Just having that kind of endorsement from DEC U.K., after the higher-ups in the U.S. threatened us one month, then invited us to participate in DECWorld, was sweet revenge for the brothers. Soon after, DEC U.S. negotiated a similar agreement with MEC. After extensive testing and training, they would also sell Version 3-E as a DEC Classified Software product.

Replace Me, Please!

BEFORE I MOVED TO THE EAST COAST, I told Dad we needed to find someone to manage the technical documentation department, specifically the MASS-11 *User's Guide and Reference Manual*. I'd been keeping it up to date on weekends after I returned from trips.

Dad and I interviewed Sherry Kappel, who responded to our ad for a technical documentation writer. Sherry's resume noted she was an editor of a community newspaper on Chicago's South Side, as well as doing freelance writing and photography. Like me, she wasn't technical but seemed highly motivated and entrepreneurial-minded. She insisted she worked well without direction, and did a great job selling herself, which impressed Dad.

I was so relieved that he offered her the job, and that she accepted and could start before I moved. I would only have a week or two to get her up to speed before I left.

Sherry recalled, "Hank said I was employee #17. I remember he emphasized the number because he was so proud of the company's growth. It had been a four-person company for so long, he said."

With Sherry on board, I was free to move. Mom accompanied me in my new white Toyota Tercel when I moved to Fort Lee, New Jersey, in February. The move was bittersweet, leaving my family, friends, my nursing job, and the beautiful city of Chicago.

Never in my wildest dreams had I imagined I'd be moving to the Big Apple. For years (at least since 1969), I had considered New York City "the enemy" after the "Amazing" Mets, and their despised (by me) pitcher Tom Seaver, snatched the National League championship away from the Cubs, then went on to win the World Series. I was sixteen, and my first big crush was on Cubs shortstop Don Kessinger.

I'm not sure how Mom felt about my moving to the New York metropolitan area. She was a Chicago gal and never gave much credence to the Big Apple being the greatest city in the world. Although she never expressed anxiety about my move or tried to talk me out of it, I think she had plenty of concerns. I was thirty, and my passion was growing the family company. I had no social life. I'm sure she wanted grandkids. *And if I met someone in New York City, would I stay there?*

I think she also worried about crime, even though she hadn't worried about me attending nursing school on Chicago's dangerous west side in the '70s. In the '80s, New York City was still recovering from the fiscal crisis of 1975. Subways, residential buildings, and monuments were covered in graffiti.

Rolling Stone magazine called 42nd Street the "sleaziest block in America" due to all the porn shops and "peep shows" from Eighth to Park Avenue. I walked down 42nd Street every day, from the Port Authority bus station to the Midtown banks. And the parks of New York, including the now-pristine Bryant, Union Square, Madison, Tompkins Square, and Riverside, were rife with drug dealers, hookers, and strung-out junkies.

Despite all this, I loved selling in New York City. The avenues (Third, Lexington, Park, Fifth, and Avenue of the Americas) and streets (Broadway, 42nd, 57th, and Wall Streets) that I routinely walked up and down were vibrant and exciting.

I remember once, while walking from one appointment to another on Park Avenue, wearing my new navy wool suit, I raised my arms like Mary Tyler Moore did in her popular TV show of the same name. It felt so free and so liberating to think that I, an RN, was doing business with some of the most successful banks and Fortune 500 companies in the world, and that they rolled out the red carpet for me!

Hiring Frenzy

S HORTLY AFTER MY MOVE, DAD BEGAN hiring like mad; the company quickly grew from ten full-time employees to sixty. By the end of the year, MEC had a vice president of marketing, a marketing manager, four outside sales reps, six sales support staff, seven trainers, four documentation writers, an accountant, and five technical support staff.

Our programming staff had grown to four, though Surender remained the sole programmer for the word processor. Bonnie had three support people and two office helpers. And Pam's training staff was growing. The previously empty warehouse behind the 400 building now bustled with people. Dad kept leasing adjacent suites, knocking down walls, and creating new workspaces. It was an exciting time for everyone in the home office.

MECollection: Pam Nelson

We were a small but growing department needing multiple training manuals to be written. Eventually, we trainers also tested the software for bugs, and proofread Release Notes for product updates. I eventually became Manager of Training and was responsible for hiring, overseeing, and training the outside trainers. Almost overnight, we quickly grew to fifteen trainers—training either at company sites or in-house. We also developed specialized courses such as Train-the-Trainer.

Dad couldn't say enough great things about the new employees he had hired. He handed out *The Third Wave* to each one and reviewed MEC's corporate philosophy—to create an environment in which employees could be creative and work to their highest potential. If they weren't a good match for the position they were hired for, they needed to let him know. He'd help them find something more suitable to their strengths.

Some who were hired as trainers cross-trained in technical support and found that more to their liking. And vice versa. Later, a handful of trainers were moved into sales. Some excelled; others preferred to remain trainers. MEC was a game of musical chairs—do what you love and everyone will benefit was Dad's philosophy.

I wasn't around to witness this explosive growth or meet most of the new hires. I couldn't imagine sixty employees taking up the space that I mostly had to myself in 1981—writing that beginner's book and going round and around the table in the warehouse, hand-collating the books.

Besides seamless transfers of documents, of critical importance in 1984 was getting out preliminary technical documentation for our soon-to-be-released IBM PC product. For that job, Dad hired freelance writer Kathy Nichols from Pflugerville, Texas.

MECollection: Kathy Nichols

I first met Hank in 1979 when I was at NASA's Johnson Space Center in Houston working for one of the contractor companies. Their work involved electronic/computer drafting for the Shuttle Avionics Integration Laboratory (SAIL). They had these big drafting machines hooked up to a PDP-11. They hired me to create a User's Manual and other documentation for their system because their alleged user guide was 'crap'—said the engineer who trained me on the drafting machine. I was told to find a word processor for the PDP-11 because standalone word processors were too expensive.

I found MASS-11 and then went up to Hoffman Estates for three days of training with Hank. To this day, I believe it was Providence that I had Hank all to myself. We had some great conversations and some delicious food in Chinatown. During one of our conversations, I told Hank that my boss in Houston was cheap and had told me, "By the way, you'll have to build your dumb terminal; here's the Heath Kit, some tools, and a soldering iron." So, I built that terminal on my own and it passed the smoke test.

I guess Hank was impressed because, in the next iteration of MASS-11, he asked me to come up to Chicago to learn the new features and to take the program tape back to Houston. MEC would pay for everything so my boss was fine with it. The training didn't take long, and then Hank started talking to me about working remotely for MEC. He gave me a copy of 'The Third Wave' and we spent hours excitedly discussing it over dinner at Wing Wah.

That entire visit, we talked about Toffler's vision. Hank knew I had three kids, ages ten, six, and four—all in daycare and that I'd always felt a little guilty. So, Hank made me an offer I couldn't refuse. I told him, 'Yes! I want to hang ten on that third wave.' I finished the User's Manual for the contractor, taught the 'drafters' how to use MASS-11, and then went to work for MEC.

Hank was a clever man; he stole me right from under that contractor's nose. He also paved the way for my long career as a freelance writer and, after all my kids could drive, a stint as an IBM employee.

He offered me a few contract jobs in Texas, mostly local training. I once trained a crusty old rancher and his son in Robinson, Hank's hometown. He had a PDP-11 with MASS-11 on his ranch just to manage his cattle inventory. It was summer, and as they say in Texas, it was stinkin' hot!

I would come up to Chicago once or twice a year to write release notes, depending on product release dates. These trips lasted one to three weeks and they were always great fun!

Once, before Carol joined MEC, she took me on an historic walking tour of Oak Park, where she lived in the '70s, and showed me all the Frank Lloyd Wright-designed homes. It was never 'just business' when I visited.

Surender and I coordinated our trips to Chicago so we could hash out the details of each new release. In later years, after MEC hired additional programmers from India—M.S. Yadav and Arun Agarwal—I enjoyed eating Indian food with them on Devon Avenue, Chicago's Little India.

When Hank called me in 1984 and asked if I could write the preliminary documentation for their new IBM-PC product, specifically an IBM User Guide, Reference Manual, Installation Guide, and Self Study guide, I was excited. MEC had a decent-sized documentation staff by then, so I was grateful he'd thought of me, a freelancer from Texas, for this challenging project.

I already had an IBM PC A/T and thanks to Hank, I had a modem and dial-up access to the VAX and MASS-11 at one of MEC's Austin clients. Later Hank sent me a laser printer. Once a week I'd print out a camera-ready copy and send it to MEC by FedEx overnight. With my tools, I felt like the avant-garde of a coming army of Third Wave, remote workers— MEC, MASS-11, and little old me! I wasn't surprised that MEC was doing so well in 1984.

Another Texan Dad hired, as our fifth trainer, was Debbie Burk, who would eventually become our second training director.

MECollection: Debbie Burk

I was twenty-eight and recently divorced when I started with MEC as a trainer. Before MEC, I worked as a customer relations rep for Mobil Oil. A former co-worker called me about a training position after she joined MEC, and arranged an interview. I flew to Chicago to interview with Pam and Hank.

When I accepted the job and told my parents I was moving to Chicago, they freaked out. My mom helped me move. It was February, and it took days because there was a blizzard all the way. The roads were frozen; we got stranded. We were able to drive 150 miles a day at most. All my furniture was in a Van Lines truck.

Mother and I finally arrived, but the moving truck was still stuck in the blizzard, so I had no furniture in my apartment. I slept on the floor for several days! I was young and naive and afraid to ask Hank to put me up in a hotel. I now know they would have in a Texas minute if they had known.

In 1984, with a growing payroll, purchases, and trainers and sales reps turning in weekly expense reports, the brothers placed an ad in the paper for a bookkeeper. Until then, they were handling the small payroll, as well as accounts payable and receivable, haphazardly and by hand. Christine Walsh applied and was invited for an interview.

MECollection: Christine Walsh

It was a most unusual interview in that they gave me a 'test.' They asked me to go out and find an accounting package that would be suitable for their needs, which they described in detail to me. I did a lot of research and purchased a product called Jewel, which, according to the product literature, fit all their criteria. I showed them how Jewel worked; they liked it and hired me.

I installed the software on an IBM Tower system and started entering all the payables and receivables data. The product didn't work as I expected, and I was very upset! I called the company, got my money back, and scrambled to find another system.

I selected a product called Open Systems. It was dirt cheap but provided ninety-five percent of the functionality MEC needed. Hank and Everett wanted fancy reports, and I told them, "You're gonna have to pay through the nose for it." They tried to talk me into using Excel, but I declined, and they respected that. We used Open Systems as long as MEC was in business.

Besides spending on accounting software and personnel, Dad invested in an in-house print shop to print our growing list of documentation projects. He purchased a printing press and two Pitney Bowes collators. He also hired two experienced pressmen, a cameraman, and an inexperienced and out-of-work neighbor to help the other two.

To keep the printer equipment, and any other hardware in the office, humming, he hired the seventy-one-year-old Ed Szozda. Ed could always be found wearing a tool belt with a wrench in his hand. In addition to being *Mr. Fixit*, Ed was a baker, and often brought his culinary concoctions from his native Czechoslovakia to share with the staff. He was always smiling and told visitors to the office how grateful he was that Dad had hired him past retirement age, enabling him to fix things as long as he was physically able to.

Also hired was neighbor Annette Swoger to ship demo tapes as well as sales and marketing materials.

MECollection: Annette Swoger

My husband and I were friends with Hank and Joanne when the company was just getting started. They both had soft spots in their hearts for people who needed work. Joanne was the one who found out who was out of work; Hank then offered them jobs. Some worked out; some didn't.

At the time I was unhappily working at the Jewel Tea grocery store doing stock. I told Joanne, who had taught me how to drive and was helpful whenever I was having a problem.

She said, "Annette, you just need to come work for us." The office manager, Bonnie, hired me. Hank told her, "She's my neighbor," so there'd be no question that I'd be hired. Besides neighbors, there were lots of (non-Karels) family members at MEC. Word just got out that it was a great place to work. And it was!

First Sales Meeting

IN AUGUST 1984, OUR FIRST SALES MEETING was held at a country club near MEC's headquarters. It was attended by both the inside and outside sales staff, our new marketing VP, her new male assistant, and our trainers. The new hires from DEC had a distinctly corporate look. They had perfect hair and manicured nails, and they wore suits and accessories from upscale stores. The rest of us looked like geeks who had mixed and matched outfits from Zayre's discount store. The DEC hires had set a high bar style-wise.

Dad wanted his employees to look their best when meeting the public, conducting training, or attending a sales meeting. He was appalled when a couple of trainers came to the sales meeting in casual attire: jeans and a T-shirt dressed up with a scarf around their necks.

He approached Pam, our training director, about his concerns, after the first day of the sales meeting. She told him most trainers couldn't afford the business attire he expected, let alone the accessories.

"The truth was, in those days looking good was important, and expensive," Pam recalled. "With four kids and a husband who painted houses for a living, I certainly couldn't afford the look Hank expected. And I told him I doubted the other trainers could either."

So he implemented a generous quarterly clothing stipend. "You are representing MEC, and I don't want my training staff looking like they can only afford to shop at the Salvation Army." This, from a man who rarely wore a suit, and who was married to a woman whose motto was 'Never Buy New!'

At the sales meeting, Dad praised the new sales hires from DEC, as he did with all new hires. "Our sales are off the roof since you ladies jumped ship," he said. With the hiring of the new sales reps, Dad and Everett agreed that salespeople would earn a flat $50,000 a year. No commission. Just a generous base (for that time). I was finally considered a sales rep, and my salary doubled overnight!

Dad once again reminded all of us about MEC's philosophy of giving employees free rein to 'do their thing' in the field. Ours was a new way to sell. No high-pressure sales managers breathing down your neck to achieve your sales quotas. No micromanaging from the home office. He trusted them, he assured them, to go into battle for MEC.

I was quiet for most of the meeting, just observing how everyone acted and interacted with Dad. It was my first sales meeting, after all. I was struck by how the new sales reps, and marketing people, fawned over my father, and how he relished their flattery.

Dad went over key sales points with us, and he encouraged them to milk the large corporations we were already in—Sandia Labs, Hughes Aircraft, Lockheed, Grumman, and Boeing.

"There are hundreds of VAXes in these companies," he said. "Go for the add-on business. Easier to build upon than start from scratch."

We then reviewed all the accounts that had had demo tapes for over three months, and he encouraged them to give him a ring if they needed help with closing.

Lost a sale? If MASS-11 was not chosen, find out why. Call him with the details. *Cold calling?* Not necessary, he said. MEC had more leads than we could handle. The inside salespeople would handle that. *Customer Pain Points?* Know what your customer needs. Make sure you are doing solution selling. Don't promise anything until you run it by me or Everett, was his final reminder.

We also went over individual accounts. It was similar to an end-of-shift nursing report. We reviewed the status of each account, what potential there was, what other departments might benefit from, what were frequent objections and how could we overcome them. We each gave short reports, listing those clients we were about to land, those throwing up objections, and those who were long shots.

"Any questions?" he asked, at the end of the first day. "Suggestions for improvement? How can the home office staff help support you better?" A few grievances were verbalized, mostly about support, shipping errors, and the phone system.

"We'll address these issues as soon as this meeting adjourns," Dad promised.

On the final day of that sales meeting, Bonnie was given a new role, as a dedicated inside support person for the outside sales force. Sales reps were only to interface with *her* going forward. She would get answers for them immediately, they were assured.

"We're also installing a new phone system so none of your calls get dropped," Dad told them. Bonnie would be in charge of overseeing that as well.

Surprisingly, at the meeting, nobody discussed the need for MASS-11 temps. Or local trainers. Or *premium* support for those who needed more hand-holding. All three were a big concern of *my* customers in New York City, but since nobody else brought these issues up, I didn't either. Maybe it was a New York City thing. But the availability of temps was certainly on *my* mind, and those of my prospective clients.

Dad was proud that the majority of his sales and training staff was female, and that he was providing well-paying jobs for them, and providing a work/home life balance by letting them work out of their homes. IBM only hired males to sell their products.

After the meeting, a *corporate* sales goal was established: MASS-11 would be installed in fifty percent of Fortune 100 companies by January

1, 1985. Everyone agreed on that. With a steering committee guiding product development and a motivated sales staff driving sales, MEC was poised for even greater success!

Calling All Temps

I N MANHATTAN, THE USE OF MASS-11 was exploding, mostly in commercial banks, investment banks, and Big Eight accounting firms. After deciding on the hardware/software combination of VAXes and MASS-11 for their office automation needs, many were just beginning to implement their new systems.

A number of them expressed concern, not because MASS-11 couldn't meet their word processing needs, but because now they needed temps who *knew* MASS-11. Most of these financial firms operated word processing centers 24/7. Want ads began to appear in the *NY Times* classifieds: *MASS-11 Temps Needed. All Shifts. Top Dollar.*

"Nobody knows it," the more nervous managers lamented, or, "Nobody has heard of it." New Yorkers also needed a lot more hand-holding than our engineering, aerospace, and pharmaceutical customers.

"Do you have local trainers and support?" was a question I was often asked. I told them we had an excellent training staff based out of Chicago, but they'd say, "We can't afford to put your trainers up in midtown hotels for weeks at a time."

Then, out of the blue, their concerns had the potential to be addressed. First, I was approached by Anne Hamilton, the VAX system manager at Andrews and Clark, an engineering firm in Midtown. I had trained her and her staff on MASS-11 a year before. At her request, I met her for lunch, and she said she'd be interested in starting her *own* business to provide technical support and training for my Manhattan customers. *Would MEC support her aspirations?*

The second company to approach me was Tiger Temps, a Manhattan-based temporary help agency that provided temps for investment banks, specifically the Mergers and Acquisitions (M & A) departments that were gravitating towards MASS-11. The most sophisticated and time-sensitive documents on the planet were produced in these M & A departments and often resulted in multi-million dollar deals.

Tiger Temps had bought a copy of MASS-11 for the PC at the request of one of our investment bank clients and wanted to learn more about us. I met with the three partners—Jay, Jeff, and Pat—in their first-floor office at 91st and West End, on the Upper West Side. Graffiti covered the first floor of the white limestone facade; inside, the place was bustling with mostly artsy-looking young temps, as many men as women, learning and practicing on several types of standalone word processing equipment.

Jay and John were an enthusiastic couple in their early thirties; both guys had theater backgrounds. Pat had short gray hair and wore owl-framed glasses with thick lenses; she, a former secretary, appeared to be in her sixties. An odd trio they made, but all were friendly and eager to get going with learning MASS-11 and making it one of their supported products.

They told me their temps were typically actors who needed to be free during the day for theater auditions but were available to work the overnight shift on Wall Street. They made top dollar generating those high-priority M & A documents, filled with columns of numbers, in time for morning delivery.

When they told me the hourly rates they paid their temps, I gasped. They made a lot more than me! I kiddingly asked if they'd hire me, and they replied, "Of course. If you're willing to work nail-biting, hair-raising night shifts." I'd already done that as an ER nurse, I told them. They said investment banks were so desperate for skilled MASS-11 temps that they would pay much more than they'd pay for a Wang operator; those were a dime a dozen.

"MASS-11 is perfect for the types of documents they produce," Jay explained. "It's the best word-processing software we've seen. We'd like to be able to provide them with the best-trained temps as well, those who understand the sheer power of your product."

I called Dad with these latest developments. "Tiger Temps is the answer to our prayers here," I said. "And so is Anne Hamilton." He understood the need for temps but wasn't as sure about the need for Anne's support services.

"For starters," I said, "the managers here are neurotic. They need their hands held by someone east of the Hudson River. To them, the rest of the country doesn't exist.

"And, besides local support, they want local trainers too; they don't want to pay for high-priced hotels and airfare for MEC's trainers. Both Anne and Tiger Temps can provide that.

"How soon can you fly out and meet them?" I asked.

He flew out within the week to meet with Anne over breakfast, and then a late lunch with the three owners of Tiger Temps. And he was impressed.

"Tell me again how you found them?" he asked. "They're all smart and shrewd business people looking for a win-win relationship with us. They're my kind of people."

"They found me!" I replied. "Thoughts become things, Dad. It works for you all the time."

MECollection: Anne Hamilton (A.M. Hamilton, Inc.)

I had been thinking about starting my own consulting business for a couple of years; I just needed to find my niche.

MEC was a company I had great respect for, and I saw its potential in Manhattan. After speaking to Hank about my desire to be a separate company under the MEC umbrella, and assuring him I would be an asset, not a rival, we agreed. My business would primarily provide an extra layer of tech support to those who needed it. They would still have to have a maintenance and support contract with MEC.

Hank was relieved that we could help him deal with what he called 'headache customers'; he gave me full freedom to support clients who needed lots of hand-holding, such as banks and law firms. I decided to start my own consulting business, A.M. Hamilton, Inc. in 1984, shortly after meeting Hank, to support MASS-11 users.

Despite MEC having a full training staff, Hank also agreed to let me provide training to the New York City financial and accounting firms who balked at paying to put up MEC's trainers.

Once I had Hank's confidence, I also supported the growing tech team in MEC's home office if they had printer questions or VMS questions.

Hank even used me to help land sales. He once sent me to England to work with Glaxo U.K. to reassure them that the product would work as it was advertised. I assured him I would always try to make the product look and perform as best as it could. And I did.

For eight years, Anne was invited to speak at MASS-11 User Groups nationwide on technical support issues. We paid her expenses if we invited her to speak at a symposium. It was a win-win situation for both of us, and there was no question that she helped many corporations reach their ultimate office automation potential with MASS-11.

New York, New York!

DURING DAD'S VISIT TO MANHATTAN, probably over a bowl of noodle soup in Chinatown, I brought up another concern. "New York City customers needed to see more MEC faces than mine," I told him. "My customers love MASS-11, but they need to be constantly reassured that (a) they're not the only ones using it in New York City; (b) MEC is a solid company, not a fly-by-night; and (c) MEC's founders and programmers will be around for years to come," I said, hoping I sounded convincing.

"I imagine that's true for all of our customers," he replied.

"New Yorkers need to be 'wowed,'" I said. "We need to have some kind of big gathering where our local customers and prospects can get together and be impressed by who's sitting next to them. They need to go back to their vice presidents and purchasing agents and name drop, and tell them, 'I sat next to the office automation managers at GM, Price Waterhouse, Goldman Sachs... They're all using MASS-11. They invited us to see their installation.'"

"Yep. All our customers would benefit from something like that," he replied. "But how many people do you think would come to such an event in New York City?" he asked.

"I don't know. At least fifty," I replied. "Maybe sixty?"

"Jesus! I thought you were going to say a dozen."

Like Surender, he said, "Let me sleep on it and I'll get back to you." And he did, the next day.

"Carol, if you think you can fill a hotel ballroom with fifty decision makers, both existing customers and serious prospects, then go for it," he said.

"That's great," I replied. "We could probably get a room at the Milford Plaza for a reasonable rate."

Dad, who knew Manhattan well and, when visiting, walked and explored her streets and avenues, quickly replied, "No. Not the Milford Plaza." It was a low-budget Midtown hotel where he'd stayed in the past.

"I doubt the Milford Plaza would impress your banking customers."

After a pause, he said, "There's a new hotel next to Grand Central Terminal called the Grand Hyatt. It's not the best area, but I read this morning in the *Times* that they are offering low introductory rates. Why don't you see if you can get a small ballroom *there*."

A ballroom? At the Grand Hyatt? "The new Trump hotel?" I asked in astonishment.

"Carol, if you're telling me we need to 'wow' New Yorkers to get and keep their business, well then, we gotta 'wow 'em,'" he said.

He then added, "While you're getting rates, find out what it will cost to get rooms for at least a dozen of our staff for two nights. See if you can get a group discount. I think this could be a great opportunity to show off our sales staff."

"But can we afford all that?" I asked.

"You gotta spend money to make money," he reminded me. "And if we get even one new VAX license at the end of the day, it will pay for itself."

A few weeks later, after I'd met with the Grand Hyatt people and booked a ballroom for late November, Dad said he'd discussed the seminar with his new VP of Marketing, and she was gung ho to plan it.

"That's right up her alley," he said. "I'd like her to be the keynote speaker; your customers will appreciate that we have a VP of Marketing who spent eight years with DEC."

I'd only met her a couple of times; she was usually traveling overseas when I was in the home office. Hawaii, Australia, London, and Oslo were her most recent destinations, "negotiating deals with resellers and customers like British Petroleum and Norsk Hydro," Dad said. He didn't mention that she took her boyfriend on all those trips.

"I already have the VP of Office Automation at Chemical Bank lined up to be the keynote speaker," I told him. "She's excited to talk about their successful implementation of MASS-11." Dad was silent. Even he knew a VP from Chemical Bank tooting our horn would be hard to top.

"So let her give the introduction, then," he said. "I'm not hiding one of my highest-paid employees at this shindig." *I* would have liked to be the one to welcome my customers but, as Dad reminded me, the purpose *was* for New York City customers to see more faces than mine. She'd give the welcome address.

Another week passed and Dad said he'd put her in charge of the catering and ordering marketing materials: engraved pens, notepads, badges, and reprints of magazine reviews.

"Catering?" I asked.

He replied, "Yeah, she thinks it would be a good idea to provide a continental breakfast and sit-down lunch for everyone, as well as a cocktail reception afterward. This will give everyone a chance to network after hours. I agreed; it's a great idea."

We must have been bringing in a lot of money, I thought, to provide two meals and a cocktail hour to fifty people at the Grand Hyatt NYC!

He told me Bonnie would also be coming, as the logistics manager; she'd make sure at least one MEC employee was at each lunch table to answer questions and get feedback on the day.

"I'll have her take everyone out for a group dinner the night before," he said.

Bonnie made it clear to all, at dinner, that everyone was expected to be ready for the seminar at 8:00 A.M. Eastern time. They could help themselves to the continental breakfast we'd provide to the customers, would get a sit-down lunch along with all the customers, and there'd be plenty of food at the cocktail reception. "I don't want anyone getting mugged on the street!"

THE SEMINAR WAS A HUGE SUCCESS. We had invited people from eighty firms in Manhattan. One hundred and forty people representing seventy firms, both existing and prospective clients, attended! As promised, Dad flew in both the inside and outside sales reps, our marketing VP, and a handful of technical support staff and trainers; he put them all up at the Grand Hyatt for two nights.

MEC's trainers all looked so professional in their new suits. Pam Nelson said that they were all so grateful for the new clothing stipend.

The afternoon consisted of technical breakout sessions, and each was well-attended. MEC employees shone as they demonstrated products and answered questions. Anne Hamilton spoke, as did the Tiger Temps trio. Even *I* spoke on advanced features and how they get implemented.

It was the first time I had ever done public speaking to a large group, using a microphone, no less. I felt as if someone was talking through me. I didn't even have stage fright even though I knew there were numerous intimidating decision-makers in that audience. The words came out effortlessly, and I didn't use notes. It was surreal; everyone applauded.

At the cocktail reception, customers continued to ask questions and network with other MASS-11 users. What surprised me most was how our existing customers invited prospects to see how their MASS-11 installations worked, even if they were competitors. From that gathering, the idea of forming a Manhattan MASS-11 User Group emerged, and its members would first meet at Price Waterhouse in January 1985.

At the end of the day, our marketing VP gushed, "MEC is such a terrific company to work for, Hank. DEC would never give me the budget and resources to plan an affair like this." It was *my* affair, I wanted to say, but I didn't. She was bragging like a peacock with full feathers displayed; I was humbled, in awe, and trembling at the day's success.

For me, the event was a revelation. What had just been a suggestion a month or so earlier had fully manifested in a successful seminar, in the heart of New York City, no less. *Thoughts did become things! Dream big! Dare to be adventurous!* Everyone we had invited, and more, showed up for the day. The positivity shared in the room was contagious. We "wowed" them!

The Ideal Word Processor

A WEEK OR SO LATER, DAD CALLED to tell me he had taken out a one-year lease on an office across the street from Grand Central Terminal, one with a Park Avenue address on the corner of Park and 42nd Street.

"I was checking out the place last week," he said. "It's a small office but it's a perfect location for you."

I didn't need an office, but I understood that having a Park Avenue address on my business card was sure to impress. And I had a new self-confidence. Granted, I *was* the boss's daughter, as well as a nurse with no aptitude for technology, but I had spent the past four years helping grow the family business! My sales had paid for that seminar. And my father had faith enough in me to let me handle the hottest office automation market in the world: New York City!

I knew our success in Manhattan was just as exciting for him, and Everett, too. *New York, New York. If we could make it there, we'd make it anywhere!* It put us in a new league. Not only were we ready for prime time in New York City, but we were hearing from sophisticated and experienced word-processing users that our product was ideal for their complex requirements.

And just what made a word processor *"ideal"* in 1984? Carl

Marbach, the editor of *DEC Professional* magazine, who also owned a publishing company, wrote an article about the ideal word processing system for a large corporation, both feature-wise and security-wise. A shared system, he wrote, was the only way to go:

> *Word processing, properly implemented, is for everyone in the organization who needs to create text or documents. When the VAX is the word processor, there is plenty of power to support the functionality of a complete word-processing system.*
>
> *Both the number of documents that the user can have and their size should be unlimited, and the system should make use of the special functionality of the computer it runs on.*
>
> *Lots of system services will be provided for shared word processing systems, usually without the users even knowing they are going on. Word processing documents automatically will be included in the backup cycles, ensuring against the physical or logical destruction of documents. New releases of the operating system and improvements contained therein will affect word processing users as well as other system users.*
>
> *There will be a system manager to issue passwords and guard your security. And with most shared systems, security will be much higher than any stand-alone can provide. You will be protected not only by password, and by file protection from other users, but also from the loss of a floppy disk which is easy to misplace, spindle, or mutilate.*
>
> *The system manager will also be an in-house resource to answer your non-technical questions about the computer system. The ability to share documents and files can also be very important.*

So, after defining the ideal word processor, which did the publisher of *DEC Professional* choose to use in-house for all their publishing needs in 1984 and beyond? MASS-11!

At the fall DECUS meeting, DEC announced they would be selling and supporting *two* word processors for the VAX: their newly released WPS-Plus, *and* MASS-11 3-E, now a DEC Classified Software Product.

DEC also released All-in-1, its office automation umbrella for the VAX. We had already started work on seamless integration with All-in-1 with the assistance of DuPont. DEC had not assisted us in doing this, and the version of MASS-11 they'd be selling and supporting would *not* have this feature.

By the end of 1984, MASS-11 was installed on VAXes in 35% of the top fifty Fortune 500 companies, 80% of aerospace firms, all the nation's leading scientific research facilities, 120 universities, fourteen governmental agencies, three of the nation's top ten financial institutions, the second largest law firm in the country, and the third largest school system in the U.S.

Our success was breathtaking. Unimaginable! Just a year earlier, MEC had ten employees, and Surender and I were both "part-time" while supporting ourselves with a second job.

1985: Ready for Prime Time

EVER SINCE OUR BRITISH RESELLER SAID MASS-11 wasn't ready for prime time in Manhattan, I'd taken that as a challenge. I dreamed about opening new doors, of getting into all the pharmaceutical firms in New York, New Jersey, and Delaware; and all the investment banks and the Big Eight accounting firms in the city.

I welcomed any invitations from DEC sales reps to show MASS-11. I put the names of prospective companies under my pillow, hoping either visualization or the law of attraction would prevail. And it mostly did.

Selling in Manhattan, walking down Park Avenue, and riding up elevators to meet with the top decision-makers, had been a thrill. The successful seminar at the Grand Hyatt, our first New York City Users Group meeting at Price Waterhouse, the opening of our new office on Park Avenue, and the positive press on how MASS-11 and VAXes were displacing large Wang installations in Manhattan were all such a high. If life was supposed to be fun, I was having plenty of it!

The success of our first NYC User Group spawned the rapid formation of twelve groups nationwide. Each month, a new one started, and we had groups meeting regularly in Washington D.C., Philadelphia, Boston, Los Angeles, San Francisco, Dallas, Houston, Albuquerque, Denver, Seattle, and Chicago. At these gatherings, users could share advice and tips as well as hear about product updates from MEC's product managers. Those who attended were our most vocal cheerleaders.

We also ordered color copies of all the great reviews we were getting in magazines, such as this one, and passed them out to prospects:

> *MASS-11 itself can be reason enough to buy a VAX. Some DEC personnel, even at the remote field offices, will certify this product above and over DEC's word processing offerings. Unequivocally and without reservation, MASS-11 WP has proven to be one of the premium, flagship, big software fighting tools. This is a product that is so universally valuable and so well designed that it deserves the immediate attention of the chief executive regardless of the size of his operation. (Computers-R-Digital, 1985)*

Our largest users, who were beta test sites for WPS-Plus, assured us we had nothing to worry about.

"It's a memory hog, slow as sin, and short on functionality—a dud," all insisted. "The only thing it has over MASS-11 is that it's integrated with All-in-1, which isn't saying much."

Instead of fearing its release, we *celebrated*, because finally, customers could do an actual side-by-side comparison, come to their conclusions, and defend their decision to choose a third-party software product such as ours. An outside consultant at one large corporation had done a thorough comparison of MASS-11 and WPS-Plus and shared the results with us. That comparison somehow made it to one of the magazines, and they published it.

Shortly after its release, we placed ads targeting the weaknesses of WPS-Plus. One featured a photo of the dinosaur skeleton from the entry hall of Chicago's Field Museum: *Bigger Isn't Better*. Another featured a depressed-looking cartoon character sitting at the edge of a cliff: *Got the WPS-Plus Blues?* And finally, *A VAX is a Terrible Thing to Waste (on WPS-Plus).*

The ads had bulleted lists highlighting our strengths versus WPS-Plus's deficiencies. I'm sure the WPS-Plus developers were baffled at how much we knew about their product minutes after it was released. Once again, it was guerilla warfare, with MEC's foot soldiers pointing their guns at DEC's generals.

From the ads, demos, and product reviews, it was clear that MASS-11 was light years ahead of WPS-Plus, even though DEC's product had been designed by *a* team of programmers, while ours was designed by one—Surender.

"Too many cooks stirring the pot at DEC," our customers joked. "And designing it in their ivory tower."

Surender became a folk hero of sorts, and he was given nicknames such as "The One," "The Man," "Zeus" and "The Elvis of Dayton," by both our staff and our customers.

Everyone knew his name; a handful had spoken to him on the phone; yet few had met him in person. Ours was becoming an entertaining David versus Goliath story, with many of America's top corporations rooting for the underdog. Among our cheerleaders were the writers and editors of magazines that specialized in the DEC marketplace, reviewing both software and hardware that worked on the VAX.

Carl Marbach said, during the 2024 interview I conducted with him, "I laugh these days when people discuss how wonderful and innovative 'the cloud' is for sharing data. Our publishing company was so advanced back in the '80s, using the VAX and MASS-11. In the publishing world, we did things the industry never thought of doing using MASS-11. We had terminals all over the offices with leased lines; we created graphics, integrated data and graphics, sent them to editors, then designers all over the country."

DEC reps had orders to show their product first, and only bring us in when the situation was desperate. However, I and several other MEC salesreps were friends with many of the DEC sales reps and technical support people, and they didn't hesitate to call us in. After all, they had sales quotas and deadlines to meet.

It would have been a perfect time for DEC to raise the white flag and buy MEC. But DEC was too insular, and Dad and Everett were having too good a time running circles around them.

And Then There Were Four

I N 1985, A FOURTH KARELS WAS HIRED. My brother John was ready to become part of MEC's rags-to-riches success story. It annoyed him that he had to ask Dad for a job. It was John, after all, who had been the first financial supporter of the fledgling MEC, lending Dad his high school savings of $6,000. *He still hadn't been paid back in full*, he told me, even with not-so-subtle reminders.

After graduating from the Naval Academy and serving his time in the Navy, John moved back to Chicago. I had helped him find his 45th floor apartment at the Outer Drive East condominium downtown, overlooking Lake Michigan. It was just a few blocks walk from his civilian engineering job at Sargent & Lundy, the same firm where Dad had started his own engineering career.

With my brother back in Chicago, the two of us occasionally met for dinner and concerts downtown. We even bought a half-share in a 25-foot sailboat, one we named *Joy*, that we docked in Monroe Harbor. We often took employees, from both Sargent & Lundy and MEC, for a sailing outing on the lake.

While he was studying at the Naval Academy, I had attended all the Army-Navy games in Philadelphia, even during the gas crisis in 1977. We exchanged letters while he was at Annapolis and at sea. We had traveled together on numerous occasions, including to Europe twice. On one of the European trips, he had accepted an award from the Danish government on July 4, 1981, on behalf of his ship the *USS Jonas Ingram*.

Our Labor Day weekend birthdays were a day apart, and as kids, we always shared a "party" on the Wisconsin River, our last canoe trip of the season with family and friends.

John was brilliant, and one of the most well-read men I'd ever met. He could debate both sides of an issue convincingly, even at a young age, and he could hold his own around the campfire with all the adults. We both shared a love of history; if he recommended a book, I usually read it, and we discussed it. The same went with movies.

John showed an interest in what MEC was doing at family dinners, and at one point asked Dad if there might be a position for him. Mom and I had encouraged him; it was our family company, after all. Dad was undoubtedly expecting this but had reservations.

John was highly qualified for a managerial position, *but which would suit him?* Not sales and marketing; we already had a VP of Marketing, and sales was Dad's baby. Documentation and training already had managers. A support manager was already in place. Product development was Everett's domain.

They privately had a father/son talk about it. *Where could Dad put his son without it looking like nepotism?* Dad didn't think Everett would want a fourth Karels family member, especially another alpha male, in the picture. But he agreed to discuss it with Everett; if *he* was on board, they would hire John.

Everett, to Dad's surprise, welcomed this news, saying he was overwhelmed with product development and needed help. Our customers were moving beyond simple word processing and inquiring about a MASS-11 suite of products that all interfaced seamlessly: database, spreadsheet, calendar, and graphics integration.

Everett had also been spending a significant amount of time with customers on the seamless exchange of MASS-11 documents between the PC and VAX. He was also working on an interface with DEC's All-in-1. Electronic publishing had suddenly become the new buzzword. We were on the cusp with our ability to support high-speed laser printers with multiple fonts and right-justified proportional spacing.

John, due to his military experience, was a proven leader and well-versed in the process; he was uniquely qualified to succeed Everett as Product Development Manager.

Everett had grown tired of being in the office, where he frequently tangled with support staff. He enjoyed flying his plane, visiting clients, and attending user group meetings. John could be very useful based in the home office, dealing with everyday issues.

So, without any fanfare, John joined the family business in January 1985 and managed the development of our current and future product line.

Surender would continue to be the main word processing programmer; Ken would be working on innovative projects in North Carolina. Two Indian programmers, M.S. Yadav and Arun Agarwal, were hired to develop a spreadsheet and calendar, respectively. John's internal staff would do programming, testing, support, and write documentation for the new products.

To my knowledge, he was welcomed, and there was no talk of nepotism among the staff. He began hiring young, bright college interns and new grads. He also established procedures to do things—how new features and bug fixes would be incorporated into products, and how testing and documentation updates would be handled. He was, from all accounts, quiet, humble, and professional, and got along well with both the existing and newly hired staff. His group socialized together and had great camaraderie.

Truth is Stranger than Fiction

I WONDERED HOW THE THREE KARELS MEN, all electrical engineers by training, would get along at MEC. Dad was the alpha male with vision, energy, and people skills; Everett, the younger brother, was more the introvert—a 'tech snob' who loved to talk tech strategy with MIS managers and was dismissive of those with IQs less than his; and John, the alpha male son who had no qualms about locking horns with those who didn't agree with him, including Everett and Dad. Dad was known to eviscerate Everett behind closed doors. Would he do the same to his son if they disagreed?

Growing up, neither of us got preferential treatment. We took turns mowing the lawn and taking out the garbage. I wasn't expected to help Mom with "girl's chores" such as cooking, cleaning, and doing the dishes. We were both good students, bookworms, and didn't rebel. When John did, Dad had him dig a four-foot ditch along both sides of the yard.

While Dad and Everett dressed casually, John wore a suit and tie to work every day. Although he appeared on the surface to be straight as an arrow, he commuted to MEC from his new Rogers Park bungalow on the north side in a vintage Chicago Yellow cab, painted white. He and his new wife, who worked at a no-kill cat shelter, owned around fifteen cats, many of them blind, three-legged, deformed, and unadoptable. They also had two dogs; theirs was an "animal house."

John often told me our childhood reminded him of Paul Theroux's book *The Mosquito Coast*, which centered around an eccentric and difficult father who often put his family in peril. Parts of it did, I agreed. But *Swiss Family Robinson* was more how I recalled our childhood, filled with pets and travel adventures.

"I don't know how Mom puts up with him," John said. "He's so high-maintenance. Everything centers around him." Mom, by contrast, was low maintenance and she handled Dad's energy, ego, and eccentricities with great aplomb.

John and I recalled our shared childhood through different lenses. His was a magnifying glass, which zoomed in on every flaw Dad had, whereas I recalled our childhood with rose-colored glasses. We'd taken lots of family trips, and there were some exciting and unexpected adventures on many of them.

Dad was a self-acknowledged risk-taker. He'd almost died in a motorcycle crash at eighteen, and at twenty-five, when Mom was pregnant with me, he'd ignored signs that he had acute appendicitis until it burst, which landed him in the hospital with near-fatal peritonitis.

On weekend canoe trips, our family was the only one without tents. We slept on a tarp under the canoes, exposing ourselves to mosquitoes and rain. We could afford canoes and camping equipment, so why not tents? None of us dared to complain.

On the first day of our first canoe trip in the Canadian Boundary Waters, Dad took a dare from a fellow canoeist. Instead of portaging [carrying] the empty canoe on the path, he paddled it over Basswood Falls! I was the only one to witness it as I rested on the trail watching the falls, not expecting to see my father go over them. Then his canoe split in half, and when I didn't see his body pop up at the base of the falls, I began screaming. Others ran down the trail to see why.

"My Dad went over the falls! He hasn't come out of the water yet!" I screamed. And then, as if in slow motion, we all saw his body shoot up from behind a large boulder and tumble down the falls. He had been pinned against it and somehow managed to pull himself loose. He'd lost his shoes and glasses, but he survived.

"Just some pain in my ribs," he'd said after he swam to shore. "A swig of port should help!"

The trip continued, and despite his certain pain, Dad carried our two canoes over each portage, up to two portages a day, as well as the two canoes of the four single women on the trip. When we got back to civilization, after taking our hot showers at the outfitters, Dad went to the local doctor in Ely, Minnesota. He was X-rayed and told he'd fractured eight ribs!

John often reminded me of these traumatic events from our childhood. One was the first time we went spelunking as a family in southern Indiana and couldn't find our way out of the cave. Another time we were paddling across Basswood Lake in Canada when a thunderstorm erupted, and high waves almost capsized our boat. Mom and Dad paddled alongside us, but the fear was real. For the most part, I'd forgotten, or repressed, those memories.

I hoped he'd get past these old grievances and that all the Karels men would get along at MEC.

Rave Reviews

THE DOCUMENTATION DEPARTMENT, UNDER SHERRY, was growing at a rapid pace. By the end of the year, she had hired three additional writers to produce sleek *Quick Reference Guides* and cards for both the PC and VAX, for all editors: MASS-11, DEC's Gold Key, and EDT.

Our documentation received rave reviews from the press that year. From an article in *Digital Review*: *"Hands-down this is the best documentation I've seen for any word processing system."*

Besides documentation, Sherry and her staff introduced a four-color glossy magazine called *Status Line*. The first issue featured an article on "The Brothers Karels," customer success stories, *Tips and Tricks* for using MASS-11, as well as photos and bios of new employees. She reserved a page for the newly formed National MASS-11 Users Group to share their ideas. *Status Line* was a fabulous marketing tool that confirmed MEC was a major player in the office automation market.

The magazine also featured *Letters to the Editor* such as this one, from the Assistant to the Deputy Chief for Administration of the U.S.D.A., a customer Dad had sold MASS-11 to in 1980:

I want to congratulate 'the Brothers Karels' on MASS-11 for the PC; it is a truly outstanding product! And congratulations to Sherry Kappel and the new MEC crew on Status Line, which is great, and for the continuation of the Karels' policy of listening to the user. MASS-11 has provided the central core for our busy, heavily automated administrative and systems management office now for four years. Recent comparisons with other systems have shown that even the old version still outperforms current competition. With the receipt of MASS-11 for the PC, my high expectations of an even better system were more than realized.

Three *Status Lines* were published in the next year and mass-distributed to customers and potential clients. They included profiles of successful and powerful users such as SOHIO, Baylor University, MIT's Whitaker Lab, Research Triangle Institute, Coopers & Lybrand, and GM Research. Our marketing materials reflected the image Dad wanted to portray. We might be small, but we didn't cut corners on quality.

MECollection: Sherry Kappel

My experience at the community newspaper was a kind of prep school for MEC. As a documentation writer, I had complete access to Surender and spoke with him several times a day.

We had our own MEC business goal to eliminate the costly process of typesetting and sending copy to an outside offset printer, so we could produce our own documentation in-house using our products. But we had to use the typesetter until we had certain features like pagination, proportional spacing, indexing, table of contents, and support for laser printers in the product.

So in some ways, we were developing a product to meet our needs, but in doing so we met the needs of so many existing and potential customers with the same goals. At the time that was such a sweeping change in technology. I remember when I started, we used an impact printer and gave the output to our typesetter.

At MEC, we were always trying out the latest technology. It was expensive and high-end, but it had to be that way. That's what our customers were using and we had to be compatible.

When we started producing our own camera-ready copy, Hank invested in laser printers to produce the camera-ready output, and offset printers so he didn't have to take it to an outside printing press.

As new laser printers proliferated, the support department became inundated with calls about printers, including calls left in the middle of the night from Europe and Asia. Dad asked a DEC rep from Alaska if she could recommend a technical person who could handle support for the West Coast, Asia, and Australia—someone who could work independently out of their home and didn't mind waking in the middle of the night to answer frantic calls about printers not working.

She recommended Sharon Fisher, the "best tech person I've ever worked with. She's brilliant!" Dad met with Sharon, a single mom who wanted to live closer to her ill mother in California. Dad hired her and paid for her move from Alaska to California, where she could work from her home. Sharon was a "printer whisperer" and worked closely with Surender and tech support staff from printing companies such as Talaris, QMS, and Hewlett-Packard to develop printer tables to support all the new printers coming out.

MECollection: Sharon Fisher

MASS-11 just blew everything out of the water with its intricate and almost infinite support for printers. Surender's code put power in the user's hands. Embedded in MASS-11 were the tools to allow end users to interface with just about everything, including going from MASS-11's 8-bit code into Xerox's 7-bit code and coming back out in 8-bit. It got us into numerous aerospace companies such as Hughes, Lockheed, TRW, Boeing, and Naval Oceanographic.

I also supported non-aerospace customers such as Goldman Sachs in Japan and England, who had heavily invested in DEC's LN03 laser printers. They appreciated that someone at MEC picked up the phone in the middle of the night (their busy day) and walked them through any problems encountered.

Growing the Company

S O HOW DID THESE TWO BROTHERS, who had grown up dirt poor in the small village of Robinson, Texas, deal with their new financial success? Besides his plane, Everett bought a modest home in the upscale neighborhood of Inverness, one known for its sprawling estates and expansive green spaces, just north of MEC headquarters.

Mom and Dad didn't give one thought to changing their lifestyle. Their split-level home in Streamwood was their castle. Both loved sitting on the back porch in the morning and evening, drinking coffee while overlooking Dad's organic vegetable garden, mounds of colorful flowers, grape arbors, and fruit trees.

The wooded area behind their house was inhabited by pheasants, ducks, raccoons, feral cats, and other wildlife that often ambled into our yard, helping themselves to the produce or leftovers that had been tossed into the garden.

Mom still enjoyed her volunteer activities with Cook County Hospital, the Elgin Humane Society, and the Elgin League of Women Voters. She also fed and provided shelter to a colony of feral cats; she was an early proponent of catch, neuter, and release.

A big house or late model car never had appealed to either. He enjoyed driving his used Bronco, and Mom refused to give up her Oldsmobile sedan, one with 150,000 miles on the odometer. They also owned a yellow pickup truck, which became a MEC vehicle.

Dad's side passion was gardening; he spent money on seeds, bulbs, bushes, dirt, sand, manure, gardening tools, and a rototiller. He planned the half-acre garden in the winter, planted it in the spring, enjoyed it in the summer, and destroyed it with his rototiller in the fall. Each year he came up with a new plan.

But Dad's main passion at the time was growing the company, and that would be due to the efforts of his dedicated sales force. Sales were *his* bailiwick, after all; he wanted to continue to build a sales force and provide them with the tools, training, and support they needed to become successful selling MASS-11.

In addition to the first three women he'd hired away from DEC, he recruited four more: one each for Northern California, New England, Texas and Louisiana, and Detroit. Each brought a distinct set of talents to MEC.

ONE OF THE FIRST SALES REPS Dad hired who hadn't worked for DEC was Natalie Kaye, who had worked for Expo Consul selling exhibit space for trade shows.

MECollection: Natalie Kaye

MEC's booth drew a lot of traffic, and everyone, both their customers and MEC employees, seemed to be having fun. That type of camaraderie with clients was what I desired, but lacked, in my career.

Weeks after MEC's big DEXPO show in New Orleans, I called Hank and asked if he had an opening on the East Coast. He knew I was a fairly good salesperson, and invited me to come to Chicago for an interview. MEC paid all my expenses. After the interview, he said, 'You're hired.' He said I would be

on probation for two months, learning the ropes from Carol.
If I worked out, I'd be helping her with customers in New
Jersey, Pennsylvania, and Delaware.

Dad had spoken with me first before hiring her. I liked Natalie and welcomed her help. It was hard giving up my pharmaceutical accounts, but I sensed Natalie had the energy and determination to be a success in that territory. She proved to be a go-getter and a great asset to MEC with her positive attitude.

With eight outside sales reps, Dad kept a close eye as well on internal staff members who might also do well in outside sales. He moved a handful of trainers into outside sales positions—offering them the same salary as he did the other reps. Three trainers accepted his offers. One moved to Washington, D.C., one to Seattle, and the third stayed in the Chicago area.

Dad also taught his sales philosophy to employees based in the home office. He believed *every* MEC employee should be in sales mode at all times. In life, he explained, we are always selling ourselves: to make friends, find a job, or a spouse.

"Receptionist, quality control, trainers, tech support," he'd tell them. "You are all ambassadors for MEC. When you're engaging with a customer, whether in person or on the phone, you must always be selling. You're selling confidence in the company and the products, as well as confidence that MASS-11 does what we say it will do."

When he'd heard, at one sales meeting, that a couple of employees were rubbing customers the wrong way with their unprofessional telephone manner, instead of singling out those employees for discipline, he enrolled the *entire* home office staff in Dale Carnegie public speaking classes so *everyone* could learn proper phone etiquette and more.

The instructors taught techniques of asking questions, active listening, being engaged in a conversation, and sounding pleasant, both on the phone and in person. Dale Carnegie trainers came to MEC's offices twice a week for six months during lunch hour. MEC provided a catered lunch for each session.

MEC was a great place for employees to socialize, make friends, and even meet spouses, whether at the Dale Carnegie training sessions, annual Christmas parties, training sessions, bowling leagues, or company picnics.

Living in New Jersey, I wasn't able to participate in any of the social activities in the home office. But I finally had time to date and eventually became engaged to the DEC sales rep who I had met on New Year's Eve.

The home office staff threw a bridal shower for me, and most MECies attended our May wedding, held at the Continental Plaza Hotel on North Michigan Avenue. The cost of the wedding was the price for a MASS-11 license on the VAX: $11,500. Mom and Dad also paid the airfare and hotel rooms for any family members who wanted to attend but couldn't afford it. The party, with a live orchestra, was as much a celebration of MEC's success as it was of our marriage.

Two days after the wedding, a dozen MECies flew to New Orleans for DEXPO, and I was on the plane with them. No way was I going to miss DEXPO at the height of MEC's success. The honeymoon could wait.

Cutting the Line

A FTER GETTING MARRIED, I TRIED to visit the home office at least every four to six weeks, to visit my family, meet the new hires, or learn new features.

On one of these visits, I was in for a rude awakening when I asked my brother if we could make a minor tweak to MASS-11 WP—to specify the thickness of an underline. It was requested by the office manager of one of the Big Eight accounting firms who referred others to MEC. This manager had done so many favors for me that I promised him I'd ask.

In the past, if I wanted to suggest a tweak, I'd have just given Dad a call. He would then call Surender, and it would probably take Surender ten minutes to program it. Instead, following the new chain of command, I brought it up with John.

Unlike Dad's office, which was cluttered with phone messages, the latest tech gadgets, marked-up books, notebooks, unopened mail, and piles of tech magazines, John's office had a spartan look: a clean desk, two chairs, a terminal, and a monitor reminded me of his spotless room at the Naval Academy. The only adornment was a painting on the wall of a sailboat on Lake Michigan.

John listened to me, his hands clasped on his desk, his intense blue eyes meeting mine, and replied, "Get at the back of the line, sister. You're going to have to get used to the idea that you're just one of eight sales reps now. And just like you, they all have 'must have' requests from their VIP customers."

Seeing the shocked look on my face, he asked, "What makes you think you can cut the line? If the other sales reps heard I gave my sister special preferential treatment, well, *now* we're talking nepotism. And you know how Dad feels about *that* subject."

His response stunned and hurt me. I wasn't a new hire salesperson getting my feet wet, as all the rest were. None of us were getting a commission. And my sales revenues had made it possible to *hire* and train new sales reps. *And him!* But I kept those thoughts to myself. *What was going on with him?*

John, with that one statement, robbed me of my joy working at MEC; he made me feel like a cheater for cutting in line. Once I came to my senses a few days later, and realized I was not, I took matters into my own hands and called Surender at home.

"Could this tweak be added to the next release?" I asked. "It's a big favor I'd like to return for one of our Big Eight accounting firms."

Surender simply replied, "Sure, that's easy. No problem."

"Sure" should have been Surender's nickname. Relieved, I called my client and told him to expect it in the next release. The undocumented tweaks, I understood, drove support people crazy, but the goodwill generated among our top customers, I felt, was more than justified.

BY THE END OF 1985, JOHN'S STAFF had programmed, tested, documented, and released a family of office automation products that included MASS-11 Manager, MASS-11 Calendar, and MASS-11 Superlist—all fully integrated with MASS-11 WP.

And the latest release of MASS-11 WP included all the features the big banks were begging for, including that undocumented tweak, which made the lives of hard-core word processing operators in investment banks and accounting firms so much easier. The new process John had implemented worked well. I just didn't like the part of it where I had to get at the back of the line if my customers had suggestions.

Butting Heads

I'D LIKE TO SAY I NEVER HAD A RUN-IN with John again. And when it came to word processing, I didn't, because I never again went to him with requests. It was over our new products. After a trade show at the Javits Center we'd both worked at, John asked me how many demos I had given on MASS-11 Manager, a fully relational database management product. I couldn't recall, I told him.

"Did you give *any*?" he asked. *Was he spying on me?* I sheepishly confessed that if anyone had asked to see the Manager at a trade show, I'd have introduced them to one of the tech guys who knew the product inside and out. I could talk about its features, however.

"You need to learn these new products, Carol," he said. "All the other sales reps are. Word processing may have been the hottest new invention in the early '80s, but it's becoming a *commodity* now. What makes us stand apart now is our MASS-11 *family* of interconnected products. Connecting words with spreadsheet data, graphics, and database text is our new niche."

I didn't argue with him. That was my sales pitch, after all. But I wasn't sure I'd be able to learn *and become proficient,* demonstrating graphics, database managers, and calendars.

I was *a words person* and appreciated what a product like MASS-11

WP offered a writer. My mind was more focused on electronic publishing being the next big wave, not the "family of products." The new goal for my clients was to eliminate the costly Compugraphics typesetting equipment and print typeset-quality documents on their laser printers.

I could speak that language: words and electronic publishing, and I could *out-demo* anyone, and answer every question with confidence. At DEC, the sales reps never gave demos; they were given by a product specialist, usually a woman, referred to in the industry as a demo dolly. Was I, after all, just a word processing *demo dolly?*

I later learned that it wasn't just *me* with whom John had these blunt, in-your-face, discussions. Behind closed doors, he confronted both Dad and Everett about a myriad of subjects—decisions that needed to be made, directions that needed to be taken, employees who needed to be promoted or booted. No topic was off-limits with John as he attacked Dad's sacred cows. Dad was used to being revered by employees and customers, not challenged, especially by a family member.

John challenged Dad's management style of giving employees numerous opportunities to redeem themselves, or moving them around until they found a position they loved. John's attitude was, if they weren't doing the job they were hired for, *then fire them!* Dad had fired two people in the home office for breaching confidence. But that was it. He didn't micromanage and was very forgiving.

I could sense his bull-dogged directness was not only wearing Dad down but bringing out the dormant pitbull in Dad as well. The two frequently butted heads behind closed doors. Dad never told me about those confrontations with my brother, but John did and often tried to get me to take his side. It put me in an awkward position; I didn't want to choose sides. I could see both of their points.

This pattern of triangulation reminded me of the three-month-long road trip my cousin Lisa and I had planned around the U.S. after I graduated from nursing school in 1974.

John, who was on a break from the Naval Academy, joined us on the leg from Chicago to Glacier National Park. Once we'd arrived, he said we should spend a week fishing and hiking. But Lisa and I had plans to keep on driving. John tried to pit me against Lisa. "I'm your brother. Family sticks together."

But I had planned the road trip with Lisa; my loyalty on that trip, I told him, was to Lisa. And so we left him behind, and he had to hitchhike home.

John often called me in the evening, questioning some of Dad and Everett's decisions. If my husband picked up the phone before me, John would vent. My husband inevitably asked why I didn't share these things with him, and often insisted, based on what John told him, that Dad was mismanaging MEC. I wasn't comfortable sharing insider MEC information with him while he was still working at DEC. My husband, I suspected, wanted to be MEC's sales manager.

I didn't agree with everything Dad did, but MEC was Dad's creation. He could hire and fire whoever he wanted. I was grateful he listened to and took my advice, and that he had faith in my efforts. He never second-guessed me, lost his temper with me, or "man-splained." He just empowered me to do my best.

In the past several years I'd watched Dad build a strong foundation for MEC that could handle the sudden success we were having. Granted, he was a work in progress, but he wasn't the hot-headed daredevil we'd grown up with. In the five years I'd worked with him, I had grown to understand how he thought and operated. He had earned my respect and admiration. I had begun my MEC journey with Dad; so my loyalty, when it came to business matters, was with him.

I recalled one particular teaching of Dad's when John and I were teens. It may have been a teaching of Hazlett's or from the ancient philosopher Epictetus, "It's not what happens to you, but how you react to it that matters." And I came to realize over time, as we siblings both worked in the family business, how vastly different were our reactions to various scenarios.

You're Fired!

I WOULDN'T HAVE BEEN SURPRISED if Dad and Everett discussed firing John, for insubordination or not adhering to the *Third Wave* way of thinking. Everett and Dad may have wanted to fire John but someone else got fired instead for insubordination: Bonnie!

To everyone but Everett, Bonnie was the mother hen who held the home office together. Whatever Dad asked of her, she took it on, cheerfully and competently. She took a huge management burden off Dad's shoulders.

But Everett saw her as a bossy "pain-in-the-ass" who had the gall to stand up to him when he wanted to stop MEC's offset printing presses to print his personal writings: his travel stories, the family genealogy stories, or his Christmas letters, among others.

MECollection: Bonnie LaScola

Things were always testy between me and Everett. While I was still in charge of support, Everett ordered me to hire a programmer, one with a doctorate, for phone support. But the man could barely speak English. He might have been a brilliant programmer, and I wondered why he wasn't hired for that position.

"Nobody will be able to understand him," I told Everett. And without batting an eyelash, he replied, "You're fired!"

He told me I was threatened by people who had degrees, and the manager of support should have a degree. Hank was in Hawaii with Joanne, and even though I had the phone number of their hotel room, I didn't want to bother him with this bizarre turn of events. So I just packed up my stuff and left. I left it to Everett to tell my support staff. I'm not sure he ever did. I wouldn't have been surprised if he'd told them I quit.

When Hank returned, he gave me a call at home. "Everett told me what happened, and he's not backing down. He's on a rampage about managers having degrees. How close are you to getting yours?" he asked.

I told him I had stopped going to college when I became 'married with children,' but I only had one semester to go. Hank said he'd pay the tuition for me to complete it, and continue to pay my salary, out of his pocket, if I'd be willing to transcribe some Ralph Hazlett leadership tapes.

I was grateful for his offer and took him up on it. Hank made himself the manager of support while I was away. Four months later I completed my Bachelor's in General Studies, and I learned a lot about psychology and leadership from reading Hazlett's teachings as I transcribed them.

Hank brought me back to the office and told me that, in addition to support, he was also putting me in charge of the printing operation. I knew nothing about printing. But I hadn't known about support either.

I asked, "What will Everett say?"

Hank replied, "I don't give a rat's ass what he'll say. You got the goddamn degree he wanted." Hank also gave me the authority to make decisions in his absence, including the *authority to say 'no' to Everett with no repercussions. I got a sense Everett firing me wasn't the only thing Hank was upset about with his brother.*

Anyhow, Hank said he and Everett would eventually be moving their own offices into the newly leased office space across the street, which would house the sales, training, and product development staff. So I wouldn't have to see Everett regularly, he assured me. He then added he was putting me in charge of the move.

Pam Nelson, the training director, recalled being stopped by Dad in the hallway shortly after Bonnie was fired.

MECollection: Pam Nelson

Hank told me that, henceforth, as a training manager, I would have to make sure the trainers I hired had a college degree. Someone had put that bug in his ear. I was not aware that Everett had fired Bonnie for not having one.

I told Hank I didn't have a degree either. Like Bonnie, I'd stopped just short of it and never made a point of finishing. Taking this in, Hank said something like, "Okay. Well, never mind." And I never heard another word about it. I think Hank was secretly relieved. As an aside, many of our trainers did have college degrees, but other qualities, capabilities, and experience had always been given equal consideration.

What Pam *didn't* know was that my father, the founder/co-owner of MEC, didn't have a degree either. *Nor did he care.* He always joked that he had a degree from the "University of Hard Knocks" if anyone asked.

Dad had far more electrical engineering credits than he needed to graduate from the Illinois Institute of Technology. But he hadn't completed two of the English literature courses required and never found the time to complete them after he was married, a father of two, hired by Foxboro, and transferred to Davenport, Iowa. He said he took the courses he needed to be the best he could be at his job—not to get a damned piece of paper.

When he was later promoted to Regional Sales Manager at Foxboro, a degree *was* required, but his boss, Al, made an exception for him due to his vast experience. A clause was included in his contract that he could never be fired for not having a degree. He left on his terms to start MEC.

1986: The Company that Delivers

WHEN 1986 ROLLED IN, IT WAS another stellar year for MEC. MASS-11 User Groups were meeting nationwide and in Europe. Those in New York City, Philadelphia, the Capitol Area, Boston, Chicago, Seattle, Houston, Denver, San Francisco, and Los Angeles met regularly.

Our support, training, and technical development departments outgrew their original office space and Dad began planning a move to a new building across the street. With input from department managers, he designed the new space, with the goal of every employee having a window.

Two highly anticipated products were released: the MASS-11 Graphics Processor (GP) and MASS-11 Mail. MASS-11 Draw, a revolutionary new vector-based drawing tool developed by Ken Crossen and his team in North Carolina, was being beta-tested at numerous research firms.

At the July sales meeting, which was held at the Palmer House in downtown Chicago, sales reps were each given a Toshiba 3100 portable computer to demonstrate all MASS-11 products at customer sites. QMS laser printers were also sent to their homes.

We used all our products in-house: MASS-11 WP for all

documentation and correspondence, MASS-11 Manager for mailing lists, form letters, and inventory, MASS-11 Calendar for scheduling training sessions and sales demos, and MASS-11 Draw for creating marketing materials and newsletters.

Our in-house print shop had four men producing two thousand books a week. Sherry was given many hats to wear including managing quality control, internal documentation, customer relations, product testing, *and* coordinating communications with programmers.

Two steering committee meetings were held in 1986. One was at the Grand Hyatt in New York City to discuss text and graphics integration. The second was held in the fall in Tampa, Florida, where they dove into office automation using MASS-11 Mail and Manager.

THE PRESS WAS HAVING A FIELD DAY testing all our products. MASS-11 Manager got favorable reviews, and MASS-11 WP continued to receive accolades, especially because we provided an identical product on the VAX and PC with seamless communication. We weren't going after the PC market, just accommodating our VAX users who were also heavily invested in PCs.

In May, an editor at *Hardcopy* wrote:

> *Word processing has grown up here at Hardcopy magazine. Mere words delivered in a reasonable amount of time just won't cut it anymore. Technology has caught up with the average business office in the way word processing is accomplished and in the finished product. The ability to network workstations and support laser printers with a full range of fonts and characters is now necessary for any one product to gain a foothold in this competitive market. Word processing must be all things to all people, and MASS-11 may be that kind of system.*

From the November 18, 1986 issue of *PC Week:*

MASS-11, from MEC, has long been considered a premier word processor on DEC's VAX series of minicomputers and the recently released PC version is no exception. Given the speed of MASS-11, its power, and ease of use, anyone serious about word processing on a PC would benefit from its use. Hardcore power users will have a field day with it. And those with scientific, mathematical, and legal word processing requirements would be hurting themselves if they did not give MASS-11 a careful look.

The Magic of MASS-11

N 1986, MEC PARTICIPATED IN FOUR trade shows: DEXPO South and West, Graphics Expo at the Javits Center, and the Pittsburgh Conference in Atlantic City. MEC's tech reps were also invited to demonstrate MASS-11 in the Scientific Solutions booth at DECWorld in St. Louis.

Dad went out of his way to compensate staff who went above and beyond with special projects, tight deadlines, or extra responsibilities— both financially with bonuses or on a night out with their special someone. Managing trade shows was one of these special projects, and for a while, he assigned Bonnie to the task.

MECollection: Bonnie LaScola

I managed at least five tradeshows. When Hank heard my husband was on the East Coast on business, he paid for him to come to spend the weekend with me in Washington, D.C., picking up the hotel bill and my husband's meals as well.

I also had to find hotel rooms for staff at trade shows. In New York City, Everett told me to put everyone up at the Hotel Pennsylvania, across from Madison Square Garden. It was economical but a bit rundown, and a couple of salespeople raised a stink. Carol always stayed at the Hotel Empire, across the street from Lincoln Center. It was also economical and a little seedy, but in a safer area, so we put everyone up at the Empire for the next show. Then one of the trainers got mugged just down the block. It was the late '80s, not the safest time in New York with the crack epidemic. I always felt responsible for everyone at those shows.

AT THE LARGER TRADE SHOWS, WE SET UP a model office, similar to the setup at the Paperless Office in 1979. Dad always wanted to show off our latest and greatest features on state-of-the-art equipment so our booth had modular Steelcase cubicles, a MicroVAX, a few PCs, and laser printers.

Shipping the Steelcase all over the country cost a fortune. Packing it and unpacking it, then setting it up and taking it down at each show, required a lot of manpower. Dad hired the firemen from the Hoffman Estates Fire Department to pack it in wooden crates on their days off and then unpack it after the show.

He also assigned a team of guys in Product Development and Support to be the 'tradeshow team' to set up and tear down the Steelcase, as well as demonstrate our products. One member of the "tradeshow team" was Bill Boehm, who recalled his good fortune of being hired to work in customer support.

MECollection: Bill Boehm

A year earlier, I had graduated with a degree in Computer Science from DeVry Institute of Technology and been hired to work in sales for NCR. It was a bad fit—my background was more technical—and they fired me.

I lacked confidence and wasn't sure where to go after that. A friend from DeVry was working at MEC and set up an interview for me. I joined the MASS-11 support team. Shortly thereafter, a couple of us broke away from the support team and started the quality control team, doing all the software testing and keeping a log of software bugs (glitches). We reported our findings to Surender via electronic bulletin board, because this was before email. I eventually was promoted to the role of MASS-11 WP Product Manager.

From 1986 on, at every DEXPO, we hired Mark Philips, a magician who incorporated the latest MASS-11 marketing message into his fabulous magic tricks, always drawing in a big crowd.

On the first evening of DEXPO West, at the Disneyland Hotel, we always hosted a hospitality suite for customers to attend, providing buckets of boiled shrimp, and fruit and cheese towers. Dad always invited all our family who lived in southern California as well. It was outrageously expensive, and Dad was unapologetic.

"This is what I've worked my ass off for my whole life," he boasted. "I love watching decision makers from Fortune 500 companies, the "brightest of the bright" scientists and engineers, and the sharpest office managers and secretaries gather at my booth to watch Mark's magic, get wowed by our products and enhancements, and then strategize and have fun at our hospitality suite. This is my dream come true, *where it all comes together. Why would I want to skimp on this?* Money is meant to be spent, not given to the IRS. And I'm having a hell of a good time spending it."

Introducing MASS-11 Draw

E VERETT HAD BEEN SPENDING much of his time, now that John had assumed many of his previous responsibilities, visiting the facilities of our largest customers. It was the best way to fully understand their corporate-wide office automation and electronic publishing strategies. He often visited DuPont in Delaware and took programmer Ken Crossen along on one of those trips.

MECollection: Ken Crossen

My true interest was graphics, and you couldn't do those on the VAX. Inspired by an early Apple MAC graphics demo, wondering if I could create a credible application in that arena, I began to write a freehand graphics program for the IBM/PC AT.

Everett took me along on one of his visits to DuPont. The engineer we met with told Everett they needed graphic design capabilities yesterday and were about to show us out the door if we didn't have a product soon.

I had in my pocket an elaborate piping diagram one of my assistants had created. I pulled it out and asked the engineer, 'By graphics, do you mean like this?' and I handed it to him.

The engineer replied, 'This is exactly what we're looking for. Tell me more.'

I told him we had developed a full-featured, mouse-driven, object-oriented freehand-drawing program for the PC that had extensive symbols libraries: organization charts, flow diagram objects, chemical symbols, electronic symbols, piping items, and computer symbols. You can create your own symbols libraries as well, I told him, including signatures, forms, schematics, and prototype documents.

He and I began an intense and exciting conversation about the functionality they were looking for in a drawing program, and I told him we'd completed most of that. He asked numerous questions about support for laser printers, integration with MASS-11 WP, editing tools provided, Lotus 1-2-3 integration, and more.

Even Everett didn't know the extent of what we'd been experimenting with in North Carolina but assured the engineer that DuPont would be the first to beta test it. That drawing in my pocket turned everything around.

Everett then spent a week with me in North Carolina, getting up to speed on the program and learning all the important buzzwords. I showed him how to create templates, and how the program could be used to document electronic circuitry, workflow, systems design, wiring diagrams, and piping layouts. I gave him an advanced course that included ways to modify drawings with fill patterns, arrowheads, and a variety of line widths.

Everett then spoke with Hank, who was very excited and gave me the green light to make it a top priority. He also gave the go-ahead for my wife Cynthia to write the documentation, with all illustrations created in Draw.

All their customers were clamoring for a drawing tool for

their schematics, flow charts, and freehand designs. We worked round the clock to get it ready for release. There was nothing like it on the PC. One of the features I was most proud of, and no other product had it, or ever did, was the ability to grab a corner and move it, without control points all over the screen. It was uncluttered, an intuitive way to edit engineering graphics, that was a differentiator.

We called the product MASS-11 Draw, and just like that, MEC entered a new world. The world of both text *and* graphics. The first review of Draw, which appeared in *Folio* magazine in September 1988, was positive, as were all subsequent reviews:

> *The bottom line is, that anyone who does technically oriented illustrations can probably make use of the program. It runs on any IBM-compatible PC. It uses a lot of memory, so 640K is a good bet. It can run from a floppy, but real men don't use floppies. It will output to virtually anything: line printer, Postscript printer, typesetter, whatever. It ain't real cheap. It goes for $695 from Microsystems Engineering. On the other hand, it is the first piece of software that I think is worth a lot more than the asking price.*

Our engineering customers, once they found out about Draw, were ecstatic. It was more than a welcome surprise. It was the next-greatest thing since MASS-11 WP!

Women's Lib at Westinghouse

G ARY MAULER, A SYSTEMS ENGINEER at Westinghouse, was one of those excited about Draw. An original member of MEC's Steering Committee, he was one of the first engineers I had trained. By 1986, Westinghouse was using all MEC's products.

MECollection: Gary Mauler, Westinghouse

The systems engineering group did a lot of writing—mostly specs and technical documentation. At the time we had an IBM mainframe, a VAX, and some military computers. In the early '80s, the secretaries had Wang stand-alone word processing systems. At that time, the engineers were all men, and the secretaries were all women. That's the way it was back then, but women's lib was changing things.

The process was, if an engineer had to write a spec: (a) he had to write it by hand, (b) submit it to the secretary to be typed up, (c) wait, wait, and wait some more for the secretary to type it up and print it out, (d) hand-write the corrections on the printout, and (e) give it back to the secretary to make the corrections.

This editing process was excruciating. It went back and

forth endlessly, using Wite-out and correcting tape, until the document was finally printed on a Daisy-wheel printer, which resembled typewriter output. I was interested in making that process easier and making the final product look more professional.

The engineers had a VAX cluster of 780s and were using the EDT text editor and line printers. When I found MASS-11, I remember saying, 'Damn! This is neat!' I was deploying VT100 terminals around the office as fast as I could, to the most efficient users, a few of whom were young female systems engineers who knew how to type. Typing was an asset if you were an engineer.

I was the only male engineer who knew how to type, having taken a class in high school, the only guy in a room full of girls. Typing, come to think of it, was the most valuable class I took in high school! But back then, if you could type, you were considered "a typist."

One of the female engineers balked at getting a terminal. If the engineers saw a woman typing, whether on a typewriter, a Wang word processor, or a VT terminal, they assumed she was a secretary.

But with women's lib taking hold, these new women engineers wanted to project a professional image. They didn't want the guys to drop stuff off on their desks and expect them to type it for them. I'd like to think the younger male engineers were more sensitive to the women's movement, but it was a cultural shift and not easy for everyone.

There was a story that Admiral Grace Hopper once told in a speech about her first job with the Navy. She said she was given a desk next to the copy machine. The older guys would walk by and drop documents on her desk, expecting her to make copies for them, and she wasn't sure how to respond.

That's what women in offices did, after all, make copies and type. Her boss saw what was going on and told her, "Just tell them to make their own damn copies!"

Our next challenge was that the secretarial pool was unionized, and engineers were not allowed to touch the Wang word processors. After I came along with the VT100s, all the engineers started hunting and pecking, creating their own documents.

The union secretaries worried that, if the engineers were doing their own typing, they wouldn't need a secretary, and they thought they'd lose their jobs. They blamed me for empowering the male engineers to type on their terminals; I suddenly became 'the bad guy' in the office.

Luckily, my manager saw the benefits of using MASS-11, that sharing documents between engineers and secretaries greatly increased productivity. Ultimately none of the secretaries lost their jobs because engineers typed their documents. They just got different types of jobs such as executive secretaries.

Once MEC gave us the option of using an EDT-like editor, the use of MASS-11 spread like wildfire around the buildings at Westinghouse. Then along came the PCs, and MASS-11 worked on them, too. We played with them, hooked them up to the VAX, and shared the data back and forth. The PCs and VAXes were very popular.

As more applications came along such as AutoCAD and spreadsheets, we were able to import spreadsheets and graphs into MASS-11. Then MASS-11 Draw came out and took off because we were able to create all kinds of diagrams, which is what engineers like to do. We started a big transition to the PC for word processing, spreadsheets, and drawings. As the engineers got more proficient at typing, they grew to like their independence using MASS-11pc. Then the powerful and fast laser printers came out, and we were among the first to use the Talaris laser printer, which MASS-11 fully supported. Now our documents looked like they came off a professional printing press!

A New Wave?

I N THE SUMMER OF 1986, WHEN I WAS four months pregnant, I got an unusual call from Dad. He hadn't called to discuss business, he said. "I just finished reading a mind-blowing book called *Ramtha*," he said. "I'll send you a copy."

It was a "trance-channeled" book, meaning the words came from a spirit, through a human in a trance-like state. The spirit was Ramtha, who identified himself in the introduction as a 35,000-year-old Lemurian warrior who, at age sixteen, had led a successful battle against the Atlanteans. He survived being stabbed multiple times; during his multi-year healing period, Ramtha achieved spiritual *mastery* and came back to Earth to share his teachings with those needing "awakening." I read the book in one sitting after it arrived.

It was similar to other New Age books such as *Seth Speaks (1972)*, *A Course in Miracles (1976)*, *Bringers of the Dawn (1992)*, and later, *Ask and It is Given (2004)*. The channeled words were often taped, transcribed, and published into best-selling books.

The spirit Ramtha selected J.Z. Knight, a dental assistant, to "channel" his words. He claimed she was his daughter in those ancient Lemurian days. (He'd also claimed the actress Shirley MacLaine was a son.) J.Z. had been channeling Ramtha since 1977 and had traveled all over the U.S., giving workshops and live-channeled sessions. She settled down in Yelm, Washington after Ramtha advised her it would be the safest place in the U.S. to survive a future apocalyptic event. The book, a compilation of the 'best-of' teachings from those sessions, was published in 1986.

Having read similar books, I didn't find anything unique about the concepts discussed. My parents taught us that God is within, that we all have divine potential. But after reading the *Ramtha* book, Dad was enamored with Ramtha's 'profound' teachings. He bought a case of the Ramtha books and passed them out to selected friends, family, and co-workers, including Everett, his sister Joyce, and Bonnie. Everett and Joyce both expressed interest.

Bonnie recalled, "I read parts of the book and told him, 'I don't need this. I'm not searching. I know who I am.' And he was fine with that."

MOM WASN'T FINE ABOUT THIS NEW DEVELOPMENT in their lives and shared her concerns with me. "Your bedroom is now the 'Ramtha Room,'" she said. "He spends hours at night in there listening to Ramtha tapes."

When she helped me move to the East Coast, before he'd discovered the Ramtha book, we had a conversation about Dad's many "influencers."

"After all these years of seeking," she said, "I think he's finally learned how to tune into and trust his intuition."

I agreed. The *Third Wave* had made a great impression on him, and MEC was still riding that big wave. Was the Ramtha book just another intriguing book? *Or a new wave for Dad?*

Special Delivery!

I
N DECEMBER, I WAS IN THE EIGHTH MONTH of my pregnancy. I'd
felt great the whole pregnancy, and lugged my 15-pound Toshiba
laptop all over Manhattan, up and down subway staircases, and
onto city buses, to give demos. Dad had hired a woman named Laurie
to assist me in the field after I gave birth. Her expertise was graphics,
and she had spent the past several months learning MASS-11 Draw.
She created sell sheets for each product using Draw, and she gave a
great demo. But she had little to no sales experience.

The plan was that, in January, she would teach me MASS-11
Draw, and I would introduce her to all my customers and teach her
how to sell MASS-11 WP. The plan was disrupted when I gave birth
to my daughter, Beth, a month early, on the last day of 1986. From
the initial contraction to birth was one hour; her premature birth
caught us totally by surprise. I didn't even have a crib yet, so she spent
her first days in a wicker basket previously used to store throw pillows.

Just two weeks before her birth I had worked the PC Expo show
at the Javits Center with John, Laurie, and Bonnie. The four of us then
closed up the Park Avenue office, storing the furniture in my garage.
It was a workout!

I had met with users at E.F. Hutton on the 29th and had lunch in the city with my contact at Coopers & Lybrand twelve hours before I went into labor. I had a 9 a.m. Draw and Manager demo scheduled with Price Waterhouse on the morning of the 31st, nine hours *after* I gave birth. I had several word-processing demos scheduled with Laurie in the second week of 1987. I hadn't made any childcare plans. I naively assumed I would continue my rigorous sales schedule after giving birth.

WORD OF MY PREMATURE DELIVERY SPREAD quickly among my customers. In the first week after Beth was born, my office phone rang all day long with messages of congratulations followed by hesitant requests for meetings or demos, *as soon as possible*, "when you're up to it," *pretty please.*

After a week of juggling the needs of my newborn and returning the frantic calls of my customers, I chose my sanity and my baby over the customers. Childbirth had birthed a new me. I didn't want to leave her side for a minute. I was intensely fascinated by her, and the experience of giving birth, so quickly and intensely, without drugs, was transcendent.

I called Dad and said, "I've given it a lot of thought this past week, and I just don't think I can do sales anymore." I wanted to say, "I don't want to do *any kind of business* anymore." I just wanted to stare into my baby's dark eyes, watch her sleep, listen expectantly for her cries, feed her, and play with her hands and feet.

He replied, "For Chrissakes, Carol, you just had a baby. Why are you even answering the goddamn phone? Take it off the hook. Tell your customers to call Laurie."

But my customers wanted to talk to *me*, not Laurie. It wasn't her fault; she had been tossed into the friendly but demanding lion's den called Manhattan. She utilized her time doing what she did best: giving Draw demos and getting the latest feedback from our users at MASS-11 User Group meetings.

She also bugged Dad about our documentation, insisting she

couldn't sell our products until the documentation had a new look. "We need new and competitive documentation similar to that of WordPerfect and Microsoft Word," she told him. "We have superior functionality, but our presentation doesn't match the quality and power of our products."

She wasn't the only one complaining. Dad became convinced by her and some others in the sales force that we needed a new look, that our three inches-thick 8.5 x 11 manuals needed more than just an update—they needed to be rewritten and designed.

I agreed and also wished we had a less clunky name, one that represented the sophistication and power of our product. Something like *Power Word*. The best name, WordPerfect, was unfortunately already taken. I'd felt for years that we should have changed our name after we moved MASS-11 to the VAX. But it was too late for that. Our clunky name had too much name recognition in the DEC world.

Dad said he'd been giving it plenty of thought, and that he'd brought it up with the documentation department. He had asked them how long it would take to do a new book, in the new format, filled with graphic images created with MASS-11 Draw. One year at least, he was told, and they'd need to hire more staff.

He was informed that they were swamped keeping up with multiple products, updates, and platforms. In 1987, the small documentation department was responsible for over forty books, not to mention marketing materials they worked on. Dad went out on a limb and said he needed the new documentation in time for the April sales meeting, or, at the latest, PC Expo in June.

"No way," he was told. That was way too long for the salespeople to be making excuses. He told Laurie he didn't get a sense of urgency on this project from the documentation department. If he permitted Laurie to hire a writer and graphic artist on the East Coast, did Laurie think it could be completed in that timeframe? Laurie was optimistic and said yes.

Maternity Leave Project

A WEEK OR SO AFTER I'D GIVEN BIRTH, Dad filled me in on this project. He asked if I would consider managing it so Laurie could devote full-time to sales. After giving it some thought, I agreed. Overseeing a project was something I *could* do while on maternity leave, I thought. He told Laurie and me, "I want this project to be *top-secret*. Not even Everett or John are to know."

Although I had agreed to a role in it, I thought it would take a miracle to complete this new manual in *six* months, let alone four. *And wouldn't the office staff wonder what I was doing with my time?* Dad said it was none of their business.

Laurie wasted no time looking for a freelance writer and graphic artist. She placed an ad in the local paper, one that included my address and phone number for replies. I received one resume for each position, both from local women. The writer lived in neighboring Palisades Park; the graphic artist lived in Passaic, a thirty-minute drive. When Laurie dropped by to review the resumes with me, she asked if I'd called either, and I said I hadn't. She briefly reviewed both.

"Call the graphic artist for an interview," she said. "But *don't* call this writer."

"Why?" I asked. "She sounds like she has lots of experience."

"There's a coffee stain on her resume," she pointed out. "We can't have someone sloppy like that. This particular project is four months, but it's just the tip of the iceberg. Many potential writing projects are waiting in the wings. We must accept only the best," she insisted, "even if it takes a few weeks to find the right person."

We then met with Barbara, the graphic artist from Passaic, in my living room. Her resume indicated she had a master's degree in museum presentations, and experience designing exhibits for the Smithsonian in Washington D.C. When we met, she said she was married to a minister and had a six-month-old daughter. She was looking for a position where she could work out of her home.

I liked Barbara as a person, and that we shared an interest in history. Laurie liked her portfolio and her qualifications as an artist.

"We'd like to hire you," Laurie said. "How soon can you start?"

LAURIE'S ADVICE TO WAIT for the perfect writer was sage. A second resume arrived the following week, from a writer named Hilde Weisert, who lived in Teaneck, two miles from me. Her resume was crisp and clean, and her writing credentials were impeccable. She noted on her resume that she was also a published poet.

I called her, and the four of us—Barbara, Laurie, Hilde, and I—met the next day, also in my living room. The two babies were present, on a blanket on the floor. Hilde and Laurie were both unmarried and childless; they were good sports about our babies crying (Beth cried the most) and needing to be fed throughout the day.

Hilde admitted she had no experience writing technical documentation, but she appeared to have a strong work ethic, a sense of humor, and a perfectionist mindset. She expressed an interest in learning more about text and graphics integration. She got along well with the three of us, said she didn't mind meeting us with the babies present.

We hired her on the spot and told her we'd set her up with all she'd need—software, a PC, and a laser printer. We agreed to meet weekly at my house to review what had been completed and to outline the next week's work. Barbara would bring her daughter Bethany to these meetings, and Hilde would bring her sheepdog, as well as lunch for all from Louie's Charcoal Pit, a Greek diner in Teaneck.

Laurie had pulled together what appeared to be a dream team for me to manage to accomplish this seemingly 'mission-impossible' assignment. Our babies and Hilde's hound rounded out the team.

Dad and Mom flew in a week later to meet with them, *and* their new granddaughter. "I'm predicting," Dad told Barbara and Hilde, "now that I've met the both of you, this project will be a success. But if it ain't finished in time, don't sweat. Nobody but those in this room will know. I'm not promising anything to anybody."

But they both rose to the challenge. My "maternity leave project" was a success due to their hard work, Dad's faith in us, Barbara's prayers, and the weekly prayers that her husband, Reverend Doug Cross, asked from his congregation. We miraculously completed the book in time for the April sales meeting.

MECollection: Hilde Weisert

It was just crazy to think how hard we worked on that book those four hectic months. But it was so much fun when we all got together at Carol's house. We reviewed what I'd written and Barbara's images—while Barbara and Carol simultaneously attended to their babies' needs.

Barbara created at least a thousand images from scratch using MASS-11 Draw. I remember one stormy night, a couple of months into the project, she called and sounded frantic on the phone; she thought she'd lost all her images, thinking that lightning might have wiped out her hard drive. She drove to my house in her nightgown and trench coat, her PC covered by a Hefty garbage bag to protect it from the rain. We eventually figured it out and everything was restored in a few hours. But that was a hair-raising experience! Back in the office, Hank picked a recently-hired employee, Sarah Browning, to be my intermediary in the office.

MECollection: Sarah Browning

I started when they were hiring and growing the organization at a pretty good clip. I was twenty-four, and hired to inspect everything that was shipped.

When Hilde came to present the new books to Hank, and said she needed someone who could print drafts in-house and assemble them to circulate for review, Hank picked me. That was still in addition to my inspection responsibilities (every order, every day).

Hilde sent files on floppy disks by FedEx, along with printed instructions. I would open the package, call her on the phone, review the contents and what she needed me to do with them.

At the successful conclusion of the project, Dad told me to take everyone out for a celebratory dinner. The four of us, with our husbands, dined on an Italian feast at the historic Stony Hill Inn in northern New Jersey.

The project was just the beginning of a years-long collaboration among us. Barbara continued to work with Hilde on documentation, and she worked with me on marketing projects.

After the book was complete, I formally left sales and, at Dad's request, started working on marketing projects from my home.

"You can keep your Toshiba laptop and QMS Laser printer," Dad assured me, and just as he promised when I moved, "you can make trips home with little Beth whenever you want. Mom can watch her when you're in the office."

Writing, training, sales, and now marketing. I was grateful for the opportunity. I had no interest, or talent, for programming, support, product development, or managing an office. I recognized that if I'd worked for any other company in 1987, I'd probably have had to resign. Working from home wasn't an option with other companies then, and wouldn't be accepted widely for another three decades.

But telecommuting to promote a product I loved *was* an option for me, a new mother, and I gratefully took it.

A Sales Surprise

I ATTENDED THE SALES MEETING IN APRIL 1987, where the new PC manuals were distributed. The printing crew had worked overtime, Dad said, to get them ready. Everyone was shocked and elated that something they had only recently requested was a reality. No more excuses for not getting sales.

The only one who wasn't happy about the "top-secret" project was my brother. He took me aside at the meeting and said, "Dad was disrespectful of the documentation department. He should have given them the option of hiring someone to do it."

He also shared another grievance with me, this one about Anne Hamilton. "Why does she have access to our programmers?" he asked, "when those in MEC's support department have to go through the proper channels? Dad is being disloyal to our support and training staff." I respectfully disagreed and my "lack of loyalty" further strained our relationship.

Besides the manuals, Dad made an announcement that was a surprise even to me. "From this day forward," he proclaimed, "we're implementing an optional commission system for sales reps. You'll get a certain percentage of each sale. No base. Just a straight commission. It's not retroactive. If you made a big sale last month, it doesn't count.

It's your choice—base or straight commission going forward. But we did the numbers, and all of you will come out ahead financially if you choose the commission system."

As he explained the new system, I slowly came to realize how much more, *a lot more,* I could have been making the past few years if I'd been paid commission instead of a salary. *Would I have willingly given up my big customers on the East Coast to the new sales reps had I been on commission?* But it was too late to change my mind about sales. And I wouldn't anyhow, with a newborn.

That announcement was followed by another. He was also offering a $1,000 savings bond to the top salesperson of the month.

Why hadn't he put that bonus in place for all the years *I* was selling? I could have used an extra thousand dollars now and then. Why did he wait until after I'd left sales?

I summoned up my courage to ask him these questions in private, after the sales meeting. He didn't hesitate when answering. "It wouldn't look good if my daughter won it every month," he said. *So that was it?* He thought it would look like nepotism if I did well?

"You never needed motivation because it's your family's company," he said. "But outside sales reps need incentives, and a few of them are telling me commissions and bonuses are what they need to light their fires."

Despite my sales success, I had always assumed the others he'd hired were bringing in more business than I was, perhaps because, whenever anyone inquired about how sales were going, he'd reply that MEC was doing better than he ever expected, due in large part to the sales superstars he'd hired.

He'd hired several more that I met for the first time at the sales meeting. I grew to understand that Dad just liked boasting about his outside sales force.

Dad didn't have time to oversee everyone in the field, so he assigned a young guy in the marketing department the job of making joint sales calls in the field and reporting back to him. And that guy, who had little experience with sales, knew exactly what Dad wanted to hear.

"Everything's great Hank! Our customers are excited about all our new products. The new sales hires are pounding the pavement and opening new doors! There are dozens of big orders in the pipeline. Next year is going to be phenomenal for MEC, Hank!"

Bonnie recalled, "That's what your Dad wanted to hear. He always believed that his employees would do their best, give their all. He loved both getting and giving praise. He never put anyone down. By praising them, he was giving them the chance to do better."

New Competition on the VAX

SOMETIME IN 1987, WE HAD GOTTEN wind that WordPerfect was about to release their best-selling PC word processor on VAX/VMS. By then, their PC product had overtaken WordStar as the #1 word processor for the PC in the world. WordPerfect employed 350 people, with a hundred just for support. When it was released on the VAX, it was received with great fanfare by the press.

Digital Review writer Nell Margolis wrote an article entitled *War of the Words Heats Up in VAX Market*:

> *If you're wondering what to watch, now that the Kentucky Derby, the Preakness, and the Belmont Stakes are over, you might tune in on the VAX word processing software market. The pace in this market has quickened considerably, in no small part due to the February arrival of PC superseller WordPerfect for the VAX.*

The article went on to list all the features WordPerfect Corporation was promising for VMS. Dad and Everett didn't seem too concerned about WordPerfect's encroachment on our VAX territory until one magazine declared that WordPerfect was *the* Word Processing 'Product *of the Year.'* For the VAX!

Dad and Everett declared war on both WordPerfect and the magazine that had coronated them. Our customers went to battle for us and wrote letters to the editors, many of which were published, claiming the comparison was rigged in favor of WordPerfect simply because of its success on the PC.

"Take a closer look before jumping on the WordPerfect bandwagon," one wrote. "It's all hype, no truth."

"It doesn't even support PostScript output," another wrote, "a must-have in the VMS marketplace."

A series of questions to the editor ensued. *Had the editors tested it with a variety of printers using multiple fonts and proportional spacing? Had they checked the performance with multiple users? Was it integrated with DEC's All-in-1? Could you use it to create scientific equations?*

Knowledge is power. These were all questions we had put in their minds when they were evaluating MASS-11 versus WPS-Plus. Just as with DEC's product, the answer was *No* to all for the WordPerfect product as well.

So just as they'd helped us in discovering the shortcomings of DEC's WPS-Plus, our loyal customers joined us in the battle against WordPerfect on the VAX. Their findings were often shared at MASS-11 User Groups, so attendees could take them back to their managers and reassure them that MASS-11 had been the right office automation decision.

Two of our largest customers did take a closer look, in their efforts to standardize on *one* product that would meet all their office automation/electronic publishing needs. They held "showdowns" to select the product with the best *functionality*, not the best *public relations*.

At GM Research in Warren, Michigan, an eight-member task force spent a year evaluating twenty major PC word processors, including

MASS-11, WordPerfect, and MS Word. This study included twenty focus sessions, and ultimately, MASS-11 was selected for their 1,600 VAX users and hundreds of PC users.

And the World Bank, in Washington, D.C., selected MASS-11 as their standard for six thousand PCs (no VAXes) running on a Banyan network, after a year of evaluating WordPerfect, MS Word, and MASS-11.

Both of these companies sent out press releases regarding their decisions to choose a relatively unknown PC product over the #1 rated product in the world, but no major magazine reported on it.

The Big Move

T HE HIRING OF NEW EMPLOYEES CONTINUED at a rapid pace throughout 1987 until we just outgrew the old 400 building. We went from two suites to eight suites, a total of 22,000 square feet. Dad had successfully negotiated with the landlords to lease a new building across the street to provide office space for training, product development, and technical support.

MECollection: Bonnie LaScola

The new office space was one massive open area. First Hank worked with Pam Nelson to design a space for the trainers as customers would be coming to MEC for Train-the-Trainer classes. The trainers were the first to make the move in 1986.

He then worked on the space for tech support, product development, and sales, with input from department managers. His objective was for everyone to have a window, and to use the interior spaces for conference rooms and training.

After all the walls, utilities, and inside offices were complete, it was time to move the Steelcase modules. He wanted the relocation to be seamless with minimal work loss.

The staff would end their Friday in one building and begin in the other on Monday. To accomplish this, he came to my husband and me to handle it.

Mike and I, with the help of some of our production and shipping staff, worked that evening, and all day Saturday and Sunday, to tear down the Steelcase, move it across the street, and rebuild it according to the new layout. All the employees had to do on Monday was set up their computer equipment in their new space. It was rough, but Hank believed we could do it, and we did.

In the new building, Pam Nelson and her staff of nine held Train-the-Trainer classes in the new training suite. The Train-the-Trainer classes were both innovative and very popular.

Sherry Kappel, who was pregnant with her first child, continued to be our documentation manager, while also being in charge of quality control, intra-office communication, and tech support.

My brother John continued as Product Development Manager, interviewing and hiring developers at a rapid pace. And Everett spent much of his time on the road, meeting with customers and attending MASS-11 User Group meetings nationwide.

Bonnie was in charge of all operations in the 400 building, while Sarah was the go-between, running back and forth between the buildings coordinating the efforts of the documentation writers, printers, and shippers.

Achieving the Promise

T HE BROTHERS OFTEN SAID THAT MEC'S SUCCESS had a lot to do with the Cold War, which lasted from 1948 to 1992, a war that led to an unprecedented arms buildup in the U.S., including nuclear bombs. President Reagan's commitment to the idea of "peace through strength" led to the modernization of military forces.

During his two terms in office, the size of the U.S. Army grew by two active divisions and saw the development of new weapons systems, including the B1 bomber and MX (intercontinental ballistic) missiles. He had also urged the development of the Strategic Defense Initiative (SDI), a high-technology, anti-ballistic missile shield, to protect the U.S. from nuclear attack. It was also known as "Star Wars."

Aerospace companies, military contractors, and atomic labs such as Sandia, Fermi, and Lawrence Livermore had been some of MEC's biggest customers, and they kept purchasing more VAXes and MASS-11 to produce all the technical and scientific documentation required to bid on government contracts. Our customers all told us the combination saved them millions of dollars, and thousands of hours in preparation time.

In June 1987, Reagan gave his Berlin Wall Speech where he told

Mikhail Gorbachev, the General Secretary of the Communist Party of the Soviet Union: *Mr. Gorbachev. Tear down this wall!* It was the beginning of the end of the Cold War. Our aerospace customers at the time were Boeing, Hughes, Lockheed, McDonnell Douglas, Northrup, and Martin Marietta. Aerospace subcontractors who used MASS-11 were Raytheon, GE, and Westinghouse. All, including MEC, would be affected by his historic words.

Inflation was rising, and economic growth slowed in the first three quarters of 1987. But MEC was still growing; our sales force had expanded to fourteen. We created a new 4-color, 8-page corporate brochure called *Achieving the Promise* that included testimonials and examples of the types of typeset-quality documents we could produce.

With the release of the MASS-11 Graphics Processor and MASS-11 Draw, we began participating in shows more focused on electronic publishing, including the Seybold Publishing Conference and Graphix Expo.

OUR CUSTOMER BASE WAS A WHO'S WHO OF THE FORTUNE 500. In a 1987 interview with the editor of *DEC Professional*, Dad was quoted as saying, "Our philosophy is simple. We listen and respond to the needs of our users. The result is a family of office automation products that address the industry's current trends—today and tomorrow."

MEC's strategy of listening and responding to customers was paying off with both sales and (now) great testimonials featuring real scenarios from decision makers. They were all office automation and/or electronic publishing pioneers and influencers, achieving the promise of what office automation could offer.

Our success stories, I felt, were our best marketing tool, and we began producing a new four-color glossy magazine called *Profiles* for prospective customers. Each issue featured four prestigious corporations that had standardized on MASS-11. These were typically installations with hundreds to thousands of MASS-11 users on VAXes and PCs.

MEC's in-house and freelance writers wrote the stories. Besides *Profiles*, many of our clients agreed to be interviewed by the press. One was Dr. William Gilbert, System Manager at MIT's Whitaker College of Health, Science, Technology and Management, which supported over two thousand MASS-11 users.

"I am favorably impressed not only by MEC's attention to its product line but by its attention to its users," he said. "This is an incredibly responsive company." And, of course, he was right!

The stories in *Profiles* and the testimonials all helped us connect with customers and prospects. And on the topic of connecting, *connectivity* was the next big request from our users—connecting with PCs, networks, laser printers, email systems, fax systems, and electronic publishing systems. These were all fairly new concepts in 1987 and revolutionary in scope.

DEC was a pioneer in networking and had its proprietary email system. But it held out for as long as it could before supporting non-DEC hardware and software.

Once again we counted on our steering committee members to guide us. They became our beta test sites for connectivity as well.

Meanwhile, Back in the Office

WORKING OUT OF MY HOME on the East Coast, I had few in-person interactions with people in the home office, and hadn't met most of the new hires.

John hired several college students that summer of 1987. One was the late Iris Chang, who began her summer writing code but, by the end, was writing words. She wrote two instruction manuals that summer. Because of her writing experience that summer at MEC, she changed her college major to journalism and, a decade later, wrote the bestselling book *The Rape of Nanking*.

Programmer Josephine Koo was another recent college graduate John hired, with a degree in computer studies and math from Northwestern.

MECollection: Josephine Koo, Product Development

MEC was my first real job. I was hired by John when I was 21. I initially worked on the word processing product, but became the programmer for MASS-11 Calendar. I appreciated working for all the Karels men: Hank (who was warm and friendly), Everett, who was intimidating but for whom I had a lot of respect, and John. I never knew John had a sibling.

I was always willing to work, and I was often there on weekends by myself. I often wonder how did we communicate at that time, before Internet and emails. We were upstarts and technology was changing so quickly back then.

As for the social life at MEC, I remember the Christmas parties and doing aerobics in the office with co-workers, after working hours, to "The Firm" VHS workout tapes.

MECollection: Sarah Browning, Shipping

In the early days, Everett's wife Doris helped out duplicating and packaging VAX/VMS tapes for shipping, one or two days a week. So each day she would deliver all of her orders to the two guys in the shipping department.

One of the guys was legally blind, a result of an accident. His mother worked for MEC and told Hank about her son's situation. Due to his condition, he was unhireable, she'd said. So in Hank's inimitable style, he hired her son for the shipping department, and bought a machine that magnified the orders enough that he could read the packing list. We got organized about where things were, and he memorized locations.

MECollection: Leslie Ciborowski, Training

While training customers in-house, sometimes we'd encounter a bug. If the programmers were in the office, we'd take a break, report the bug, and it would often be fixed in real time by the time we resumed training.

There was always laughter in the office. And you never had to bring lunch—there was always food everywhere, for the Train-the-Trainer classes or the in-house staff training sessions. If Surender or other programmers were in-house, Indian and Thai food was brought in.

MECollection: Julie Golden, Product Support

John hired me in 1985 to test MASS-11 Manager, the new database. I was nineteen, had a 2-year degree in programming, and responded to an ad he had placed in the Chicago Tribune. Soon after, Bonnie brought me into the Support Department.

I talked customers through so many crises, including one who was irate that their printer wasn't working. As it turned out, it wasn't plugged in! I dealt with a lot of PC questions, and technical questions from the sales people in the field. I reassured them that our products could do what we promised. As stressful as support was, everyone got along so well. We were all so young. Bonnie was a go getter and always stood up for us. It was a great atmosphere to work in!

Photo Gallery

Everett, Johnie (mother), H.A. (Hank), Joyce (sister) in Robinson, Texas

My family hosted Japanese businessmen through the International Hospitality Center. My parents wanted us to be exposed to other cultures. We also hosted Filipina nurses and Indian doctors from Cook County Hospital on holidays.

The Brothers Karels featured in "Status Line,"
our marketing magazine, in Fall 1984

A pamphlet prepared for the Open House at the
Paperless Office at the Watergate Hotel May 3, 1979.

Everett in front of MECAir in Las Vegas, Fall 1983.

*Carol Karels at the first MASS-11 Symposium, held
at the Grand Hyatt in New York City in November 1984.*

MEC's marketing magazine "Status Line" showed all the computers MASS-11 supported: Digital VAX, Rainbow PC, and IBM PC.

Everett and Surender at DECUS 1983. MEC was the only third-party vendor invited to exhibit in the Scientific Solutions booth.

Carol and Hank Karels at DECUS in St. Louis 1983

First Sales Meeting held at MEC's headquarters in 1984.
Hank and Everett seated in first row

*Sales meeting held in April 1987. Hank is sixth from left in back row;
Everett is sitting far right.*

PC Expo at Javits Center in NYC 1986

One of a series of ads targeted at Digital's WPS-PLUS. MASS-11 was touted as a publishing partner for the VAX.

DEC UK releases a six-page color brochure touting MASS-11 as "the USA's foremost name in word processing software."

MEC's technical support and product development team.
Manager John Karels is in the center of photo wearing a tie. Circa 1988.

The "new look" of our documentation started in 1987
for MASS-11 WP, then Manager, Menus, and Draw.

Hank Karels at the height of MEC's success in 1990.

The last sales meeting held in May 1992. Hank is second from left in back row; Everett is standing far right.

A Partial List of Corporations Using MASS-11 for Office Automation

Aerospace

Aerojet
AIL
Allied-Bendix
Ball Aerospace
Beech Aircraft
Bell Helicopter
Boeing
Computer Sciences
Douglas Aircraft
Fairchild
Ford Aerospace
GE and RCA
Goodyear Aerospace
Honeywell
Hughes
JPL
Lockheed
LTV
Lucas Aerospace
Martin Marietta
McDonnell Douglas
NASA
Northrup
Raytheon Company
Rockwell International
Singer Kearfott
Smith Industries
Sperry
Sundstrand
Teledyne Brown
The MITRE Corporation
TRW
United Technologies
Westinghouse Electric

Automotive

Chrysler
General Motors Research
Mercedes Benz
Volkswagen

Chemical

ARCO Chemical
Dow Chemical
E. I. DuPont
ICI Americas
Nalco Chemical
Raychem

Computer Industry

Compuserve
Control Data Institute
Emulex
Intel
Intergraph
Motorola
Precision Visuals
Racal-Milgo
Texas Instruments

Engineering

Allen Bradley
Babcock and Wilcox
Buckhart-Horn
Cleveland Pneumatic
Giffels
Greiner Engineering
HNTB
John Corolla
MDA
Montgomery Engineers
Morrison-Knudsen
NKF Engineering
O'Brien Kreitzburg

Entertainment

Boston Children's Museum
Boston Computer Museum
Island Records
Lorimar Telepictures
Screen Actors Guild

Financial Institutions

Arab American Bank
Australian Stock Exchange
Bancohio
Chemical Bank NY
Colonial Management
Coopers and Lybrand
Dean Witter
Donaldson, Lufkin, Jenrette
Goldman Sachs
Integrated Resources
J.C. Bradford
Manufacturer's Hanover
Northern Trust of Chicago
Rabobank
Smith Barney
World Bank

Food and Beverage

General Mills
Kellogg Company
Lawry's Foods
Pepsico Research
Pioneer Data
Texas Beef Producers
T.J. Lipton

Government

Atlanta Regional Commission
Chicago Public School District
LA County Health Dept.
LA Dept. of Sanitation
Chicago Sanitary District
New Zealand Parliament
NYC Parks Department
US Bureau of Reclamation
US Fish and Wildlife
US Postal Service

Insurance

Aetna
Middlesex Mutual
Phoenix Mutual Life
State Mutual
Title USA

Laboratories

Argonne National Labs
Fermilab
Lawrence Livermore
Los Alamos
Sandia National Labs

Manufacturing

Allen-Bradley
Bally Manufacturing
Celanese
Davidson Instrument
Eastman Kodak
Firestone Research
Fleetwood Enterprises
EG&G
Ferrante International
FMC
General Instruments
Gillette
Magnavox
Sanders and Associates
Universal Instruments

Medical

American Acad. Orthopedic Surgeons
American Heart Association
Beth Israel Boston
Bishop Clarkson Memorial Hospital
Cedars Sinai Hospital LA
Cleveland Clinic
Healthnet
Lackland AFB Med Center
Mass General Hospital
Maxicare
Med Foundtn of Buffalo
Sloan Kettering Memorial Hospital

Petroleum

BP America
Champlin Oil
Cities Service Oil & Gas
Ethyl Technical Center
FINA Oil
Mobil Research
Roy M. Huffington
Schlumberger
Shell Oil
SOHIO
Sun Refining

Pharmaceutical

Abbott Laboratories
American Cyanamid
Becton Dickenson
Betz Labs
Burroughs Wellcome
E.I. DuPont
Eli Lilly and Company
E.R. Squibb
Glaxo Inc.
Johnson and Johnson
Lederle Labs
Merck, Sharpe & Dohme
Merrell-Dow Pharmaceuticals
Pfizer
Research Data Corporation
SmithKline Beecham
Wyeth-Ayerst Labs

Publishing

Boston Globe
CCMI/McGraw Hill
Fort Worth Star Telegram
Professional Press
The New Yorker Magazine

Research Centers

Alcan International Ltd.
Alberta Research Council
Atomic Energy Commission of Canada
Brookings Institute
Fox Chase Cancer Center
Georgia Tech
MIT
Research Triangle Institute
Salk Institute

Telecommunications

Alcatel Network Systems
Ameritech
AT&T Long Lines
Bell South
GTE Airfone
Hughes Network Systems
Mountain Bell
United Telephone Co. of Florida

Utilities

Bechtel Power
COM/Energy Massachusetts
Detroit Edison
MMWEC (Massachusetts)
Norsk Hydro
Ontario Hydro
PA Power and Light

MASS 11®

A Partial List of Corporations Using MASS-11 for Office Automation

Part Two

The Unimaginable

MEC'S SUCCESS HAD JUST BEEN a figment of Dad's imagination in 1977; a decade later, his dream of running a profitable company using Toffler's principles of telecommuting, and giving employees freedom to create at any time of day, had become a reality. It was his ultimate dream come true.

And being a mother was *mine*. Balancing motherhood with work was manageable as long as I could continue to work out of my home. Working for MEC, I didn't have to choose between being a full-time stay-at-home mom or having a career.

I could do both, and not just because I was the boss's daughter. At MEC, a number of women worked part of the time from home. I flew back to Illinois with Beth once a month, and Mom relished the opportunity to spend time with her first grandchild.

My parents both wanted to travel more for pleasure. MEC was doing well enough financially, and Dad felt comfortable with the managers he'd hired to keep things running smoothly in his absence. Mom and Dad's favorite destinations were Hawaii and the Canadian Rockies.

But the unimaginable happened in late September of 1987 while both were vacationing in the Canadian Rockies. After a hike in the mountains, they went for a massage. Both were lifelong fans of bodywork. The masseuse said Mom's liver was greatly enlarged, and her tan was more likely from jaundice than the sun. She encouraged them to cut their vacation short and to get the necessary tests and treatment back home, not in a foreign country.

Mom insisted she felt fine. Nonetheless, they changed their flight before dining at the Lake Louise lodge, where they had spent their honeymoon. Dad didn't call me until after they had returned home and had made an appointment with Dr. McNeil, our family doctor.

"I didn't want to worry you," Dad said. "We both thought the masseuse was sounding an alarm unnecessarily. But Dr. McNeil took me aside and told me privately he suspected she had cancer of the pancreas. He gave us an appointment for blood work and an x-ray next week."

Besides being horrified by this news, I was enraged by Dr. McNeil's lack of a sense of urgency. I asked Dad to take her to the emergency room immediately. He assured me he would as soon as we hung up. I then sobbed for the rest of the weekend.

My best friend Elsie Flores, a classmate from nursing school, was visiting me with her infant daughter Christina at the time. Mom thought of Elsie as her second daughter and often treated her to lunch after I had moved East. Elsie was in shock too, but so supportive that weekend, helping with Beth. We all flew back to Chicago two days later.

When I arrived at Sherman Hospital in Elgin, Mom had already been admitted to a surgical floor. Her skin and eyes were yellow and she was furiously scratching her arms and legs. The biopsy was inconclusive, but her labs indicated a blockage in her bile duct, which accounted for her jaundice and itching.

Surgery was scheduled for the next day. The surgeons asked a barrage of questions. *Did she drink alcohol?* No, Mom insisted. Just an occasional sip of port on canoe trips.

Was she having severe abdominal pain? No, Mom replied. Just occasional heartburn relieved by a half-teaspoon of baking soda in water, a remedy she'd drunk most of her adult life after dinner.

They explained to me and Dad that they would do an exploratory laparotomy. "If we see cancer, the surgery will be an hour at most. Open and close, followed by palliative measures. If it's benign, we'll do what we can to relieve the obstruction so she won't be itching all the time. If we have to take out her pancreas, she will be a diabetic requiring insulin injections the rest of her life."

Four hours at the most, they assured us. The worst-case scenario could be eight hours. Any more than that under anesthesia would be hard for her, they said, with no guarantees of the outcome.

MOM WAS WHEELED INTO THE OPERATING ROOM at 11:00 a.m., and taken to the Recovery Room at 2 a.m.! Her surgeon came out twice with updates. The first, at the two-hour mark, was that her pancreas was hard as a rock, and they had to carefully dissect it so as not to nick an artery. That might take hours.

The second update, which was at the eight-hour mark, was that her heart had briefly stopped, but she was doing fine now. At fifteen hours, she was closed up and taken to ICU. The surgeon said it was the longest surgery ever performed at Sherman Hospital. There were so many mysteries, he said. *How could she not have been in severe pain with a calcified pancreas?*

What followed after the surgery was equally a mystery. Mom was in the ICU for three days and then discharged from the hospital ten days later. The nurses tried to teach her how to test her sugar and inject insulin, but she showed no interest. So Dad had to learn. We all figured she was just worn out from being under anesthesia for fifteen hours.

Dad took care of all diabetes-related activities once she was home, and even learned how to cook a diabetic diet. But he said she turned her nose up at the food he offered her.

"It has no taste or smell," Mom said. He also noted she showed no interest in her pets and didn't want any visitors, including her sister.

It soon became apparent that she was not just exhausted and disinterested due to a difficult operation and recovery. *She had a different personality.* Her doctors had no explanation for that, or her behavior change, after it continued for several weeks.

"Is it possible she had a mini-stroke when her heart stopped?" I asked the surgeon when she went for her first post-op visit.

"There's nothing to indicate that," he said, "but anything can happen during or after fifteen hours of anesthesia."

INITIALLY, DAD WENT HOME EVERY DAY to make lunch and give her her lunchtime insulin, as she continued to refuse to test her sugar or self-inject her medication. Then he started bringing her into the office, asking the staff in the warehouse to give her simple tasks and keep an eye on her. *But what tasks could she do?*

She occasionally escaped from the office and was found walking down the road toward Dunkin' Donuts. The responsibility of monitoring her whereabouts became a burden on the staff, which affected their work.

After a few weeks, neighbor Annette, who worked in shipping, took Dad aside and said, "Hank, I hate to tell you this, but Joanne goes through the staff refrigerator and eats our lunches. She unwraps a sandwich, takes a bite, and puts it back on the shelf. If she likes it, she eats their entire lunch. She does it right out in the open. Everyone's afraid to say anything, but I felt you should know."

Annette's comments answered some questions Dad had. "Eating everyone's lunches is why she never wants to eat what I've made for her," he fumed. "And sneaking out to Dunkin' Donuts explains why her sugar is so high before dinner." After that, he had to hire a caregiver during the day.

JOHN SAID IT WAS A MIRACLE that Mom survived that fifteen-hour operation. "I've done some reading about her disease," he said. "She was hours from death, Carol, before her surgery. They took out half her abdominal organs. Most surgeons would take a look at her 'hard-as-a-rock' pancreas and close her up, and declare it was time for Hospice! But they did the hero doctor thing and kept her alive. But it's not her. That woman is not our mom!"

John had been reading about more subjects than pancreatitis, he told me. He handed me a paperback book called *Strangers Among Us*, by Ruth Montgomery.

"This is what I think happened to her," he said. The author described how an *original* soul, the one you are born with, can leave a body due to trauma, an accident, or while under anesthesia, and enable a *different*, or *lost* soul, to just "walk in."

"This explains why her personality changed," John said. "Because it's not her. She's a walk-in!"

Shaking his head, he muttered, "Dad's in a cult; Mom is possessed. This is *not* how our lives were supposed to turn out, Carol!"

ALL I KNEW IN THE FALL OF 1987 was that life would never again be the same for me and my family. She was our pillar of support, our confidante, our fun-loving mom. As a result of her illness, Dad lost his focus. She was the person he could lean on, ask her opinions, and whose spot-on instincts he could trust. That person was no longer there for him. Increasingly, Ramtha filled that void.

Unleashing Publishing Potential

THE YEAR 1988 WAS THE MOST PRODUCTIVE for our programmers. We released a new version of MASS-11 WP that provided an on-screen preview of text and graphics, a thesaurus, and several other desktop publishing features.

DEC was happy because we were making progress on our All-in-1 integration kit. We also endorsed DEC's Compound Document Architecture (CDA), which supported "live links" to text, graphics, images, spreadsheets, charts, and tables—a huge deal!

And MASS-11 Graphics Processor (GP) supported a dozen popular graphic formats. All of these features enabled our users to create massive, complex documents with a few commands.

Another exciting announcement was that MASS-11 Draw 5.0 would support freehand design, the first product of its kind to do so. A WYSIWYG (what you see is what you get) on the screen product was also in the works, for release in mid-1989 on the PC, VAXstation, and Macs. MEC was on a roll!

In 1988, Sandia Labs, which was an early user of MASS-11 on both VAXes and PCs, selected MASS-11 as their standard. They had been using eighteen different word processors and, after a year of intense testing, narrowed the field down to MASS-11 and WordPerfect.

A twelve-hour showdown, with representatives from both WordPerfect and MEC participating, resulted in a decisive win for MASS-11. It would eventually be installed on 350 VAXes and 4,500 PCs.

Also that year, we took our office automation and electronic publishing show on the road, with product symposia held monthly starting in New York City, followed by Dallas, Albuquerque, Cincinnati, Boston, Philadelphia, Chicago, Anaheim, Washington, D.C., and Research Triangle Park in North Carolina. The symposium in New York City drew 140 attendees from eight states, and numerous reporters interested primarily in MASS-11 Draw attended.

From *Personal Publishing* magazine in April:

MEC, a company best known for its library of products for Digital Equipment's VAX minicomputer line, may have a winner for desktop publishing with version 5.0 of its MASS-11 Draw for the IBM PC.

Another journalist wrote:

Perhaps the best testimonial to MEC is that all manuals are produced with MASS-11 products. Pictures on nearly every page, created with MASS-11 Draw, complement the examples. While other companies have produced elegant manuals for their products, it usually means that offset typesetters worked on the product.

In 1988, we signed a nationwide agreement with Olsten Temps. Tiger Temps continued to thrive as they supported our East Coast customers, both with temps and training. They had used every type of word processor known to man and told us, once again, that MASS-11 was the best!

In early May, our steering committee met in Chicago. The main topics of discussion were Postscript support, Mac support, and

MASS-11 Draw. It was the most well-attended ever, with twenty corporations represented.

Everett was interviewed by *Digital Review* as its "Newsmaker of the Month." He was also interviewed by *Business Week* because of a "noticeable trend" in corporations replacing their dedicated Wang systems with VAXes and MASS-11. Both of these interviews reinforced our stature in the e-publishing world.

Misunderstandings

N MAY 1988, WE LOST TWO valued employees, Sharon Fisher and Sherry Kappel. Sharon, our printer guru and technical support person on the West Coast, was a proponent of Toffler's "electronic cottage" philosophy. As a remote support person, she handled most of the support calls from our aerospace clients in California, and all the middle-of-the-night support calls from our overseas clients. But Everett made a decision that all outside support staff had to relocate to the home office.

MECollection: Sharon Fisher

Telecommuting was ideal for someone like me. I worked around the clock and my personality wasn't well-suited to an office environment. I got along great with Surender, and even though we were three time zones apart, we collaborated on numerous printer table issues by phone. But when Everett made all outside support staff move to Chicago, I did, but I was unhappy. After a few months, I quit and moved back to Spokane with my daughter.

Sherry left after giving birth to her daughter and learning her office responsibilities had changed. Unlike Sharon, Sherry felt she did her best work *in* the office, surrounded by writers and tech support specialists who sought out her advice and vast knowledge about our products. Her managerial responsibilities, before going on maternity leave, included documentation, quality control, technical support, and intra-office communications. She worked closely with both Everett and Surender.

MECollection: Sherry Kappel

Hank and I never really discussed what I would be doing after I gave birth, but I had child care lined up, and I assumed I would return to my previous managerial roles. He mistakenly assumed I would want to work out of my home, as Carol did, after she gave birth. But I felt my value at the office was way more.

While I was out on maternity leave, Hank and Everett put John, who was Product Development Manager, in charge of support as well; the departments were then merged to include testing and quality control.

When I returned from maternity leave, I put Hank and Everett in a pickle. Although my salary was the same, they had given many of my responsibilities away. When I returned, I was bored out of my mind. So I left MEC and went to work for Anne Hamilton. Ironically, I worked out of my house for her.

After I quit, I got a call from John, and he asked if he could meet with me at my house. He said, "Sherry, I hope that your leaving MEC had nothing to do with me." I explained the situation to him and he was very cordial and understanding. And I believe he saw the injustice in that decision. But the new merged department was already in place and functioning well, I was told. There was no turning back.

Under John, product managers were assigned to each of fifteen products. The newly merged Product Development and Support group held regular meetings to review the progress of new products and updates. Product managers also conducted weekly training sessions for all support personnel with topics such as "Digitizing Signatures and Logos with Draw," "How to Create a Symbols Library with Draw," and "MASS-11 and Postscript."

MASS-11 product design reviews were scheduled before each product release; the status of bugs, comments from all the beta test sites, and the latest documentation were all reviewed at this time. It was an efficient process meant to reduce errors and post-release anxiety among both customers and support staff. Nothing was perfect, but our customers seemed pleased.

Redefining Publishing

T HE LATE '80S WERE EXCITING TIMES, with breakthroughs daily in office automation and electronic publishing. MEC was leading, not following. Our largest customers were the first to discover the power of MASS-11 and take advantage of all that our products had to offer.

Paul Neshamkin, VP at Drexel Burnham Lambert Investment Bank, recalled the electronic publishing scene in 1988:

> Drexel's mortgage-backed securities department had been producing research reports by doing the typing and filing in-house, then making repeated trips to the in-house typesetter and, occasionally, to an offset typesetter. However, management found that producing client reports externally was time-consuming and expensive and posed a threat to data integrity. Each month, the department wrote as many as thirty weekly and bi-weekly reports for distribution to more than 5,000 clients.
>
> Members of the department staff had heard about MASS-11 from their counterparts in the legal community. The bank staff grew to love MASS-11 because it could effectively integrate

statistics, charts, and tables into text. Right-justified proportional spacing, tables customized to support long statistical charts, and similar file structures on the VAX and PC versions of the product were also seen as attractive features. Reports that used to take days could be done in hours. One user described MASS-11 as a sports car—very manageable and easy to do very difficult things with. Moving in-house would also improve the department's quality control.

Dr. Will Gilbert, Director of the Computer Facility at MIT Research Labs, recalled, "MASS-11 was way ahead of its time in the '80s. Because of this, my computer facility was the go-to place for word processing. It was the beginning point for many millions of dollars in grant funding awarded to MIT, as well as being the vehicle for many of the business plans used to found Cambridge-based biotech companies, which sprung up in the 1990s."

DESPITE TESTIMONIALS AND GLOWING REVIEWS from the VAX-centric magazines, we had less success getting recognized by the PC media giants: *Computerworld, PC Magazine, Infoworld,* and *PC Week.*

MASS-11 Draw was being positively reviewed, but our word processor was rarely included in their side-by-side product comparison charts. When we called the editorial offices of the mostly Manhattan-based PC magazines, the typical response was, "We already have thirty-five-word processors for our annual issue focused on word processing."

Another response was, "MASS-11? Never heard of it." Even though we could check off every box on their lists, we were at a disadvantage because we weren't sold in retail stores.

Many decision makers at our largest VAX/PC installations, who had confidently bet the farm on MASS-11, were now being questioned by corporate brass about having put all their eggs into one-word processing basket, especially one *they'd* never heard of.

"If it's so great, why isn't it listed in any 'Best of PC Word Processors' lists?" was the most common question asked.

Our users were begging us to beef up our PC public relations—to get the PC press to acknowledge MASS-11 for the powerful product it was.

"Help! We love you guys and want to buy more of your products," our customers pleaded. "The higher-ups here have no idea how much we need you!"

We were no "off-the-shelf" product like all the others; ours was more a boutique product that had been largely designed by and custom-tailored to our clients' specific needs.

IT DIDN'T MATTER TO THESE PC MAGAZINE EDITORS that the World Bank and GM Research chose us as their standard on PCs. Or that Sandia Labs in Albuquerque, New Mexico, chose MASS-11 over WordPerfect for their 8,300 secretaries, engineers, and scientists.

Our products may have had superior functionality, but we were no match for WordPerfect's mega-marketing machine and advertising dollars. They had the largest booth at every PC trade show, with paid actors shouting about all their new features and tossing out freebies to the audience.

To remedy this situation, we hired a Manhattan-based ad agency/PR firm. Their mission was to increase our product visibility by hounding the PC press for interviews, product reviews, and inclusion of MASS-11 in their product comparisons. I would be the liaison and meet with them weekly. I felt optimistic about our relationship.

One Step Beyond

I N MAY, MY PARENTS TOOK A FIVE-DAY VACATION. At least that's
what Dad told everyone. What he told me was that he and Mom
were flying to California, where he'd drop her off so she could stay
with her sister Pat for the weekend. He would then fly to Colorado,
where Ramtha was holding a first-ever, three-day retreat at Estes Park.
Ramtha followers would be attending from all over the world, he said.
On Monday morning, after the retreat, he would return to California
to pick up Mom, and both would be home by Tuesday evening.

Dad said nobody at the office would know his whereabouts, or the
purpose of the trip, not even Bonnie. He was only telling me in case
there was an emergency.

They didn't return until Friday. I picked them both up at the
airport, and Dad swore me to secrecy when he explained the delay in
their return.

"The retreat was mind-blowing," he said. "The first night, on the
mountain, we saw spaceships hovering right above us. The second day,
just as we were getting deep into the teachings, we got bomb threats
and had to evacuate. JZ told us the retreat would continue at her home
in Yelm, Washington, where she had a barn that could accommodate
all of us. We each had to make our plane reservations to get to Yelm

and then back home. Because of the interruptions, the retreat didn't end till Thursday. Fortunately, Pat didn't have other plans and kept Mom a few extra days."

Spaceships, bomb threats, and evacuations. "What else was discussed at the retreat?" I asked, as if I wasn't fazed by what he'd told me. I was hoping to get an insight into what was in his head. "And will there be any more retreats?"

"What I *can* tell you," he said, "is that we weren't drinking alcohol or taking LSD or any other hallucinogenic drugs, which I'm sure is what you're thinking. Ramtha wants our vessel to be pure. And yes, there will be future retreats. I signed up to be a student at the Ramtha School of Enlightenment. I spoke to Everett about it and he also wants to sign up. There will be at least two two-week required classes a year," he explained, "held in Yelm, that we will both be attending together."

"What will you be studying that's not already in the Ramtha book?" I asked.

"The book is just the tip of the iceberg," he said. "But I can't tell you anything more. That's part of our agreement when we sign up for the teachings. We're not supposed to discuss what goes on with anyone, including family."

"So basically, what happens at the retreat stays at the retreat?" I asked.

"For now, yes," he replied.

Dad said he worked out a deal with Pat to watch Mom whenever he went. With Dad muzzled, I only learned about the goings-on at the retreats from occasional articles in the *National Enquirer* sent to me by my aunt Lee. The articles included photos of actress Linda Evans, a Ramtha devotee, sitting in the front row of the arena where the teachings were held.

They also mentioned that Ramtha students walked blindfolded around a field while loud rock music blared. Food and sleep were limited. Ramtha instructed/advised his followers to stock up on food, munitions, and survival gear. He also encouraged them to build underground shelters, and move to the Yelm area, which would be one of the safer areas during an earthly catastrophe: nuclear, asteroids, or pole shift. Other than what I read in those occasional articles, I was in the dark for the next several years.

A Revolutionary Powerhouse

ELECTRONIC PUBLISHING WAS THE NEW office frontier, and MEC was at the forefront of this as well. In 1989 alone, we held symposia on electronic publishing in Washington D.C., New York City, New Jersey, North Carolina, Saint Louis, Atlanta, Seattle, Philadelphia, Sunnyvale, and Dallas, each drawing upwards of a hundred guests, both existing users and prospects eager to integrate their data, graphs, and charts into one final document, while bypassing an expensive typesetting machine.

The symposium in New Jersey was our first *industry-specific* one, focusing on pharmaceutical firms. Natalie, our pharmaceutical sales rep on the East Coast, suggested it be held at a hotel near Newark Airport to make it easier for out-of-state and international clients. Representatives from a dozen international pharmaceutical firms were among those who attended.

Most were looking for new and improved ways to prepare their lengthy and complicated New Drug Applications (NDAs), which combined information from multiple departments and required hundreds of revision cycles.

An NDA could be 100,000 to 400,000 pages in length, each one full of tables, graphs, drawings, and scientific equations. The paper required to print a new drug application could fill a semi-truck; it could take years to complete one.

Most of the attendees already used MASS-11 but were seeking information on more advanced features just released such as live links, variable referencing, and user-defined keys. These were the features that could further speed up the process of getting their new drugs to market.

Live links let users break the various parts of documents into pieces and, with live-link calls (commands built into documents), enable the "construction" of these lengthy NDAs in a relatively short time. When the user was ready to assemble the finished document, they could "call" all of those pieces together by simply typing a series of commands into the document.

Variable referencing enabled the user to cross-reference text to pages, tables, and figures. It allowed them to build a file of constants (working drug name, for example) that were attached to a variable. If those drug names changed throughout revision cycles and updating, the user could simply access the file containing the references and change the drug name once, next to its variable. When the document was printed, the application automatically changed the drug name to its updated version. Variable referencing helped keep documents up to date, and it cut the editing chores to a minimum.

And user-defined keys let a user store a series of commands into one keystroke, another tremendous time saver.

"These features alone made MASS-11 the hands-down best word processor in the world," noted Keith Sessions, a documentation manager at Cerner Corporation. Cerner, based in Kansas City, was a top supplier of medical information systems.

"MASS-11 was more than a word processor," he added. "It was a revolutionary powerhouse document creation system because it was a 'command-driven' product. And no product has been able to do anything like it since!"

Take My Job, Please!

A FTER FIVE YEARS WITH MEC, MY BROTHER GAVE notice in January 1989. He and Ken, our MASS-11 Draw programmer, left together and started their own company, TechView Inc., to market a product called TechEdit. TechEdit was Ken's latest programming feat, the newest and hottest object-oriented graphic design tool for engineers and information technology.

John and Ken both thought MEC was in trouble. Despite our large sales force, our sales were down. The end of the Cold War meant fewer military contracts. Aerospace companies were laying off thousands of engineers and not paying their bills, including ours.

MECollection: Ken Crossen

As the world moved away from the VAX, John and I talked a lot about the direction MEC was going in. MEC was still heavily invested in DEC and VAX/VMS while the world was moving to PCs and workstations. MASS-11 was becoming a programming language of sorts, similar to all professional photo-typesetting systems of the time, similar in spirit to but simpler than PostScript. It had become a "civilian" gateway to much of the enormous power of PostScript.

John was pursuing a different market, live display of manufacturing work instructions. That market wasn't interested in printing on paper, but rather on direct display on consumer TV/HDMI screens on the factory floor.

Besides technology, MEC had a bloated payroll and high rent while revenues were diminishing. John also wanted to get out because he intensely disliked working for his father and uncle. Hank was wonderful with all his employees, but not his son. Both were bright and did what they did well, but their management style was quite different, and they pushed each other's buttons. And nepotism was a thing with Hank. He went out of his way to tell everyone, "John may be my son but that doesn't mean he'll get special treatment."

I observed Hank fawn over others far less deserving, while being hard, almost brutal, with his son in meetings. Everett often took Hank's cue and scoffed at John's technical advice, which was only taken when seconded by their top customers. That included John's advice to get on board with Postscript.

John and I were both concerned about Hank and Everett's involvement with Ramtha as well, and we thought they were taking their hands off the wheel. We both thought it would be prudent to "rescue" at least one product in case MEC was sold or went bankrupt. I didn't want to risk losing TechEdit.

So I went to Hank and told him my concerns. He surprisingly agreed with me, and we shook on a deal, one that stipulated I would continue to make changes and updates to MASS-11 Draw, and financially take care of Surender if anything happened to MEC. I would have done that anyhow. I told him that my wife Cindy, Surender, John, and I would be full partners in TechView. John would handle the business side of things: sales and marketing. Hank told me that was a terrible idea to put John in charge of sales and marketing, but wished us well.

Gene Kratochvil, a systems engineer who'd only been at MEC a year, took John's place.

MECollection: Gene Kratochvil

MEC was my second job after graduating from Cornell College in Iowa with degrees in Computer Science and Physics. I was hired by John in January 1988, and he made me Product Manager for MASS-11 Manager, MEC's database product. I loved learning new things and was a good tester. As new products came out, I moved around—to MASS-11 Mail, then All-in-1 Integration.

Ultimately I was supporting several products. I was also the VAX system manager, and I helped our customers with installations and troubleshooting on the VAX. I had respect from all the teams since I had supported them all. I wore many hats at MEC!

I was a direct report to John for eleven months until one day he took me aside and asked, "Gene, how would you like to have my job?" Imagine the owner's son of a wildly successful company asking you that! I figured he was having a bad day, but the next day he posted the position.

I applied and got the job. I hadn't even thought about getting a salary increase, but the day after I accepted, Hank gave me a $10,000 raise! I couldn't believe it, nor could my wife. I couldn't make up a story like that, how the owner's son handed his job on a plate to me.

But I was with the company several more years, and hired dozens of really talented people to develop, test, and support our existing and emerging products on several platforms, including a WYSIWYG product.

WYSIWYG on the Horizon

OUR STEERING COMMITTEE MEMBERS, many of whom were investing in VAXstations and Sun workstations, were now requesting a graphics-based word processor, one that supported a WYSIWYG (what you see is what you get) screen display.

Our users provided us with the ideal scenario for such a product: (a) an identical file format on each platform so that data could easily be exchanged; (b) the product would have to be compatible with MASS-11 on the VAX and PC, with formatting intact, and a keyboard interface similar to MASS-11; and (c) conversions to and from other word processing software such as DisplayWrite, MS Word, and WordPerfect.

Surender was working with a Unix programmer, and both assured the brothers they could develop a WYSIWYG product that would rival all others. With this assurance, the brothers committed both finances and resources to produce the product they tentatively called WysiWord. It would take a year, maybe two. But with Surender at the helm, it would be the best! They'd done it before; they would do it again! They took out a $1.1 million loan to finance this massive and far-reaching project, one they hoped would provide revenue for the next decade.

Energy Shift

TOWARD THE END OF THE YEAR, Dad slowly began divesting himself of day-to-day office concerns, including his pet projects. He had made Bonnie the general manager of the 400 building. He gave up sales management after hiring a former co-worker from Foxboro, giving him the title of VP of Sales and Marketing.

He also hired Al Rayshich, who had recently retired from Foxboro, and made him Manager of Inside Sales and Large Accounts manager. He hired two sales managers, one for accounts west of Chicago and the other east. And he put Training Director Leslie Ciborowski in charge of training sales reps on all products, and gave her a local account, Abbott Labs, to manage.

Soon after, Barb Gossen, our longtime Inside Sales Coordinator, gave notice. She confided in me that she was concerned about MEC's future. "MEC is hemorrhaging money. Your dad keeps hiring all these sales reps, and I'm not seeing any significant new sales. It's mostly add-on business from existing accounts." Barb told me she was sorry to leave but she had a sinking feeling about MEC's future.

Inside sales was a critical position, and Dad asked if my friend Linda (Murphy) Cahoon, a high-school classmate, might still be interested in working for MEC. I had told him years before that she was a clone of Bonnie—smart, down-to-earth, hard worker, high energy, and highly motivated. I told him I'd check, for I still thought she'd be perfect in any role at MEC.

MECollection: Linda Cahoon

I wasn't ready to leave my job in special projects at Citibank when Carol first approached me at our high school reunion in 1981. But I was in 1989. By then, I was tired of the repetitiveness of the banking world and ready for a new challenge. Hank and I saw eye-to-eye on everything we discussed. He offered me a position in the International Sales group, working with customers and OEMs in England, Australia, New Zealand, Norway, and Hong Kong. I would be their conduit to technical support, so I had to know the product cold.

I learned a lot and became familiar with the types of clients who used MASS-11. They were all so excited about it, and so was I. But my position in Inside Sales didn't last long; Hank had other plans for me: The Department of Defense's CALS initiative.

In the late '80s, the U.S. Department of Defense (DOD) was proclaiming that all documents had to be "CALS compliant" by 1992. CALS stood for "Continuous Acquisition and Life-Cycle Support Initiative." Its purpose was to eliminate manual tasks and paperwork in the life cycle of its weapon systems. The DOD wanted all-digital information, which included technical manuals, training materials, engineering sketches, product definitions, operating procedures, and technical plans to be integrated into a common system, in a common format, basically to avoid what they called scattered "islands of information." The DOD estimated they could reduce document handling and conversion costs by up to half of its total $15 billion document handling budget.

Everett did some research and, recognizing that the CALS Initiative was inevitable, assigned three programmers, all reporting to Surender, to it. After looking at the specifications, Surender reported we were already eighty percent there, and that it would be a piece of cake.

MECollection: Linda Cahoon

Out of the blue one day, Hank approached me and said, 'Linda, I want you to try being our CALS project manager.' In my short time at MEC, I'd learned that you had to be three things if you were going to be any project manager at MEC: (a) very detail-oriented, (b) able to read complex government specs, and (c) able to work with different types of people. Hank told me I would also need to write documentation for users. I had done all that at Citibank, and I accepted the challenge.

I got right on it with the programmers. My job was to test their code and make sure it was foolproof. The first time they handed me the code, I failed them: the code didn't work as it should. They were in shock, perhaps because they didn't realize how thorough I'd be.

I also attended several CALS trade shows, including one where we were invited to give a presentation on how MEC was addressing it. I attended with two of the CALS programmers, as well as a tall, friendly tech guy who set up our booth. MEC's presentation was scheduled for the afternoon. I thought I'd be there as moral support for the programmers. At lunch, one of the programmers casually said to me, 'Oh, by the way, Linda, you'll be the presenter today. We have to be somewhere else.'

Somewhere else? That was why they were there, to give the CALS presentation! I had never done public speaking. I went to my room and practiced for an hour. I was very nervous when I got on the stage. The friendly tech guy sat in the first row, smiled, and gave me moral support. There were perhaps two hundred people in that room, all eagerly asking questions—as if I were the CALS expert! And I guess I was back then. I was able to answer all of their questions, with confidence. I had so many people giving me their cards after my presentation. It was a miracle that I'd pulled it off. I never knew I could do that!

I learned so much at MEC and I was up for any challenge Hank threw my way. With MEC, you brought certain skills to the job and Hank expected you to expand on those skills. He would suggest something that let you use your old skills and learn new ones. He wanted you to at least try. If you didn't work out in that position, he'd say, 'OK, that's not your forté. Let's try something else.'

I was never bored at MEC. I always worked super hard. My attitude was, someone is putting their trust in you, and you want their faith in you to be warranted. I always felt, 'I can do it!' And I did!

My high school friends Bonnie and Linda were typical of most MEC employees: up for any challenge, working hard for the company's success, and able to be productive without supervision. Most gave their heart and soul to MEC.

My father implicitly trusted his employees; he wasn't a micromanager. If they worked in the office, he expected them to be on time and do the job they were assigned based on the "deal" he had offered when he hired them. Some had deals to only work four days a week, others to leave early to pick their kids up at school. He also made unique deals with field staff: the programmers, sales reps, and trainers.

These deals were between Dad and the employee, so when Dad

got word, from either an employee or a customer that he was being taken advantage of, only Dad knew for sure if that was the case.

John insisted that Dad had a responsibility to fire those who lied about how they spent their time on MEC's dime, or had profitable side gigs that interfered with their productivity at MEC.

But Dad was committed to being a Third Wave employer, one who enabled employees to have a work/life balance. But too often there were no consequences for those few who took extreme advantage, to the detriment of MEC.

I agreed with my brother but I kept my mouth shut. But I was with Dad when we discovered that an employee was a thief, using our mailing list, our VAX, and our internal resources. He reported directly to Dad, and had free reign when it came to travel, expenses, and access to inside information and our top customers. A customer clued us in, and Dad and I went onto this employee's computer after hours. I saw the pained look on Dad's face when he realized he had been betrayed. The first words out of his mouth were, "I think we can save him."

It took me a few seconds to acknowledge what he'd said. Then I blurted out, "Why would you want to save him? You should have him arrested!" The next day, Dad fired him and two others involved, but he stopped short of pressing charges. He also discovered another trusted employee knew about this "side gig," and never told him. These betrayals of his trust, few as they were, took an emotional toll on Dad, and wore him down.

A Weekend in Charleston

I WAS RARELY INVITED TO ATTEND the highly technical steering committee meetings, so I was surprised when Dad suggested I attend the one in Charleston, South Carolina. A bonus to visiting Charleston was that we'd be able to visit with a favorite cousin and nephew Greg Baker, who lived on the outskirts of the city. Greg hadn't seen Mom since her surgery and was eager to introduce her to his new son Jared, who was Beth's age.

It was the second steering committee I'd been invited to since Beth's birth and Mom's illness; the first had been in San Antonio and had been a disaster, (taking Mom there, not the meeting) due to Mom having hallucinations. Instead of attending the steering committee, I spent the weekend taking care of her.

His inviting me to the Charleston event was prescient. I had arranged through the hotel to hire a bonded sitter for Mom and Beth during the day. Mom and Dad flew down from Chicago, Beth and I from New Jersey. We got to our hotel in the late afternoon and unpacked our things. I suggested Dad check Mom's blood sugar and give her insulin before meeting Greg and his family for dinner.

Dad opened her suitcase and it was empty! No clothes, no glucometer, no oral meds, no syringes, and *no insulin!* Dad had a fit.

Mom just stared into space, showing no emotion.

Mom had been a surgically-induced diabetic for almost two years. She was non-compliant with her diabetic diet, meds, and checking her blood sugars. If he handed her pills, she pocketed them in her cheek, then spit them out when he wasn't looking. If he didn't check her blood sugars, they mostly didn't get checked. Yet he had trusted her to pack her suitcase with all the supplies she'd need to stay alive for a weekend in Charleston.

Why was he still in denial about her condition? I wondered. We had been to psychiatrists, and they had put her on antidepressants. Nothing had changed. One psychiatrist suspected the fifteen hours of anesthesia had damaged her amygdala, an area of the brain that processes emotions, memory, and sensory perception, which kind of made sense. He inferred that no psychiatric drug might be helpful to her.

We inquired at the front desk about the whereabouts of the closest pharmacy. "It's about ten minutes down the road, but it closed at five," the clerk said.

"It closed at five?" I gasped. "Is there another pharmacy in town?"

"They *all* close at five," he replied. "They re-open at ten tomorrow."

I found it hard to believe no pharmacies were open on a Friday evening, anywhere in the U.S.A., in 1989. But I quickly realized it didn't matter what time they closed. We had no prescription to even obtain insulin, let alone syringes! So our only option was to go to the ER, explain our improbable situation, hope they believed us, and leave with some free samples to last the weekend.

So that's how we spent our Friday night in Charleston, not reconnecting with Greg and his family but in the Emergency Room. Needless to say, I cancelled the bonded sitter and spent the weekend watching Mom and Beth.

Dad, I sensed, was dissociating from both Mom and MEC. He went through the motions of looking after her, but he snapped easily. I sensed he was burned out from being the primary caregiver for both his wife, his employees, and his customers. The combination of Mom's illness, Barb's foreboding resignation, the betrayals, Everett's increasing arrogance, and decreased sales despite hiring more sales reps had all taken an emotional toll on him.

And with John out of the picture as his primo sparring partner, he and Everett were increasingly engaged in their own war of words. There were other factors as well that I didn't know about at that time.

In the Emergency Room waiting room, he listened to Ramtha tapes on his headphones. As I sat there in the ER, trying to entertain my 3-year old, I realized that MEC was a house of cards, and if Dad withdrew his, the rest would come falling. Maybe not all at once, but it was only a matter of time.

Promises Achieved

B Y 1990, OUR CUSTOMERS WERE SUCCESSFULLY using all our products on the VAX and PCs. They had "achieved the promise" we had been selling for the past decade. They were connecting with other hardware, software, and users worldwide while saving time (years), and money (millions), and getting their products to market at record speeds. Most were eager to share their office automation and electronic publishing success stories—at user groups, at DEXPO, with reporters, and in our publications.

In 1990, Surender was in his second year working on WysiWord, and our users were debating over which platform it should support first. The first was delivered on DEC's VAXstation. Linda Cahoon was the product manager; Hilde Weisert was writing the documentation.

Everett continued to attend most user groups and symposia, fielding questions and taking notes at each. He enjoyed this immensely and flew MECAir to most of these events, taking MEC staff with him. With John's departure, he became the conduit for sales reps to request features customers were requesting.

We held twelve product symposia that year and sent staff to over thirty local MASS-11 user group meetings. We also participated in two DEXPO shows, one in Boston, and the other in Las Vegas. Two steering committee meetings were held, both at MEC's headquarters in Hoffman Estates.

We owned and operated our high-volume publishing facility on the premises with four pressmen churning out all MEC documentation and marketing materials.

On the PC, our competition was still WordPerfect and Microsoft Word; MS Windows 3.0 had just been released. And on the VAX, DEC's WPS-Plus, as slow and inefficient as it was, was still a competitor, followed by WordPerfect.

KEITH SESSIONS, THE DOCUMENT MANAGER at Cerner Corporation, along with Hilde, Sherry, and Anne Hamilton, had become the "world experts" on MASS-11, especially its advanced features that played a huge role in our customers' success.

"We were all a bunch of geeks trying to go as far as we could with MASS-11," Keith recalled. "We took it to the next level as we explored the new frontier of electronic publishing. It was thrilling!"

MECollection: Linda Cahoon

At a MASS-11 National Users Group meeting in Anaheim, I discovered how excited and knowledgeable MASS-11 users were. I couldn't believe all the documentation challenges these users presented, and how, together, they had found MASS-11 solutions to achieve them. The Users Group elected officers, produced a newsletter, and had an electronic forum to exchange ideas. It was all so exciting, being on the leading edge of the electronic publishing revolution in those days.

Keith, who attended every National User Group meeting, noted, "I wasn't thrilled, however, that Everett was becoming the 'face of MEC.' He wasn't a people person like Hank. At the National User Group meetings, he could be argumentative and condescending. There were lots of smart people in the room who knew more about his products than he did, but he came across as arrogant and defensive. It wasn't like the old days. We loved MASS-11, but not Everett!"

In late June, a sales meeting was held in Chicago. Even though he had hired two former Foxboro co-workers to manage sales, Dad led the meeting.

"June was another phenomenal month for sales," Dad announced, "with purchase orders in excess of $1 million!"

He also reported that DEC had established an office automation task force to go after competitors Wang and NBI, and that MASS-11 would (finally) be part of their "official" office automation strategy.

"On June 26," he announced to the group, "we signed a DDS (Digital Distribution) agreement for our MASS-11/All-in-1 integration kit. We are the first word processing vendor to have this."

Dad and I had both worked closely with a woman in DEC's office automation group who was instrumental in getting the agreement signed.

"Bonnie will be flying to DEC headquarters next week to meet with DEC's Software Supply Business offices to finalize details," he said. "And once again, MEC has been invited to attend DECWorld in July. Bill Boehm will represent MEC. Those WPS-Plus programmers still can't get it right!"

This was all great news, but the deal with DEC should have happened in 1982, when both MASS-11 and the VAX were the hottest office automation game in town. DEC's VAX sales were slowing down as workstations were emerging as the new superstars of tech.

Al informed the group that, besides DEC, we had agreements with two international resellers: Choice Computing in Sydney, Australia, and MEC Information Systems in London. We'd also made agreements with two more national temp agencies, he said: Kelly and Snelling, which, along with Olsten, made a total of three agencies that were committed to train both temps and MASS-11 customers nationwide.

In New York City alone, thirty-four local temp agencies advertised support for MASS-11.

Our Washington, D.C. sales rep announced that his efforts to get MASS-11 products approved by the GSA (General Services Administration) had paid off, making it easier for government contractors to purchase all our products.

During the breaks, a couple of sales people expressed concerns. They had heard rumors that DEC was signing a similar agreement to sell WordPerfect on the VAX. And several said they were getting hammered by Microsoft's *Word for Windows* on the PC.

After lunch, we discussed sales goals, expectations, and accountability. Expenses would be tightened, and daily call logs, similar to nurses notes, were expected.

By the end of summer, three sales reps gave notice. They blamed Everett for not listening anymore to their customers. Their departures brought the total number of resignations of sales reps to seven over the past year. Dad quickly hired new ones, but all had to be trained.

MECollection: Leslie Ciborowski

Hank was brilliant at identifying the most successful and well-connected sales people on his travels, and recruiting them to work for MEC. We just had to train them on how to demo and sell our MASS-11 products, and he assigned that job to me. I went out with them a lot. And I learned so much from them.

"What If" Games

SHORTLY AFTER THE SALES MEETING, Dad wrote in his journal, dated June 25, 1990: *In the boom years of MEC, Everett and I used to play "what if" games to sharpen our management skills, but there was always a limit to our imagination.*

Dad kept journals about everything—his blood pressure readings, Mom's blood sugar readings, his dreams, the books he was reading, Ramtha's insights, and musings on MEC. He often wrote in his journal in the middle of the night, if he couldn't sleep, or if he woke early. His journal entry, written at 4:00 a.m., continued:

> *Certain situations were simply considered catastrophic and were too painful to even contemplate, like: What happens if: 1) 40% of our sales force quits at one time? 2) Peace breaks out and wipes out our aerospace business. 3) 'Billion dollar' firms go bankrupt, leaving us holding the bag? (Like $200,000.) 4) Our foreign distributor walks into our office and tells us that he is in technical bankruptcy and can't pay us the $300,000 he owes us. 5) The bank threatens to call our $1.1 million 'payable on demand' note. 6) Our suppliers stop delivery if any of the above occurs? 7) We ask all of our top management to take a severe salary cut.*

The first four catastrophic "what ifs" had already happened. If the bank called the loan, the result would be disastrous for MEC. The loan was taken out in 1989 to (a) finance the development of WysiWord, (b) pay monthly rent payments of $75,000, and (c) pay the weekly $80,000 payroll.

Additionally, the money would provide Dad with retirement income; he had reinvested most of his salary in the company for the past decade and hadn't socked away anything in a retirement fund. We were making money hand over fist but spending it just as fast, on equipment, hiring, rent payments, and travel.

I'm certain Dad had sleepless nights about all of these scenarios. His journal entry ended with:

> A worry, once contemplated, stays with me, like cancer, sapping my energy, occupying my thoughts, eating my guts out.

Over the next three months, sales continued to gradually decline. In October, to stop the spread of rumors, the brothers gave a "State of the Company" address to home office employees. Dad spoke, Everett wrote it up, and it was included in MEC's weekly internal newsletter for those working remotely:

> Henry [only Everett called him Henry] explained that 1990 has been a year of transition for MEC. In the early months of 1990, there were rumors that DEC might choose to sell competitive products instead of MASS-11. These rumors caused several salespeople to leave us. We did sign a sales agreement with DEC in June, and they are currently selling MASS-11 products, and not, as rumored, competitive ones. But short-term damage has been done to our financial condition. While these salespeople were being replaced, MEC's

sales dipped, causing a short-term cash shortage.

Henry also described several other events that occurred during the year that had negative effects on the company's financial condition including a tripling of our real estate taxes due to the new Sears headquarters project in Hoffman Estates, the breakout of peace in Europe that hurt our aerospace business, and three unexpected bankruptcies of major customers, leaving large invoices unpaid.

On the positive side, several long-term development efforts are nearing fruition. They include our new CALS products, our FAXMail products, and our new WysiWord product. These exciting new products can be expected to produce significant revenues during 1991 and beyond.

In addition to the agreement with DEC, similar agreements are in the works with others we can't yet talk about. However, these agreements will not bear fruit until next year.

We hope that the worst is behind us, and the best is yet to come. Meanwhile, we need to temporarily tighten expenditures to keep the cash flow under control. With the help of every employee, MEC will successfully get through 1990 to enjoy the increased revenues of 1991 and beyond.

Excitement, Exhaustion, Exasperation

N 1990, THERE WERE SO MANY new computers, software products, operating systems, and workstations being developed! Topping the list were DEC's DECstation running Ultrix and DECWindows, the VAXstation, and Sun's workstations.

There were also so many acronyms: CDA, DDA, WYSIWYG, GUI, CALS, IGES, CPM, HPGL, and EPS. I'm sure I wasn't the only marketing person writing press releases about products I didn't fully understand.

Technology was light years ahead of where it had been just a decade before, when I was teaching basic word processing concepts, such as cut-and-paste and mail merge to secretaries with "deer in the headlights" looks on their faces. Those early days were like pre-school compared to the high-tech world of 1990. If I had looked into a crystal ball in 1980, when I was working full-time as an ER nurse, I could never have imagined what I'd be shown.

How our small but mighty team of programmers, documentation writers, trainers, and support staff kept up with all the different hardware, software, networks, operating systems, and formatting standards was mind-boggling. How could MEC possibly maintain this frantic development pace and stay ahead of the competition?

MECollection: Sarah Browning

Somewhere around 1989-90 I moved across the street from shipping (in the old building) to the new building to manage publications. We hired an Editorial Assistant and I also got Doris, Everett's wife, part time. She was a top-notch proofreader and relished any opportunity to talk about words.

There was Hilde writing and rearranging and learning the intricacies of the software and making it work for us and all the users as fast as she could.

Each major new release affected bunches of books and hundreds of pages, and it seemed there was always a new release in progress. New functionality meant new chapters, new vocabulary, new screen shots, references to the new stuff throughout, etc.

Many changes weren't really documented at all, just "discovered" in alpha testing, or the night before the books were supposed to be in the darkroom.

No matter what, there was always some drop-dead date by which the whole product: media, multiple books, installation instructions, had to be ready to throw in a box and ship. And when the whole operation was hell bent on getting something out the door, it was a thing. Excitement, exhaustion, exasperation.

We believed in what we were doing. It would pay off.

Viva Las Vegas!

A T THE END OF NOVEMBER, THE STEERING COMMITTEE met at MEC for the second time that year and got a closer look at WysiWord. *Fantastic!* was the consensus. They hadn't seen any graphical user interface product as comprehensive, all agreed. Everyone was upbeat and optimistic about WysiWord's chances of success. Versions were promised for the VAXstation, PCs with MS Windows, Macintosh, and Sun workstations.

Despite the best intentions to 'tighten the belt,' we sent fourteen employees out to Las Vegas in early December for four major events: DEXPO West, the MASS-11 National Users Group meeting, DECUS, and the Southern California MASS-11 Symposium. We used all these venues to introduce WysiWord to the public and demonstrated it on the VAXstation, PC Windows, and Macintosh at each event, to great fanfare from both users and the press.

Our pre-show press releases paid off. That week, WysiWord was favorably reviewed in both *Digital Review* and *Digital News* magazines, and the reviews brought many prospects to our booth.

I made a point to stop by WordPerfect's booth at DEXPO, where they were demonstrating the VAX version of their product. The booth was smaller than ours and manned by two tech guys. I was wearing my badge, but they didn't look closely at it. I asked about the more advanced printing features they claimed they had in their ads.

Both admitted their marketing people had jumped the gun on Postscript support and proportional spacing. "We're getting hammered on that," one said. "We're still trying to figure out the nuances of the VAX, especially when it comes to printing. We know how important those features are to you VAX users, however."

I appreciated their honesty with me, but they shared that information with the wrong person. I lived for nuggets of competitive information like that; that one was pure gold! I left their booth with a spring in my step and a smile on my face, feeling confident they wouldn't make a dent in our VAX sales. I told Dad the good news. He replied, "They're all a bunch of liars." In retrospect, our "war of the words" with WordPerfect was probably the last thing on his mind.

Dad talked about marketing with me, but for the most part, I didn't know what was going on behind the scenes financially with MEC, other than the "State of the Company" message that all received.

Perhaps it was just as well. I enjoyed being a key player in our successful family company, but the ability to take big risks, make enemies, get knocked down, and then get back on your feet was not for me. Since I'd been hired, we'd been on a straight-up trajectory of success through hard work, wise decisions, listening to our customers, and great negotiating. It never occurred to me that it wouldn't last.

We'd developed a family of hot office automation products, our profits had snowballed, resulting in MEC hiring more people, investing in more equipment, and expanding our headquarters ten-fold. Although I was probably one of the more frugal employees at MEC, I'd never experienced them having to pull back the reins and tighten the belt since the lawsuit in 1980.

For financial reasons, we'd stopped working with our Manhattan-based PR firm, which meant I had even more marketing responsibilities on my plate. With help from two women in the office, I was writing ads and press releases, setting up all the symposia, writing our monthly internal sales newsletter, editing our customer newsletter, and producing our four-color glossy magazine.

Barb Cross continued to work with me on all these projects, as well as with Hilde on WysiWord documentation. She made my marketing words and Hilde's technical documentation come alive with her artistic talent. She was overdue for a well-deserved raise, but all raises and bonuses were on hold. I prayed she wouldn't leave, or worse, get laid off.

Everett had also replaced our accounting/auditing firm with a man who, like him, had graduated with a degree in engineering from Northwestern. Unlike Everett, the man was computer illiterate. He'd never used a spreadsheet, preferring to do his calculations with a pencil and paper. *How could an accountant in the era of Excel not know how to use a spreadsheet?*

A few employees who worked with him questioned that decision, and why he spent so much time behind closed doors in meetings with Everett. My brother, who was no longer with the company but seemed to know more than me when he called, told me he suspected Everett and the new accountant were playing with the numbers.

I didn't know how John came to this far-fetched, in my mind, conclusion. I suspected John was "hitting the bottle" more than Everett was "cooking the books." But both possibilities saddened me.

1991

I N 1991, THE SOVIET UNION BROKE UP into fifteen independent states. Defense cutbacks and a recession led to massive layoffs at DEC, Data General, Apple, and Tandem, as well as the military contractors in the entire Northeast.

Electronic desktop publishing had become one of the fastest-growing areas of computer technology, with corporations demanding more and more from their desktop systems every day. Phase 1 of Wysiword was complete; a beta version was released on PC Windows, Macintosh, DECstation, Intergraph workstations, Sun workstations, and IBM R/S 6000 workstations. It was a phenomenal effort on the part of our programmers, led by Surender. Our remaining sales reps were demonstrating it all over the U.S., and the product was getting good press.

DEC's marketing efforts to promote MASS-11 WP were taking off, but not yet *paying* off. Their manager of Network Applications Support and Electronic Publishing groups wrote the following in the May/June 1991 issue of their *Product Insight* magazine. The article was entitled "Special Focus on Office and Electronic Publishing."

For the first time, DEC's word processing users can move
beyond word processing into the realm of high-impact

PostScript publishing. By selling and supporting the popular MASS-11 word processing application, DEC enhances its unique ability to provide users with an even wider selection of leading products for a seamless, networked publishing solution. Features such as open architecture, multiple editing styles, advanced printing capabilities, statistical editing, group authoring, and hot links, all have made MASS-11 a popular layered application in VMS environments. It is installed on more than 7,000 VAX systems and over 500,000 PCs worldwide.

Their efforts, unfortunately, were five years too late. WysiWord, not MASS-11 Classic, was the hot new product they should have shown interest in. But they hadn't, for it ran on too many non-DEC platforms.

MEC NEEDED A FINANCIAL "HAIL MARY" pass in 1991 and the brothers began seeking outside investors. They prepared a one-page sheet entitled "MEC Investment Opportunity" with a brief chronology. *Our 16th year!* The sheet noted we had $9 million in annual sales, and that MASS-11 was installed on seven-thousand VAXes and 500,000 PCs worldwide—all sold via our direct sales force.

They also prepared a first-ever organization chart which listed one-hundred and thirteen employees, including both part-time and consultants. This was down from 140 a year earlier.

Both Intergraph and Ashton-Tate showed a strong interest in WysiWord. Intergraph was a billion-dollar computer-aided design (CAD) company, the second-largest CAD vendor after IBM. Located in Huntsville, Alabama, it had 10,000 employees, making it one of the largest employers in the state. They had MASS-11 installed on many of their three thousand VAXes; they had bundled it into the CAD product they resold on the VAX. Everett made several visits and told Dad, "This could be a multi-million dollar deal."

ANOTHER POTENTIAL INVESTOR WAS ASHTON-TATE, the third largest software publisher in the world, with its database product dBASE. Their revenues in 1990 were $230.5 million. Ashton-Tate had been looking for a WYSIWYG word processor to complement their wildly successful dBASE; they found us after reading a great product review in PC Week magazine. They'd looked at several, and, after Everett and Surender flew to San Jose to give them a demo, they were most impressed with ours.

They offered $3 million, and, after speaking with Surender, the brothers agreed. *Three million dollars!* That would save MEC's neck! Surender recalled the conversation the three of them had. "We could all retire comfortably on that!" Dad, Everett, and Surender were all feeling optimistic in that first week of June 1991. MEC desperately needed one of these deals to go through.

The decision maker at Ashton-Tate said they'd like to send two programmers to MEC to review the code with Surender, "just to make sure it's clean."

The employees in the home office rejoiced. Ashton-Tate was visiting! All were told to wear their most professional clothes that day and to make sure the office was spotless. Bonnie would be in charge, as both brothers would be out of town, and unreachable. Surender would be on his own.

"I was terrified," Surender recalled. "The stakes were so high, and it all fell on me. But the two programmers were pleased with what I showed them, and they left saying they'd tell management that WysiWord was foolproof. We could expect to hear from Ashton-Tate's management within the next week, they said, and get the $3 million check soon after." The brothers rejoiced once they heard from Surender.

Shockingly, the deal with Ashton-Tate fell through a few weeks later, when Ashton-Tate was swallowed up by an even bigger software giant, Borland, makers of Turbo Pascal, Sidekick, Turbo C, Quattro

Pro spreadsheet, and Paradox database. The men we were negotiating with had no clue this was going on behind the scenes.

MEC'S ONLY HOPE NOW WAS INTERGRAPH. Everett was certain they wanted to bundle it into their workstations and resell it as they had with MASS-11 on the VAX.

"This deal could eventually be worth millions," he repeatedly told Dad. "We just need to provide a UNIX version. But our UNIX programmer is well along with it."

Dad wanted to meet Everett's contacts at Intergraph, "just to make sure we're all on the same page." But Everett was adamant that Dad keep his nose out of it. "I've told them you're semi-retired," he said. "I know the players and the situation better than you."

It wasn't like Dad to "just go along" with Everett when it came to such an important negotiation, especially one his retirement depended upon. Everett didn't have the negotiating skills Dad did, and he had a history of often stretching the truth about what had been discussed with potential clients.

But Dad let Everett "do his own thing." If he was going to retire, he figured, he'd have to give Everett some slack and trust him to do the right thing and make the right decisions. Running MEC on his own, without Dad's "interference," had become Everett's "Ramtha challenge."

Semi-Retirement

WHEN ASHTON-TATE EXPRESSED INTEREST in WysiWord, Dad thought the coast was finally clear to take his hands off the wheel and semi-retire. He was itching to get his hands in the soil and plant his garden. But the garden he was planning was in Washington state, not our backyard in Streamwood, Illinois.

Unbeknownst to most employees, both Everett and Dad had bought property near the Ramtha estate in Washington State in 1990. Everett's land included a horse stable, which he rented to local horse owners, many of whom were wealthy followers of Ramtha who had acquired property outside Yelm. He had also purchased a home next to Dad's property.

Soon after Dad acquired his land, he paid cash for a local contractor to custom-build a new house, one Dad had designed. It resembled our home in Streamwood, he told me—a split-level one with two small bedrooms and a larger master one.

One difference was that the *new* house would have an Armageddon-safe bunker, one he would eventually stock with canned goods, water, grains, and guns. Ramtha advised all his followers to be prepared for inevitable disasters, and Dad listened.

The builder suggested that Dad also include a master bath and walk-in closet in the master bedroom to increase the resale value. Dad declined. He later told me, "I wanted Mom to feel at home in it. I didn't want her complaining about missing the old house, or fussing that the new one was too fancy. And I told him I didn't give a damn about resale value. This was going to be our forever home." As soon as the Yelm house was finished at the end of June, Dad put our Streamwood home on the market.

In September, while Dad was planting blueberry bushes at his new home, Everett laid off several people, including the former Foxboro manager Dad hired to replace him as VP of Sales and Marketing. The man's title had changed numerous times at the whim of Everett—from VP of Sales and Marketing, to President, to VP of Operations in a few short months.

Two weeks later, Everett informed Dad that Intergraph had pledged $500,000 for WysiWord. Feeling financially confident with that news, Dad met with a representative from a retirement investment firm recommended by trusted Ramtha friends. "Karolyn" convinced him to invest his retirement money in a tax-sheltered offshore trust, one called Anderson Ark and Associates (AAA), owned by two brothers, Keith and Wayne Anderson. Dad invested what he had, after purchasing his new home with cash.

In October, Everett told our new accountant to cut my salary in half, effective the next paycheck. He didn't inform me; I just noticed it when I got my paycheck, and called Dad. When Dad asked him about it, Everett replied, "She's family. When we're struggling to pay the bills, the family gets their pay cut first."

I later learned Al's pay was cut, as was Surender's. Like me, neither received advance notice. But we were all considered "family."

MECollection: Hilde Weisert

Both Hank and Everett disappeared around this time, and left the reins to four women who were appointed to do functional specs. This group included me and Sarah Browning

in Publications. It was a very strange period, but also thrilling.
I just remember it was all women seemingly running the new
building at the end.

Dad's "retirement" lasted four months. In late November, Everett
called Dad to tell him he was faxing some important paperwork from
the bank. "I just need you to sign in two places and fax it back,"
Everett said.

"What am I signing?" Dad asked.

"It's just a bank formality," Everett replied, "regarding the loan."
Everett had faxed just the pages with the required signature lines.

"Fax me the *entire* goddamn document, not just the page where
my signature is needed," Dad said.

After reading the whole thing, Dad learned the bank wanted to
use Dad's and Everett's homes as collateral for the loan.

"Jesus Christ, Everett!" he fumed. "What the hell is going on back
there? Why do they need *my* house as collateral? Didn't you tell the
banker that we're expecting $1.5 million in receivables in December?
At least that's what you told me last time we spoke. And that we're
close to getting a half-million dollars from Intergraph? Or did I just
dream that you told me these things?"

"NBD (National Bank of Detroit) is calling the shots now," said
Everett. "All they care about is that we didn't make the last loan
payment. And that we haven't paid rent in two months."

NBD had recently bought out the Bank of Elk Grove, MEC's local
bank of ten years. The Bank of Elk Grove was one of many small local
Midwest banks that NBD gobbled up in the late '80s; the new bank
didn't care about MEC's stellar financial past. All they knew was that
the loan payments weren't being made.

Dad had no choice but to sign. But his trust in Everett was eroding.
Could he trust him that a deal with Intergraph was real?

The brothers read up on everything they could about finding

investors; they found a promising company called the Caserta Group, based in New York. Shortly after Thanksgiving, both flew out to meet with the owner, Peter Caserta, and discussed their dire situation. They met for several hours and were impressed by Caserta's knowledge, vast connections, and promises to find the perfect investor. Peter Caserta estimated that MEC was worth $15 million.

Caserta said there was no guarantee of a buyer, but they had several foreign investors interested in a company like ours. By the end of the day, the brothers had handed over a check for $30,000. Caserta insisted Dad come out of retirement.

So Dad made it his own "personal Ramtha challenge" to rescue MEC. He packed his bags and returned to Chicago, leaving Mom in the new house with a young caregiver from Australia. In addition to his clothes, he brought a sleeping bag. Having no house to live in and no cash to stay in a hotel, due to his recent investment with Anderson Ark, he moved into his old office at MEC. Buoyed by Peter Caserta's assertion that MEC was worth $15 million, he was energized and determined to turn the MEC ship around.

The next week, Dad met with the banker and explained they were now working with Caserta, and that potential investors would be looking closely at MEC in the next few months. She gave him a three-month reprieve on the loan. He met with the landlords, who brought the $70,000 per month rent down to $30,000.

On December 5, the steering committee met at MEC. On December 10, a small MEC crew was sent to participate in DEXPO Anaheim and the National Users Group, where customer Keith Sessions announced that his new 600-page manual on MASS-11 was nearing completion. Nobody was informed about MEC's worsening financial situation or the "big deal" with Ashton-Tate that got away.

The brothers were counting on that promised end-of-the-year half-million-dollar payment from Intergraph, one which could be used to pay down the bank loan, our vendors, the rent, *and* make payroll. But we never got a check, and they wouldn't return Everett's calls. Finally, angry and frustrated, Everett asked Dad to call them. He did, and they hung up on him.

Their last resort was the anticipation of $1.5 million in receivables in December, projected by the West Coast sales manager. Instead, only $500,000 came in.

That was their emergency backup plan.

1992: Downward Spiral

I RECALL ONLY ONE NIGHTMARE I'd had as a child. It was a recurring black-and-white one that involved large, razor-thin panels of glass, all moving slowly and smoothly on a conveyor belt, until the conveyor belt came to an abrupt stop, and all the glass shattered into millions of shards around me. I always woke up in a sweat, feeling shattered myself.

That was how I felt in 1992. MEC's plane was spinning out of control, and I felt many of the doomsday emotions I felt when flying with Everett from Las Vegas to Omaha years back. This time, I doubted an emergency landing would save us.

Despite the doom and gloom forecast, most employees continued to give it their all, many working well past sixty hours a week, getting a partial paycheck or none at all, and not knowing if or when the metaphorical guillotine would come crashing down on them.

In January 1992, Dad flew to New York, and the two of us met with all of our top customers and Anne Hamilton, to inform them personally of the financial situation we were in. Dad told me not to worry about him and Mom, that Mary Neff, a lifelong family friend who always came on our family canoe trips, had his back financially.

Back in Chicago, he made countless phone calls to loyal customers all over the country, explaining our situation. He also asked if any major purchase orders were in the works.

Not really, he learned. Most companies were dealing with their own financial crises, tightening their belts, putting purchasing plans on hold, and struggling to pay their bills. A good number were converting to MS Word or WordPerfect, as it was easier to find staff and temps who knew those products in rural areas, he was told. And they were cheaper. Some were converting to Interleaf or DECwrite for more sophisticated publishing needs.

Dad saw the writing on the wall, and called me to let me know, ahead of time, that more layoffs would be inevitable. Barb Cross, our graphics designer, was on the list, he said. He said he was sorry.

In those months that Dad placed his card back in MEC's deck, it became clearer to him that our enemies were no longer DEC or WordPerfect. We were fighting on a new front: Microsoft and the lending bank were the new enemies.

MECollection: Sarah Browning

In 1992 there were six of us in Publications, after one of many reorganizations. Hank and Everett weren't really around much at all. That also may be why it was kind of surprising when it really was the end—there had been so many disruptions people got used to it.

I feel like the last part came kind of quickly, and began somewhere between the introduction of Microsoft Word for Windows and Hank's "retirement." These are the two events that in my mind mark the beginning of the end.

I had gone to bat for the first two people I had to lay off - editorial assistants, one who worked on training materials and one who worked on marketing materials, both of whom had been hired hoping we'd be moving into producing video instruction soon. One had been there a year, one a little less. I went to Everett and pushed hard for them to get some kind of severance, even if it wasn't much. He authorized two weeks' severance for one and a week for the other.

The most recent addition had been added to our department not long before, having worked prior to that in a testing and documentation capacity in product development.

Anyway, I met privately with the two and delivered the bad news. Then I quietly told the remaining couple of people what was going on. The new one immediately ran and told all his buddies over in product development and Everett had to quell a panic over there. He called me in to chew me out and I remember it was obvious how hard it all was for him. I felt pretty conflicted about who I should be looking out for at that point.

On my last day, I was called into a meeting with Everett, along with six other women. We were dismissed together. I had been there five years.

Surender was trying to find a way to save the valuable software that he had developed—software that I had written books about, trained on, sold, marketed, and used daily over the past decade. MASS-11 WP was his magnificent creation. He talked about taking the source code and starting his own company. But the bank said no; the source code was a company asset.

On Valentine's Day, the week that both brothers celebrated their birthdays, we were threatened with bankruptcy. By the end of the week, the bank called and gave us a ninety-day reprieve. Dad wrote this in his journal:

February 25, 1992, Thoughts on Bankruptcy, Black Tuesday
Today I woke up around 3:30 a.m. and did my exercises. I felt fine until around nine when, once again, the full

realization of what we were being forced into by the bank once again hit me. The knot in my stomach started acting up again. My mind quit functioning properly. All I could think about were the employees who would lose their jobs and even their homes.

They are all good people, in fact, the best. As the team has shrunk in size, the quality has steadily improved. These people are truly dedicated to MEC. They are even willing to work for nothing for twelve weeks to pay off the bank loan and help us get rid of the personal guarantees. I call that real dedication.

By 10:00 AM, my head felt like it was in a vise. My temples were painful to the touch; my forehead ached. Our bankruptcy lawyer had told us as much as we could afford at $250/hour to know about bankruptcy: Chapter 11, Chapter 7, and personal bankruptcy. It all sounded ominous. But now that I was about to enter into bankruptcy, it somehow didn't seem quite as sleazy as I had imagined it to be. To 'go bankrupt' used to leave me with the feeling that somehow the person involved was a poor manager, a bad risk, a person one shouldn't trust, a person to avoid if at all possible.

I felt none of these things applied to me, and now that I reflect on the matter I am convinced that no one else in a similar situation feels any different. How could I have been so harsh in my judgment of all those entrepreneurs out there who have declared themselves bankrupt?

Potential Buyer(s)

O UT OF THE BLUE, IN MARCH 1992, a potential buyer, "Bob," showed up. Bob said he would give the bank enough money to keep them off our backs, and in exchange, Dad and Everett would sign over their stocks to Bob and give up their positions in the company. Bob would also be the escrow agent, and said the deal had to be top secret; the bank was not to be told until the deal was done.

Al noticed a clause in the bank contract that MEC would have to notify the bank if ownership changed. So Everett notified the bank. When Bob heard, he was furious and called the deal off.

Surender did some investigating on his own. Bob's company was not listed in the Yellow Pages, so Surender called the State of Illinois to do a company search and learned there was no such company, but one with that name had been dissolved twice!

Surender planned to approach Everett over the weekend to discuss a plan to take over the maintenance side of the business. But another potential deal had surfaced. There was a French firm that developed modeling and simulation (M&S) software that was willing to invest $2 million for 49% of the company.

A consultant had been hired by this French firm to find a midsize U.S.

company with a proven sales force to market and sell their software product, one that was only sold in Europe. The consultant and his wife had spent six months researching the U.S. market and seeking potential partners. After spending several weeks interviewing our staff and customers, they thought MEC would be the perfect company. He told Dad to prepare the MEC staff with the good news.

Dad wrote a letter to Mom at 3:00 a.m.:

> *The only downside to this deal with the French, dear, is that if it goes through, I must remain in the company as the chief executive officer of their American division. But at least we won't be in the poor house if there is such a thing anymore. The last thing I did before leaving Yelm last November was purchase a large tent for the very real possibility that we might have to live in one until I could get started again after going bankrupt. That doesn't look like it is going to happen now, but I may have to live out of my office for the rest of my life!!!*
>
> *Actually, dear, living in the office is not too bad a deal. I have a couch to sleep on, a refrigerator, and instant access to my work, which takes most of my waking hours. Somehow things seem the opposite of what they should be.*
>
> *You want to live in Chicago, and I'm in Chicago. I want to live in our new home in Washington, and you live there. Maybe we can switch roles.*

The deal was that the French company would pay off our debt and invest heavily in MEC. We sent a sales rep and a product manager to France to learn their product. They requested we hold a sales meeting in Chicago where their marketing and technical reps could meet with all our staff and begin preliminary training. And then, in the middle of negotiations, our West Coast sales manager resigned.

Dad's Letter to Mom, May 17, 1992:

Hi Dear,

Just a quick note to tell you hello and share some bits of life with you. Four motels in as many cities in four days. This trip was prompted by our West Coast sales manager leaving. I've been visiting our West Coast sales reps, our trainers, and our customers. This whole thing has had a demoralizing effect on our people. But the trip had its bright sides too.

I visited Cedar Sinai Hospital in Beverly Hills, one of our largest MASS-11 installations with five thousand users. I saw the devastation wrought by human hands [the Rodney King riots] to the L.A. area. Half of their employees were affected by the riots and couldn't get to work.

But I also saw one of nature's true miracles while there. In the middle of a side street coming onto Beverly Boulevard, there is a triangle of concrete for pedestrians to stand on when the light changes. On this concrete island was a lonely traffic sign, and at the foot of this sign a small crack in the concrete. And out of that crack is growing a mature tomato plant about 2 ½ feet high and two feet in diameter. And get this! It was full of blooms and had small tomatoes on it! It showed no signs of abuse.

I covered almost five thousand miles in a little less than five days. Plus working all day, every day.

This weekend I returned to the bicycle nature path along the Fox River [in Illinois]. What a little dream world when you get off the beaten path! I counted all the baby ducks. The mothers are fiercely protective of their children and immensely proud of their new families. What is amazing is that we lived so close for so many years without ever trying it out. And it was right under our nose the whole time.

Love, DAD

A sales meeting was held on May 21, when we all learned about the family-owned French company and the product that they wanted us to market and sell. At the meeting, the consultant stated there were no competitors, to his knowledge, in the U.S. The M&S business was a virgin marketplace with unlimited opportunity.

But, "just for good measure," he assigned me, the boss's daughter, the task of verifying this statement. I hoped he was right. The consultant hinted he would be the new manager of sales, and everyone was excited, including Al, who wanted to retire.

After returning to New Jersey, I began the search for M&S competitors. I must have looked through a hundred back issues of computer magazines, looking for articles and ads. No luck. And there was no such thing as a Google search to help me.

Then I called my brother and asked if he knew anything about that market. He said no, but he vaguely remembered that one of his programmers worked for a company called Istel that made that type of software. He remembered them being bought out by AT&T.

The next day, John serendipitously received an invitation in the mail to an AT&T/Istel seminar on their M&S software called Witness. He faxed it to me and I immediately signed up Dad, Al, and a tech support rep for the Chicago seminar. I called Istel and asked for product literature and they faxed it within minutes.

I called *Managing Automation* magazine and they faxed me a Buyers Guide listing all the M&S vendors. DataPro also sent me their books on M&S.

This was no virgin market in the U.S.! One competitor had a thousand employees. Another sold their products through IBM. Others sponsored annual M&S user groups that were attended by major Fortune 500 firms.

M&S had been around for years in the U.S. The French product was state-of-the-art but at least two competitors had the same feature set, perhaps more.

I discussed my findings, which could kill the deal, with Dad. If they knew there was stiff competition in the U.S., would they still be interested in purchasing MEC? Dad said to give them everything I found. And so I did.

I later heard they were very disturbed that the consultant had spent over six months investigating the U.S. market without finding any competition. It was baffling to me as well that they had gotten that far in negotiations without knowing much about the M&S market in the U.S.

Dad's Letter to Mom dated May 30, 1992:

When I spoke to you last Saturday, dearest, I gave you the impression that MEC had been sold to the French firm. That still hasn't happened, and the delay is slowly eroding our company. We simply have no money to work with and the people we owe money to, including our own, are growing weary of waiting any longer. They all have their resumes out and they are quitting one by one.

We lost four sales reps in four weeks. Our guy in southern California resigned Friday. He was ashamed to tell me he had taken another job because I had previously explained to him how crucial it was for him to at least stay until we had signed a deal with the French firm. The 'due diligence' phase we are currently engaged in may just drag on so long that we bleed to death while being 'saved.'

Last week was one of the most intense I believe I have ever been subjected to. It started with a client demanding their money back on a job our now departed sales manager had taken the order for back in December. At the time, he was the 'hero of the day,' bringing in a big order just before Christmas. But he had committed to have everything up and running by

December 31. He didn't tell anyone back in the office about that. That gave us less than a month to complete the project and it stuck a nice bonus in his pocket.

Of course, nothing worked as was promised and the customer is demanding his $50,000 down payment be returned immediately. He is threatening to sue us for consequential damages. Little does he know we don't have $50,000 to give back! No one looked to see if the job could be done, much less if we could do it in less than thirty days. This was what was going on all over the company after I 'retired.'

The moment I got to Denver and checked into my hotel room, I had a message to call Everett. He wanted me to call the landlord immediately. When the landlord called him, he told the landlord that I was handling the situation and that I would get back to him. I wasn't worried, even though we owed him over half a million dollars. Our attorney had just extracted a verbal commitment from the landlord not to rock the boat for six weeks until we could get the deal signed with the French firm.

So I phoned the landlord immediately, suspecting nothing serious. He informed me that since we hadn't paid any rent since around October of last year, he had leased our building out from under us, and he wanted us out of the building by June 1! So much for verbal commitments from landlords.

So now, I not only had the customer threatening to sue us for their $50K, giving me a knot in my stomach, but the landlord as well. I returned to Chicago to talk the landlord out of kicking us out of the building. The French firm showed no interest in helping us out of our fix.

So I visited the landlord alone and got him to renege on his commitment to the other client. I had to commit in writing to pay him $62,000 over the next thirty-one days in two equal *installments. The first installment of $31,000 is due on June 1, a day from today. Everett and I will split it, and I will use my IRS refund for that. I was saving that for a rainy day. I don't have a clue as to where the second payment will come from.*

Dad's letter to Mom dated June 10, 1992:

Dear One,

Well, I am finally getting settled in, living in my office. I have very few needs. The 'home' I live in costs $31,000 a month in rent. This is a drop from the $70,000 we were paying until May 30 of this year. Or I should have said we were 'supposed' to pay because we haven't paid any rent since October of last year.

I only have to cross the hall to go to the bathroom, or I should say the 'men's room,' because even though this mansion contains eight large 'bathrooms,' there isn't a single tub or shower in the whole building. And I have no one to blame but myself since I designed it.

I remember it clearly: 'Hank, why don't you put a private bathroom in your office with a shower stall?' 'What for?' I asked. 'I got a home to take a bath in.'

I don't get distracted by TV, radio, newspapers, or any media for that matter. The only paper I take is the Wall Street Journal. One of the reasons that I type my letters to you is that I am also taking a course in typing to increase my speed. It also gives me a chance to keep a sort of diary of this period of my life.

I also spend a lot of time thinking about the beautiful home we own in Washington state. I haven't been back in about four months. This is all a very humbling experience for a proud man who believes in paying his debts. But it looks like we'll have a

signed deal with the French in early July.
    Love, Dad

Dad wrote to Mom in July:

The moment I got back from the landlord I had a personal letter from your caregiver on my desk. I was expecting an upbeat letter about your progress. Instead, she informed me she would be returning to Australia in September; she needed to make some money. Free rent, Ramtha's tuition, and access to Everett's property to give horse-riding lessons aren't cutting it for her anymore. She wants cash, which I don't have.

After August I have no one to take care of you. I can't do it and I don't know anyone else willing to do it. Carol isn't an option; you can't even walk up her front steps. [Moving her to New Jersey wasn't an option unless we sold our house. And my husband would never go along with that plan.] You can't take care of yourself so I have to start seriously looking for a place that can take care of you properly.

I don't even want to think about my options if this deal doesn't go through. You might think that you can continue living your life the same as now. I just don't think that is realistic under the present circumstances.

Well, dear one, in the past I have tried not to burden you with my problems, but occasionally I have to tell you what is going on or you start thinking everything's coming up roses and that I'm an old scrooge for being such a tightwad.

We have had it tough before and we have made it through some very difficult times. I'm sure we are going to get through this one too. It is important though that you don't place impossible demands on me at this time. I will need your help

and encouragement to see this thing through.
    I will always love you,
    Dad

In all those months of negotiation, the French hadn't invested a dime in us. Nor were they aware that the bank was taking more and more each week, leaving barely enough to make payroll. Everett hadn't paid the sales reps their travel expenses for almost eight months, so many weren't even making business trips. Medical and dental expenses hadn't been paid for months either. [MEC was self-insured.]

The bank debt was $750,000, we owed the phone company about $30,000, and American Express $50,000. Most of our vendors hadn't been paid anything for months. UPS and FedEx stopped our services, and we couldn't order paper from our supplier. Surender and I hadn't been paid for weeks. Everything on Dad and Everett's "what if" list had manifested.

THE FRENCH DEAL FELL THROUGH IN MID-JULY. The bank took over and said they would find a buyer, whether we liked them or not. And within weeks, they did: three CPAs who had formed a friendship during their ten years at a Big Eight accounting firm and a lawyer friend. They understood business, money, and law. And they knew a bargain, with desperate sellers who had run out of cash.

On September 11, 1992, MEC, which was worth $9 million and had 144 employees at the start of 1991, was sold for its assets, with the agreement that the new owners would pay off any outstanding debts to the IRS. The fact that Wang went bankrupt and WordPerfect lost its first-place status to Microsoft Word in 1992 didn't make any of us feel any better.

Dad summed it up in an email to me dated February 23, 1993. He blamed the National Bank of Detroit primarily, for calling the loan:

The company that bought MEC is required by contract to pay the taxes, but if they don't there is no way to make them other than suing them. It takes money to sue and I don't have the money to hire a lawyer. The new owners were counting on that. That is why I have to sell my house to pay the IRS. If you want to write a book, you have one right under your nose.

Our demise was no accident. It was very carefully crafted by the National Bank of Detroit, commonly known as the 'whore of the banking industry.' They bought community banks and called all the notes. Then they took the proceeds and put cars on the lots all over America. NBD was owned primarily by the automotive industry. Tens of thousands of small businesses like ours were driven out of business by NBD. Or, using a very unjust law favorable only to banks that would buy you out in what was called an Asset Buyout, and leave all their debtors sucking gas. Enough! I get depressed just thinking about it!

Everett blamed Microsoft as he summarized MEC's demise in a one-page document entitled "The Final Days":

Microsystems did pretty well in keeping up with the rapidly changing computer industry for thirteen years between 1978 and 1991. However, the nemesis of the software industry, Microsoft, succeeded in putting an end to us in 1992.

Around 1990, Microsoft released the first version of its Windows operating system (O/S) for personal computers. Along with the O/S, it also released a suite of office automation products that ran under Windows. These products included a word processor, a spreadsheet, and a database manager.

The Windows O/S was an instant success in the market because it dropped the required IQ level for operating PC products from about 115 to 100. This opened up the computer market to many millions of new users. There was only one fundamental problem with Windows. Microsoft did not release any tools that would allow other software companies to write application programs for Windows for two years after the release of Microsoft's applications. This gave Microsoft a two-year head start in marketing its office automation products. It wasn't until late in 1992 that Microsoft finally released the Visual Basic tool set for Windows programmers. By that time, the entire office automation market belonged to Microsoft.

Keith Sessions, who had just released his massive, 600-page tome *MASSLore: A Power-Users Guide to MASS-11*, concurred. "MASS-11 was an amazing product for its time," Keith noted, "but when Microsoft released Word for Windows in January 1989, everyone in the industry went on high alert. You didn't have to be a fortune teller to see that, eventually, Microsoft would drive a stake in the heart of all competitors, including MASS-11, and even WordPerfect. Despite the power of MEC's existing character-based product MASS-11 and the promise of a WYSIWYG product, I thought to myself, there's no way MEC can compete with Microsoft's unlimited resources."

MEC was an experiment in intention and manifesting and, for most of its existence, a successful one. If getting rich was the Karels Brothers motive, they would have hired a business expert to find a buyer either at the beginning of its success in 1982, or at its peak in 1987.

The goal wasn't to sell MEC and get rich; it was to dare to dream big, to develop the best word processor in the world, and in the process have fun, be adventurous, empower employees and customers, learn about the secrets of the universe, spend as fast as you made it, and try not to go broke in the process. Engaging in battles along the way was frosting on the cake.

Our formula for success was listening to our customers and delivering the goods with breakneck speed. Most of MEC's employees and clients remember the exhilarating ride up, not the heartbreaking ride down! As the boss's daughter and one who documented the successes of MEC in real-time, both remain vivid in my mind.

Dad blamed the bank for our demise; Everett blamed Microsoft. But as mentioned earlier, MEC was a house of cards. Although there were many talented, hard-working, enthusiastic, and dedicated employees, Dad was the glue who held it all together.

Sarah Browning, who managed publications, concurred. "The whole operation that came after Surender said "Sure, I can do that" needed Hank's practical strength and the balance it provided."

When Dad pulled his card from the deck, focusing his attention on the secrets of the universe, among other things, MEC inevitably came tumbling down.

EVEN THOUGH MEC WAS SOLD, our customers continued to use MASS-11 for over a decade. For the thousands of MASS-11 clients worldwide who used MASS-11 to "achieve the promise" of producing complicated documents that supported the invention of new drugs, weapon systems, and scientific breakthroughs, the experience was nothing short of liberating.

Word processing transformed the lives of secretaries, engineers, authors, scientists, and investment bankers. And me! It changed the way I thought, created, and expressed myself. It freed me to change my mind and make revisions to my words without penalty and without stopping my thought process. It made it possible to work out of my home for three decades and make a living as a writer.

The employees I spoke with, thirty years after MEC's demise, expressed similar sentiments, whether they were part of "The Little Engine that Could" chapter of MEC or "The Runaway Train."

From all of them, I got a sense of family. In many ways, MEC was similar to the lessons learned in Louisa May Alcott's *Little House on the Prairie* books. 1) Surround yourself with good people. 2) Be generous. 3) Be loyal. 4) Stand up to bullies. 5) Be a happy warrior. 6) Have a positive attitude and, 7) Share your success stories.

And so I have.

Although the Karels brothers never became personally wealthy, the new owners did. They created conversion software from MASS-11 to MS Word, which they sold primarily to law firms. And they renamed MASS-11 Draw to SysDraw, created thousands of network drawings with it, and sold it to Visio for $3 million. Visio was later acquired by Microsoft for $1.3 billion!

So yes, MEC's legacy lives on. The decision to take three months off from ER nursing back in 1981, to write that MASS-11 beginner's manual was an unexpected opportunity of a lifetime—one that was simply beyond words!

Travel MECollections

ONE OF THE PERKS OF WORKING for MEC was the opportunity to travel—all over the U.S. and the world. Almost every employee with knowledge of our products was allowed to attend a trade show, symposium, or user group.

When Dad was in a city such as New York, London, or Seattle, he enjoyed walking the big city streets, checking out the latest technology, bookstores, and local food. He had discovered some favorite hole-in-the-wall Chinese and Indian places and always returned to them. He invariably bought a guidebook, took copious notes, and encouraged his traveling employees to do the same.

His dream of taking a trip around the world, when he had been at Foxboro, had finally come true. The Navy took my brother to Europe, Africa, and the Middle East. I too saw a lot of it while working at MEC. I traveled Monday through Friday for at least five years, as did most of our trainers.

Even the programmers escaped their electronic cottages for destinations far and wide. "All expenses paid" to travel were the big perk for the programmers: Surender went to Delhi at least once a year to visit his family and recruit new programmers, taking Ken and Ken's family (several times), Everett (twice), and Dad (once). On trips to India, everyone stayed with Surender's family and was given tours of Delhi, the Taj Mahal, Kathmandu, Lake Dal, Kashmir, Pahalgam, and Agra.

Everett made several trips around the world, with stops in Europe, Asia, Australia, and India. His daughter Lisa, now an RN, noted, "My father was always an adventurer. He always researched places he visited and wrote about his trips afterward using MASS-11 WP and the graphics integration feature to include photos and maps. He loved to travel and always advised me to go to the local markets and not the tourist traps. He once took me on a business trip around the world. He was also on a spiritual journey, and Ramtha served both my Dad and my uncle Henry on their seeking paths."

Trainers spent their weeks non-stop on the road, in places as varied as the Mojave desert, the oil fields of Manitoba, the atom-smashing research labs in New Mexico, and overseas destinations such as Paris, London, Oslo, Auckland, and Sydney.

One trainer spent a week training our Australian dealer in Sydney, then flew directly to Anchorage, Alaska, for another week of training at an energy corporation, giving her the distinction of flying the entire length of the Pacific Ocean on one flight (8,500 miles), while crossing both the equator and the international date line. She also transitioned from early summer in Australia to early winter in Alaska! *Imagine trying to pack for that trip!*

Trainers always had to be on their toes and prepared for any weather conditions, flight cancellations, or customer cancellations. They also had to be comfortable eating alone in a small-town cafe where nobody knew their name but everyone stared at you between sips of their soup. Eating alone, whether in local cafes or big city restaurants, became second nature to me and most of our trainers.

MEC's second training manager Debbie Burk recalled her days on the road with MEC. "I was training a new trainer in Boston. We took the ferry to Martha's Vineyard for the weekend and rented mopeds. She said, 'You're the coolest boss I've ever had!' and I told her it was thanks to Hank's generosity. Another time I traveled to London to conduct training for a new client. Everett and Bonnie flew in the next day for a meeting with yet another client. After completing the meeting, Everett rented one of those big black taxi cabs with a driver for the day, and we visited all the tourist sites in London."

As a bilingual (English and French) trainer, Pam Nelson was offered at least one overseas trip. "Hank asked if I'd like to train a class of French engineers in Paris – in French! I did speak French, having grown up in Paris, but I was not familiar with French *computerese*. Despite *that* handicap and the fact that my baby was only two months old at the time, I'd learned by then to just say yes. With Hank's permission, I hired someone to fill me in on French computer terminology and went to Paris, pumping my breasts along the journey, so I could resume breastfeeding upon my return."

Trainer Kathy Rayshich discovered her favorite place in the world while on an overseas training assignment: New Zealand! "I spent ten days at the University of Waikato. My hosts were very gracious, and I was treated to many home-cooked meals. Several of my students volunteered to be tour guides and took me all over the island in my free time. After my training, I took a one-week personal vacation in Fiji since it was so close. But I returned to New Zealand many times with my family after I started my own business."

If an employee wanted to tack on a few extra days of sightseeing or bring a family member along, it was at their own expense. MEC picked up the airfare, hotels, and three meals a day for the trainer.

Anita Fron recalled bringing her mother with her on several training trips. "I brought her on my first MASS-11 Manager training class in Anchorage, Alaska. She also came along when MEC sent me to London. We always shared a hotel room. She went sightseeing while I did my training, and we'd have dinner together in the evening.

"We were in London during a heat wave. I had jetlag; the room was hot, with no AC or ventilation. There were five to six terminals in a closet. I couldn't think straight and I believed I would faint. After London, my mom and I took the train to Scotland, where I taught thirty-five people at a chemical company in a much bigger room, but still with no AC and no ventilation. As a trainer, you just dealt with it."

It wasn't just trainers who spent time on the road. Product managers, trade show managers, and inside sales reps—all had opportunities to travel—to meet our customers, demonstrate new features, and have fun!

Bill Boehm, WP Product Manager in 1987 recalled, "Once I had to personally deliver a tape update to Price Waterhouse in San Francisco: fly out and back in one day. Nowadays you could just do a digital update, but back then we didn't have that capability."

Barb Gossen first dipped her toes in an ocean while traveling for MEC. "I went to DEXPO twice, once in San Francisco. When Hank and Everett found out I had never seen the Pacific Ocean before, they drove me to the beach just so I could take my shoes off and step in the water. I was in business attire and wearing nylons, but I did it."

Exploring cities on foot made Dad feel free, while for Everett, flying his plane, anywhere and with anyone, was his passion. An article on MECAir written in MEC's employee newsletter provided insights into its "popularity" as a means of travel:

> Sort of like jury duty, every MECie runs the risk of being asked to take a trip with Everett in MECAir. We thought we would look into what goes on during these infamous MECAir trips and let you know what to expect if you get asked.
>
> One thing MECies are finding out is that there is no such thing as a routine flight on MECAir. Somehow, Everett manages to intermix a touch of terror into every boring trip. During some trips, he adds a dash of lightning as spice. On others, he treats his passengers to heart-stopping views of 747s in mid-flight.

Often, when someone new was hired from out of town, Everett would offer to take them out to breakfast. Little did they know, when they accepted, that they'd be boarding his plane and heading north to Kenosha, Wisconsin, where they'd dine in a coffee shop adjacent to the local airport.

He typically enlisted his passengers to help get the plane ready for takeoff, or even take the wheel at some point. Barb Gossen recalled visiting Surender with Everett. "It was my second time on a small plane, and I was instructed by Everett to untie the wings before takeoff. It was very windy that day, so I thought it safer to just untie one until we were ready for takeoff. Somehow the message that the other wing did not get untied did not make it through to our pilot, Everett. It might have been a very short trip if not for the fact that he began his taxi very gently. . . "

On yet another MECAir trip to Dayton, this time with Bonnie, Everett asked her if she wanted to take the wheel but, she recalled, "I told him, at four-foot-ten, my legs were too short. I couldn't see out the windows or reach the pedals. So he taught me how to fly using the gauges. I learned to fly *with gauges* before sight!"

Surender's son Rajeev recalled when Everett took him, Surender and another family member up to watch the launch of a rocket off Cape Canaveral. "It was the thrill of a lifetime!"

And for many, so was MEC.

MECollections

O NE OF THE FUNDAMENTAL, RECURRING THEMES in the story of MEC that so often struck those who worked there, and that I've already mentioned often in this book, was how profoundly its way of treating staff differed from that of more traditional corporations. Here are some insights into that difference.

Surender Goel

I felt so lucky to have been associated with MEC. I enjoyed it all, especially my friendship with Hank. I was able to work independently out of my home in Dayton. I'd wake at five, have my coffee, and work till 11 PM. I had the flexibility to help my kids with homework after school, to attend their school functions, and to get in a round or two of tennis in the afternoon. MEC paid for me to go to India two times a year, sometimes with Ken, often with Everett or Hank. We stayed there 2–3 weeks with my family. If it wasn't for MEC, I probably would've gone crazy—still programming at NCR, which was not very interesting. MEC was exciting!

Bonnie LaScola

I had a great childhood. My parents were loving and nurturing, but other than getting good grades at school, I didn't face many challenges. After I married a man with two children, I had to learn how to handle all sorts of things. But until Hank, I never really believed I could actually do it. Why Hank believed in me so readily I'll never know. He did, though, and with each new assignment, I started to believe in me too. He taught me how to stand up for myself and how to solve problems. I learned how to manage: things, people, and myself. I always remember him saying, "Bonnie, that's not how I would have done it, but you got it done, and better than I could have!" He allowed me to be the best I could be. I will always be thankful to him for helping me find the strength I had in myself.

Ken Crossen

Hank's genius was having the confidence of knowing he was right. He was fearless. He was a perfect small-company guy. He was an expert on pressing the flesh daily. He wanted everyone to be empowered. Hank was a caregiver on some level to his employees, warm and full of wisdom. He invited loyalty the old-fashioned way. Fortune was with him, and he had that "magical sauce." He was like a father to me, giving me advice that has served me well to this day. He understood my nature, which was basically "leave me alone and let me do my thing." He respected that.

He took a chance on me, Surender, Carol, and Bonnie. None of us were proven entities. He gave us the tools and freedom to be successful. Bonnie was a brilliant gatekeeper for him.

James Meade

Hank was interested in human motivation, but not so much in motivational psychology or motivational seminars. He was interested in getting people to do more than they ever dreamed of doing. He created the right conditions, then left them alone. When he designed the new building, he followed one simple design principle. He wanted everybody in that building to see the sun. They would have dignity, and all that sunlight would create an environment where they could "hear themselves think."

Everett created the castles in the air; Hank put the foundations under them. Everett had the outrageous ideas; Hank made sure the weapons were ready and in working order, and gave the final order to attack. Who knows if either would have succeeded without the other? Together they succeeded. Against all odds. And what were the odds, when they started their company, that they would succeed in the same marketplace with IBM, Digital, and Wang?

Kathy Nichols

Hank and Everett were visionaries—way ahead of their time. I always did my best at all my jobs in my fifty-seven years in the workforce, but I will never forget that Hank Karels was directly responsible for the course change of forty-four years of my working and volunteer life.

Pam Nelson

Hank was a mentor and I learned valuable lessons from him, such as (a) how important it is to cultivate insight into people such that you can put them in the right positions. It can make the difference between shining and failing; (b) how important it is to set the right expectations, never over promise on a deadline, and never promise anything you can't deliver and; (c) to always be open to expanding your capabilities by saying "yes" to whatever challenges come your way. These, and other lessons, have served me well. He could be strict, and sometimes loud and intimidating, but he was always fair and took great care of his employees.

Gene Kratochvil

Hank was the ultimate boss, even though he disliked that term. The way he handled even the most difficult situations was genius. He always asked, when there was a problem, "What other options do we have?" When I was the hiring manager, I would love to sit in on interviews with him. He asked such insightful questions and learned their life stories. He didn't hire based on degrees and resumes but from those interviews. He had great instincts. I also enjoyed working with Al Rayshich, who was a manager of managers.

While at MEC I developed a new appreciation for writing. I would test a feature, then write up what didn't work. I typically wrote cryptic one-liners. Everett taught me good writing structure and how to write a good summary description.

Anne Hamilton, A.M. Hamilton, Inc.

Hank was such a generous man. He just said, "Do what you need to do," and he gave me the resources I needed and just let me do my thing. He was a good role model to me for dealing with people. I kept my consulting business going until 2016. I kept in touch with Hank on the phone even after MEC was sold. We always talked around his birthday. It was mutual respect. I'm so grateful to him for the opportunity for me to start my own business.

Kathy Rayshich Cartwright

As a result of my time spent at MEC, both training and selling, I had the confidence to start my own business with my husband. We've been in business for over thirty years and I attribute much of our success to the business lessons I learned from Uncle Henry, and my father, Al Rayshich.

Barbara Gossen

Hank wanted all employees to be confident and caring on the phone or in any face-to-face encounters with customers. To achieve this, he arranged for the Dale Carnegie course to be held in-house at MEC, and all employees were encouraged to attend. This several-week course was also a very helpful life skill thanks to Hank's foresight and desire for self-improvement for all.

Leslie Ciborowski

Working at MEC was a priceless experience. Everett with his plane and maps; Hank with his herbal cures for everything including putting garlic cloves in his ears when he had a cold. Hank was a great and unique businessman!

I learned a lot from him on what to do, and what not to do, as I managed trainers, trained sales reps, assisted with demos at trade shows, and managed a local Fortune 500 account. I was honored that Hank asked me to be part of the Steering Committee. All of these experiences helped me in the growth of my own training company, which has been in business for 31 years.

Christine Walsh, Accountant

Hank was way ahead of his time when it came to meeting the needs of the employees, especially the women. We had two pregnant females and Hank asked me to purchase a chaise lounge for them to rest and elevate their legs. He also offered 9–3 "mother's hours." He was an example of entrepreneurialism at its finest. He did try to empower everyone. He handed you the reins and said 'Go for it!'

Natalie Kaye

The years I worked for MEC were among the best in my life, and were an integral part of my growth. I was grateful for the mentoring and guidance I received from Hank and Carol. There were many lessons I learned at MEC that helped me start my own business and continue loving my work to this day!

Annette Swoger

If Hank thought you needed anything, he would do anything to make it happen. I know a handful of employees betrayed his trust and took advantage of his generosity, which just broke his heart. He had total trust in them; it was hard for all of us to see that.

Bill Boehm

I have nothing but wonderful memories and enormous gratitude for MEC—the people I met, the skills I learned, and the opportunities given to me. I hope Hank knew how much I appreciated what he did for me.

Sharon Fisher

Working with Hank and Surender was a wonderful experience, each for different reasons. Hank understood my nature, and was able to get the best out of me. Surender and I were on the same wavelength technically and it was always a joy problem-solving with him on the phone. Joanne was one of the finest women I've ever met, and always concerned about the wellbeing of me and my young daughter.

Sarah Browning

The brothers gave every idea a shot. Hank tried to design an operation that could bring a physical product to a designated market as efficiently as possible. Everett wanted robotics and software that designs itself. He wanted ideas, programming breakthroughs. Hank wanted to hold it in his hand, like a trophy, surrounded by his grinning teammates. There were aggressive moves, especially by Hank. Bringing the whole printing operation in-house, centralizing editorial, hiring the blind guy. It was kind of his trademark, being the risk taker. He was adventurous and winning his favor seemed worthwhile.

Rajeev Goel, Surender's eldest son

I remember Uncle Henry visited us in Dayton when I was about eleven. I was already doing some rudimentary programming and he asked if I would create a program for him. I showed it to him the next day and he handed me a $100 bill. I had never seen that much money in my life! It made me realize I could make money as a programmer! And I have!

What Came Next

Everett

Everett was kept on as a consultant for the new owners for a short time. He sold his home in Inverness, and he and Doris retired to the home they purchased in Washington. There he used MASS-11 and MASS-11 Draw to create a monthly black-and-white magazine called the *Nisqually Eagle* that included his musings on technology, flying, and travel. He and Dad occasionally crossed paths at the Ramtha retreats. He was involved with Ramtha until his death in 2000 at the age of sixty-three.

Surender

After MEC was sold, Surender also stayed with the new owners for a short period, then left to start his own business. "The thrill was gone!" he said. He still lives with his wife Manju in Dayton. Two sons, Rajeev and Ajay, and their families live nearby. Both are programmers and successful entrepreneurs. His daughter Nirupa is a neuroscientist in British Columbia. Surender has seven grandchildren, and plays tennis daily.

Dad

Dad was kept on for a brief time by the new owners. They reneged on their promise to pay back taxes and provide him a salary for a year, forcing him to sell his new home to pay those taxes. He spent the rest of his life living in in four refurbished shipping containers. One was his library, one his kitchen, one his personal area, and one was for storage. He also had a well, a vegetable garden, a rock fountain, and an underground shelter, which he stocked with survival supplies.

He took violin and art lessons, painted over a hundred watercolor and oil paintings, kept a journal, read dozens of books on energy medicine, frequency therapy, and naturopathy, and started at least two more businesses focused on alternative health. He made enough to live comfortably in his containers and travel.

He said his three-week trip to India with Surender, at age seventy, was the best trip he'd ever taken. Then, at age seventy-seven, just months before he died, he used part of his Navy pension to take a trip of his dreams: a two-week rafting trip through the Grand Canyon, in a wooden dory, no less!

He was active with Ramtha's School of Enlightenment until his death in 2006, often attending sessions with his sister Joyce, and two nephews. He acknowledged that he had not only manifested MEC's success, but also its demise. He never dwelled on the past, but lived totally "in the moment." He counted Al Rayshich and Surender Goel as his closest friends.

Mom

A month before MEC was sold, we moved Mom into an assisted living facility in the small, former logging town of Castle Rock, Washington, just west of Mount Saint Helens. She lived there for ten years. In 2002, she was sent to the ER after having a psychotic episode which left her unable to walk, then transferred to a family-run nursing home in the nearby town of Longview. A month later, I received my first handwritten letter from her in eighteen years! Her writing resembled chicken scratch but her "Mom voice" came through in the letter.

I called the facility nurse, who told me Mom was a wonderful addition to the place, chatting with everyone, and making others laugh. She'd already made many friends and was like a social worker to staff members, she'd said, giving them advice. She also noted that all the nursing home cats slept in her bed. This report sounded too good to be true! Beth and I flew out immediately.

It was the first time my seventeen-year-old daughter met the fun-loving grandmother she had never known. Mom was wheelchair-bound, made eye contact, and with a twinkle in her eye, asked endless questions about our lives. We brought her up to speed over lunch at the local Chinese restaurant. Beth told her she was an EMT and was planning to study nursing after she graduated high school. Mom asked about MEC, and I told her of its demise.

"Without you," she said, "MEC wouldn't have gone anywhere in those early years." This was the mom I grew up with, always giving praise.

She asked about my husband, and I told her that chapter of my life was over, and she had no comment.

We also drove down to The Grotto, a 62-acre national sanctuary/shrine to Mary, in Portland. The Grotto's mission was to offer a sanctuary of peace, prayer, and natural beauty for all people. Mom said she'd always wanted to visit it.

Beth pushed Mom's wheelchair as we walked the grounds: the cave with a reproduction of the Pieta sculpture, the Peace Garden, and the Chapel of Mary, which featured a stunning stained glass window depicting the Resurrection of Christ. As we wandered through this beautiful sanctuary, with rays of light dissecting the darkness of the evergreens, I acknowledged Mom was resurrected. Her recovery was a miracle!

When we returned to the facility, I told the nurse how Mom had been for the past eighteen years. "What medications is she taking?" I asked. The nurse said that besides insulin, she was only taking two drugs. I was unfamiliar with both of them.

"They're new psych meds," she said, "just recently approved by the FDA. One is an antipsychotic and the other an antidepressant. She's on the maximum dose for both."

Drugs were responsible for Mom's miracle? It broke my heart that we all needlessly suffered for all those years when two new psych meds could have helped her. I later learned that MASS-11 was used to create the new drug application for one of them. It might have taken years longer to get released if not for MASS-11, I thought.

Later that year, I took Mom and Dad out to lunch for their fiftieth wedding anniversary. The two conversed with affection. Then Mom asked Dad if they could return to Chicago, and live in a high-rise overlooking North Avenue beach. "You achieved your dream. Living downtown overlooking the lake has always been mine," she said.

Her comments shocked both of us. I don't think she quite understood that she was an invalid needing full-time nursing care, and that Dad was essentially a pauper living in four shipping containers in a forest a hundred miles north of her.

They continued to live separate lives, she in the nursing home and him in his containers, until they died, within six months of each other, each age seventy-eight.

John

After my brother left MEC, he had a tumultuous business relationship with Ken marketing TechEdit; the partnership ended in a fierce legal battle which John lost. Defeated, John became a recluse of sorts. He left his wife, built a primitive cabin on a scenic plot of land west of Madison, Wisconsin, and lived off the land. The only staples he bought at the store, he told me, were orange juice, kimchi, and beer. His companions were his border collie, a cat, and three goats. He told me that he wished he'd become a farmer at eighteen, that he felt happiest living in the woods, taking walks with his pets, and drinking beer on his front porch until he passed out.

Despite being a recluse, he still hungered for battle. He got involved in local politics, sent a multitude of letters exposing corruption in local government to the editor of the newspaper, and once wrote to me: "My town is like the Hatfields and the McCoys, everybody warring with each other. It wasn't like that before I came, ha ha!"

John died in 2010 of alcoholic cirrhosis of the liver with encephalopathy; he was fifty-five.

And me? I too was kept on for several months by the new owners, until I was laid off along with a handful of others they had kept on. It was a huge relief to get that phone call.

"We're sorry, but we no longer need your services."

I had no desire to find a job in office automation or electronic publishing. Nothing could surpass the thrill of working for MEC. And I never considered returning to nursing. I was a writer and I had plenty to write about. But it was too soon, and too painful, to write about MEC.

MEC was Dad's creation, and I was proud of my contributions to its success. But birthing a child was my miraculous creation, and any new career would have to fit in to the new life I created around her.

I volunteered a lot in my adopted town of Leonia, New Jersey, and never discussed my previous MEC life with new friends. I didn't keep up with technology trends. I lost track of former MEC co-workers. But I joined a writers' group, used MASS-11 daily, and wrote another million or so words, including my nursing memoir and three other books.

At seventy-one, I still work part-time as a Home Health nurse, after returning to the profession at age sixty-two when I moved to San Antonio, Texas to be near my granddaughters. And I enjoy it! I've even had a few patients who fondly recalled using MASS-11 at

Lackland Air Force Base and BAMC.

But I still love writing, and I wrote *War of the Words*, using Google Docs, in the spaces between seeing patients. One day, while writing the book in my nursing scrubs, my 9-year-old granddaughter Hallie asked, "What's your new book about?" and I told her it was about starting your own business and being an entrepreneur.

"Do you think I could be an entrepreneur someday?" She had been watching "Shark Tank" on TV with my daughter and was thinking of starting a lemonade stand.

I told her she could be what she dreams, and reminded her of all the heroines in her favorite Disney movies and the positive, uplifting, and adventurous lyrics she had memorized: "When You Wish Upon a Star," "A Dream is a Wish Your Heart Makes," "Just Around the Riverbend," "I See a Glimpse of What I'm Meant to Be," and "A Whole New World."

Thoughts become things, I told her, so think amazing ones!

Noteworthy

In August 1992, the former $3 billion Wang Laboratories filed for bankruptcy.

In 1994, Novell acquired WordPerfect Corporation in a stock swap valued at $1.4 billion. Each of the two owners, Alan Ashton and Bruce Bastain pocketed $600 million. Their marketing and sales manager, Pete Peterson, who was largely responsible for their business success, was let go before they sold.

In 1994, Peter Caserta and ten others from the Caserta Group were indicted on federal charges of operating a confidence swindle that bilked dozens of small companies out of millions, companies that the banks had turned their backs on. After pocketing MEC's $30K, they came up with no potential investors.

In 1996, Novell sold WordPerfect to Corel, Inc. for $115 million.

In 1997, MEC's new owners sold components of MASS-11 Draw, renamed Sysdraw, to a startup company in Seattle called Visio for $3 million.

In 1998, Compaq acquired Digital Equipment Corporation for $9.6 billion. A few years later, Hewlett-Packard acquired Compaq.

In 2000, Microsoft acquired Visio (the company that purchased rights to MASS-11 Draw/SysDraw) in a stock swap. The trade was worth approximately $1.5 billion.

In 2000, Corel purchased Borland [the company that purchased Ashton-Tate] in a $2.44 billion stock swap.

In 2000, the three partners of Anderson Ark Investing (AAA) were tried in Federal Court in Seattle for a tax scam that "ripped off Uncle Sam for $120 million." I have no idea how much my father invested, and lost, with them.

Evolution of Office Automation: MEC in a Nutshell

Microsystems Engineering Corporation
Industry: Office Automation Computer Software
Founded:1975
Founders: Hank and Everett Karels
Defunct: 1992
Fate: Acquired
Headquarters: Hoffman Estates, IL
Key People: Hank Karels, Everett Karels
Principal Programmer: Surender Goel
Principal Graphics Programmer: Ken Crossen

Products: MASS-11 WP, MASS-11 Manager, MASS-11 Spreadsheet, MASS-11 Draw, MASS-11 Graphics Processor, MASS-11 Express, MASS-11 Mail, MASS-11 FAXMail, Internodal Mail, WysiWord, TechView, All-in-1 Integration.
Number of Employees: 140
Motto: "The Company that Listens" "The Software that Sells (DEC) Hardware"

MEC's first software contract was with NASA in 1975, developing systems for use with the space shuttle. In 1976, they expanded into the commercial market, developing specialized business systems for the DEC PDP-11 minicomputer. In the course of their contacts with a wide variety of customers, the two brothers realized there was a market for a good word processing product on the PDP-11 that DEC was not meeting. MEC created MASS-11 (Microsystems Administrative Support System) in 1978 to meet this need for legal and insurance companies. MEC's first word processor for the PDP-11 was released in 1978 and was sold through DEC's dealer network.

MEC targeted Fortune 500 companies and solicited product design advice from corporate MIS Managers, with the promise of timely implementation of features. Hence, their nickname "The Company That Listens." By 1987, their nickname was "The Software that Sells (DEC) Hardware" and MASS-11 products were installed on over 4,000 VAXes worldwide, with 200,000 VAX users and 50,000 PC licenses. MASS-11 was used in 60% of Fortune 500 companies and major banks, and 40% of Research labs and law firms. It was also used almost exclusively in most universities with VAXes.

MASS-11 WP was first released on the Digital VAX in 1981. It was the first to optimize the VAX for efficient shared word processing, making it possible for multiple users to create, revise, share, and print lengthy and complex documents. Initial customers were aerospace and engineering firms. Numerous OEMs sold it to law firms, medical companies, and state legislatures. MASS-11 soon became popular at pharmaceutical and R&D firms due to the sophisticated equation editor and ability to share tech-pub documents with secretaries and other collaborators, all using VT-100 terminals. As the product evolved with footnoting capability, end-notes, redlining, and laser printer support, more large law firms invested in VAXes using MASS-11 as their word processor. Numerous Wall Street Investment Banks and Big Eight Accounting firms based in Manhattan also standardized on MASS-11 due to its highly sophisticated column functionality and right-justified proportional spacing.

In the early 1980s, DEC was a reseller of MASS-11 WP on the VAX until they completed their word processing product WPS-Plus. DEC Office Automation management was irate that MEC released MASS-11 for the IBM PC in 1985, as they were adamant that MEC only develop a micro version for their own DEC Rainbow and Pro350. MEC then formed its own outside sales force.

Word Processing History Timeline

1964
- IBM Selectric typewriter MT/ST "word processing machine"

1969
- Mag cards for form letters. One page of text per card

1972
- Lexitron made the first "word processor" with a screen. Vydek first to use floppy disks to store text.

1975
- DEC released PDP minicomputers.

1976
- IBM controlled 80% of the "word processing" market with 150,000 standalone systems using magnetic tape readers. Early word processors had basic functionality including a spell checker and list merge.

1977
- MEC released MASS-11 (Microsystems Administrative Support System) for DEC's PDP-11.
- Digital Equipment Corporation (DEC) ships the first VAX 11/780.
- The first IBM PC released.
- Lanier CRT (cathode ray technology) with built-in keyboard and floppy disks.

1979
- MASS-11 WP was sold through dealerships on the PDP-11.
- Satellite Systems, Inc. (later called WordPerfect Corporation) shipped SSI*WP product for Data General minicomputer for

$5,500.
- WordPerfect 2.0 released on IBM PC $495.00.
- Micropro released WordStar, which was the first commercially successful word-processing software program produced for microcomputers and the best-selling software program of the early '80s.

1980

- Alvin Toffler published *The Third Wave* and introduced the concept of office automation in the electronic cottage.

1981

- MEC programmer Surender Goel completely rewrote MASS-11 for the DEC VAX VMS in native mode. After the product was ported to DEC's VAX VMS, the name MASS-11 was retained, even though support for the PDP-11 product ceased. Demand for MASS-11 surged when VAX users, primarily scientists and engineers realized they could type their research documents and share them with secretaries, greatly enhancing turnaround times for revisions.
- MEC actively sought the advice of its engineering and research customers in developing an advanced scientific equation editor.
- IBM PC released.

1983

- DEC became a reseller for MASS-11 WP as MASS-11 is sold to numerous Fortune 500 accounts.
- MASS-11 Version 3-C was released and included the equation editor, as well as multiple numbering styles and composite documents to meet the needs of aerospace, oil, and R&D firms. Eventually, more than half of the major oil companies in the US and abroad chose MASS-11 for the departments of their organizations requiring heavy-duty scientific word processing, including Shell, Sun, Norsk Hydro (Norway), Mobil, Standard

Oil, and British Petroleum.

- Intergraph in Huntsville, Alabama became a reseller of MASS-11 WP.
- MASS-11 WP Version 3-E was released which included features such as footnotes, table of contents, redlining, split screen editing, and indexing. The powerful combination of the VAX and MASS-11 helped open doors for both DEC and MEC to get in the doors and meet the office automation needs of large law firms nationwide.
- MEC developed its own sales force. A limited number of DEC OEMs in vertical markets also sold MASS-11 (Quorum, Shared Medical Systems, Intergraph, Legal Data).
- A Steering Committee was formed. In line with its motto "the company that listens," MEC invited MIS managers from sixteen Fortune 500 companies to meet annually with principal programmers Surender Goel and Ken Crossen. The purpose was for these managers to share their office automation strategies and offer suggestions on how MEC's products could best meet their complicated corporate-wide office automation needs. These sessions provided valuable feedback to MEC's programmers regarding existing products and future directions.
- Microsoft Word for DOS was released on the IBM PC.

1984

- MASS-11 WP ported to IBM PC/AT and DEC Rainbow.
- In response to the proliferation of microcomputers in many of its large installations, MEC's programmers developed MASS-11 for the IBM PC, the DEC Rainbow, and compatibles. General Motors Research worked closely with MEC on the development of MASS-11's PC to VAX seamless communications utility. Several major corporations that were primarily PC sites selected MASS-11pc as their standard, including the World Bank, after

evaluating it against all the major PC competitors of that time, including WordStar, WordPerfect, and MSWord. Ease of use and comprehensive functionality were just two of the reasons it was chosen.

- MEC held its first regional User Group at the Grand Hyatt Hotel in NYC. 140 people representing seventy firms, both existing and prospective customers, attended the full-day presentation. Its success spawned the formation of MASS-11 User Groups nationwide–in NYC, Washington DC, Philadelphia, Boston, LA, San Francisco, Dallas, Albuquerque, Denver, and Chicago. At these forums users could share advice and tips, as well as hear about product updates from MEC's product managers. Founders Everett and Henry Karels regularly attended. Representatives from each regional user group met annually at the National MASS-11 Users Group to vote on their top ten wishes for the product, which MEC pledged to incorporate into the next release. Listening and responding rapidly to the requests of MIS planners, department managers, and end-users helped MASS-11 evolve into one of the most feature-rich word processing products on the market, surpassing the features of the popular standalone WP products of the time such as Lanier, Wang, and NBI.

1985

- MASS-11 WP 5-C was released, which included multiple types of tabs, sophisticated column editing, line drawing, double underlines, multinational character support, and proportional spacing.
- Due to growing interest in MASS-11 WP among Manhattan's Big Eight Accounting Firms, and commercial and investment banks, MEC opened an office on Park Avenue in Manhattan for demos, training, and support.
- Tiger Temps, a temp agency specializing in the document

production needs of NYC investment banks, invested heavily in training their temps on MASS-11 to staff the M & A departments of investment banks round-the-clock. Olsten Temps soon followed, training their staff nationwide on MASS-11.

- By the end of 1985, MEC had released a family of office automation products that included MASS-11 Manager (a state-of-the-art relational database), MASS-11 Calendar, and MASS-11 Superlist—all fully integrated with MASS-11 WP.
- WordStar on the PC is the most popular word processor in the world.
- DEC released its VAX-based word processing system called WPS-Plus

1986

- MASS-11 was installed on over 4,000 VAXes worldwide and at most universities.
- MASS-11 User Groups formed in major cities across the U.S.
- Commands were introduced to integrate HPGL graphics files into MASS-11 WP documents. Also released in 1986 was the MASS-11 Graphics Processor that processed third-party graphics files, including MAC PICT and AUTOCAD into MASS-11 WP documents. Live link graphics integration followed shortly after.
- MEC tech reps were invited to demonstrate MASS-11 in the Scientific Solutions booth at DECWorld in St. Louis.
- Scientists and engineers widely rejected DEC's own WP product for the VAX due to being memory-intensive and high cost per user. By contrast, MASS-11 WP was feature-rich, extremely efficient, had a built-in spell checker, and was an affordable alternative to stand-alone WP systems such as Wang, Lanier, and NBI.
- VAX WP competitors: WordMarc, Word-11, Saturn, WPS-Plus

- There were 30 word-processing software products on the PC.

1987

- MASS-11 Draw released.
- As more VAX sites invested heavily in IBM PCs, a growing demand for desktop publishing capabilities arose. MEC's graphics programmer Ken Crossen and his programming team in North Carolina produced the revolutionary MASS-11 Draw, a mouse-driven freehand graphics editor that was fully integrated with MASS-11 WP. The product supported IBM PC XT/AT and compatibles, and the Toshiba 3100 pc. Draw included graphics primitives such as lines, circles, arcs, squares, rectangles, polygons, polylines, ovals, and curved-edged boxes. Six different text sizes, ranging from 6 to 36 points were included. Draw contained extensive symbol libraries to help users create organizational charts, Gantt charts, flow diagrams, chemical diagrams, and engineering schematics. Tools to scale, rotate 360 degrees, duplicate, undo, delete, and align objects for editing. On-screen rulers for precise measurements.
- MEC added MASS-11 Mail, a menu-driven mail utility, to its VAX version of MASS-11 WP. It allowed users to send editable documents and ASCII files to other VMS users via VAXmail or Western Union. It was available as a no-cost add-on or sold as a standalone product. MASS-11 Mail featured list management, return/receipt, and the ability to send binary files and interface with Western Union's Easylink and ITT Worldbridge.
- MEC released MASS-11pc Version 7-A that supported 43 Postscript fonts and unlimited point sizes. Other enhancements included the ability to exit DOS without leaving a MASS-11 document, Hot Print with one keystroke, spreadsheet integration, and text and graphics integration with the ability to specify graphic placement in inches.

- MASS-11 was fully integrated with DEC's All-in-1 File Cabinet.
- MEC moved Product Development, Support, and Training into new headquarters: 2501 W. Hassell Rd.
- November 1987 was a record month with over $1 million in sales.
- MEC started the development of a GUI (Graphical User Interface) Word Processor, one that would that incorporate a drawing editor and business graphics that used the native GUI of each platform: DECwindows for the VAXstation, MS Windows for the IBM PC and compatibles, and the standard interface on the Macintosh. The goal was to have graphics capabilities that enabled users to create a variety of graph types from imported spreadsheet and database information, as well as the ability to edit, annotate, and scale the graphics to fit anywhere in a document.
- MEC released new MASS-11 PC documentation that is entirely created with MASS-11 text and graphics products.
- A network version of MASS-11pc was released that supported Novell, Banyan, and 3Com networks.
- MEC took their `Gallery of Products' on the road with their Product Symposia. Everett Karels presented "Where We Are, Where We're Going."
- MEC participated in leading industry trade shows such as DEXPO, PC EXPO, Seybold Publishing Conference, and Graphix Expo. MEC's products were favorably reviewed in the leading trade media including Digital Review, DEC Professional, Hardcopy, and PC World.
- WordPerfect took 1st place over WordStar in the PC market.

1988

- MEC held ten Product Symposia.
- MEC endorsed DEC's Compound Document Architecture (CDA) which supported "live links" to text, graphics, images,

spreadsheets, charts, and tables.
- MASS-11 Version 8.0 provided "live link" text and graphics integration, an on-screen preview of text and graphics, and several other desktop publishing features. Supported graphic formats included MDL metafiles, HPGL, AutoCAD, Tektronix, Macintosh, PICT, and Lotus.PIC and IGES.
- MASS-11 Graphics Processor (GP) was released in November.
- MASS-11 WP sales to Fortune 500 accounts continued to rise
- Samna's Ami released on MS Windows

1989

- Eleven nationwide MASS-11 Product Symposia were scheduled for the year.
- MASS-11 Fax Processor completed, which worked with Biscom Inc's FAXcom 1000+, a hardware unit that was attached to the VAX. The product provided an interface that let users queue faxes, specify delayed delivery to take advantage of off-peak telephone rates, and provide accounting data for internal cost accounting and billing.
- MASS-11 Spreadsheet released, with the ability to import data, graphs, and macros from Lotus Development products, from 20/20, and Ashton Tate's dBase3. It was also CALS compliant.
- Executive Express released…
- Large-scale layoffs on Wall Street
- Word Processing became a commodity with WordPerfect and MS Word dominating on the PC. WordPerfect also on the VAX and Data General
- MS Word 1.0 was released on MS Windows; WordPerfect 5.1 for DOS was released, which became a best-seller.

1990

- MEC announced WysiWord WP at the National Computer Show; WysiWord delivered on DEC's VAXstation
- CALS Support. The Dept of Defense specified that all government

contractors comply with the CALS format (Computer-Aided Acquisition Logistics and Support) for electronically sent documents. CALS was part of the SGML standard for identifying structural parts of a document—elements such as title, author, headlines, and main body copy. The purpose was to automate the paper-intensive processes surrounding weapon system acquisition and reduce document handling and conversion costs. The DOD estimated that CALS compliance could reduce these costs by up to half of its total $15 billion document handling budget.

- CALS Forum held at MEC
- DEC established an Office Automation task force to go after Wang and NBI. Part of their strategy was to distribute MASS-11 WP as part of DEC's product offerings.
- MEC's IGES Gateway and Internodal Mail Gatew.ay link to All-in-1 released
- First MS Windows 3.0 Word 1990

1991

- MEC's family of products included MASS-11 Classic WP for VAX and PC, WysiWord for PC, Data Management products such as Manager, DDA and Superlist, Spreadsheet, Draw for PC, and Communications products such as FAXmail.
- WysiWord released on PC Windows, Macintosh, DECstation, Intergraph workstations, IBM R/S 6000 workstation.
- DEC asked MEC to Develop DEC's Proprietary Office Automation Products (March)
- DEC officially sold MASS-11 WP as an alternative to WPS-PLUS due to its connectivity with ALL-in-1, a PC version.
- Olsten Temps signed a contract to provide temp services nationwide to MASS-11 installations. Tiger Temps in NYC had already been providing temp services to banks and Wall Street firms using MASS-11.

- First investors invited to join in ownership of MEC (March)
- Defense Cutbacks, Recession in Northeast–Massive layoffs were taking place at DEC, Data General, Apple, and Tandem. Software and hardware companies were both affected. The entire Northeast military contractors were in a recession.

1992

- The bank pulled our loan. MEC sold on 9/11.

2000

- MS Word had 95% of WP market.